PRAiSE FOR DAViD LEiTE
AND NOTES ON A BANANA

A Finalist for the New England Book Award for Nonfiction
A Paste Best Book of the Year (So Far)
One of *Timeout: New York*'s Best Summer Beach Reads
One of *Real Simple*'s 25 Best Father's Day Books
One of Book Riot's Best Books of the Month

"A terrific contribution to understanding not only the experience of bipolar illness but also the experience of life: warm, funny, poignant, and human."   –Kay Redfield Jamison, author of *An Unquiet Mind*

"Excellent. . . . David Leite has managed the unlikely feat of combining a work of laugh-out-loud humor with the solemn subject of mental illness. A splendid and entertaining book."   —Dick Cavett

"Sharp-tongued, often hilarious, deeply honest. . . . This is not a book about a disorderly mind so much as it is about the astonishing resilience of the human heart. Leite has written a book for us all."
    —Marya Hornbacher, author of *Madness: A Bipolar Life*

"Ruthlessly candid. . . . The book is funny and hopeful even during some of its darkest passages, a deft balancing act that has brought Leite pre-publication comparisons with Augusten Burroughs and David Sedaris."   —*Connecticut Post*

"Belongs in the great Canon Of Mental Illness, a rending portrait. . . . It's Leite's deft portrayal of mania, written with the celerity and buzzing hagiography that are hallmarks of the condition, that gives *Notes on a Banana* its chimerical quality: equal parts memoir, case study and, for those who suffer along with Leite, both signal and solace."

—Paste

"Nothing short of masterful. . . . The author's writing is as lyrical and immersive as if it were literary fiction; elements that are rarely found in traditional memoirs. Yet, he accomplishes this feat with grace and levity. In speaking to others, Leite's story and writing style have been likened to David Sedaris, Augusten Burroughs, and Jeffrey Eugenides. Powerful recommendations for this funny and touching memoir."

—Book Riot

"A beautifully-written book. . . . Poignant and rich, as some of us who love Leite's work, have come to expect. You won't be disappointed."

—*Forbes*

"Expertly walks the line between sad and funny. . . . [Leite's] first-hand account of mental illness pulls no punches, serving up an honest and open perspective on personal and family issues that are often swept under the rug."

—*Publishers Weekly*

"A witty account. . . . Readers will enjoy Leite's ability to bring levity to a host of serious—and sometimes sad—subjects."

—Associated Press

"Exposing ourselves and our innermost secrets to the world is a tricky, delicate balance and it takes skill, tenderness, and humor. David Leite does it masterfully in his memoir. . . . Engaging, tender, warm and witty. . . . I found myself smiling, nodding my head in empathy and understanding, unable to put the book down from beginning to happy, satisfying end." —Huffington Post

"A true literary feast for the soul, presented with creative, honest prose, droll anecdotes, and all the savory trimmings of a happy ending." —Bay Area Reporter

"A tender, funny and sadly real story—one that will certainly resonate with readers." —Time Out: New York

"Though the James Beard Award–winning food writer gets intense and often dark in his colorful memoir. . . . His joy in life, family, and food remains constant." —EatingWell

"An honest look at overcoming a life fraught with anguish and obstacles. From an awkward youth through his turbulent teens and twenties, David Leite emerged as one of the best food writers of our generation. *Notes on a Banana* is the brutally forthright story of a man who found love, and finally his calling . . . in the kitchen." —David Lebovitz, author of *My Paris Kitchen*

"Leite gives voice to the devastation that is undiagnosed and mistreated bipolar disorder. . . . His triumph is rich with lessons for us all." —Drew Ramsey, MD, Assistant Clinical Professor of Psychiatry, Columbia University, and author of *Eat Complete*

"Warm, witty, sometimes heartbreaking. . . . Will engage foodies and all who appreciate candid and charming self-portraits." —*Booklist*

ALSO BY DAVID LEITE

The New Portuguese Table

NOTES
ON A
BANANA

A MEMOIR OF <u>FOOD</u>,
<u>LOVE</u>, AND <u>MANIC</u> DEPRESSION

DAViD LEiTE

DEY ST.
An Imprint of WILLIAM MORROW

HarperCollins books may be purchased for educational, business, or sales promotional use. For information please e-mail the Special Markets Department at SPsales@harpercollins.com.

A hardcover edition of this book was published in 2017 by Dey Street Books, an imprint of William Morrow Publishers.

FIRST DEY STREET BOOKS PAPERBACK EDITION PUBLISHED 2018.

Designed by Suet Chong
Handlettering by Joel Holland
All photographs are from the author's collection

Library of Congress Cataloging-in-Publication Data has been applied for.

ISBN 978-0-06-241438-0

18 19 20 21 22   DIX/LSC   10 9 8 7 6 5 4 3 2 1

FOR ALAN, THE ONE.

You are my balm, my net, my heart.

FOR MY PARENTS.

I'm still here because, thankfully,
the banana didn't fall far from the tree.

DOROTHY: *Oh, will you help me? Can you help me?*

GLINDA: *You don't need to be helped any longer. You've always had the power . . .*

DOROTHY: *I have?*

SCARECROW: *Then why didn't you tell her before?*

GLINDA: *Because she wouldn't have believed me. She had to learn it for herself.*

—*THE WIZARD OF OZ*

AUTHOR'S NOTE

This is a work of memory, and like memory, it's imperfect. I've done my best to write the truth as I experienced it. When my memory fell short in places, I leaned on the memory of others; family lore, legend, and stories; photographs and journals; medical, psychiatric, and school records; and newspaper articles to help connect the dots in my head. For small, inconsequential details that defied recollection—the interior design of a restaurant, someone's clothing, a cereal's name, you get the idea—I relied upon habits, research, and, sometimes, a hunch.

In certain cases, I've changed names. When needed, I also freely altered details to blur identities and protect certain individuals' privacy. There are no composite characters in my story, but I did conflate some experiences and bent time in one instance to avoid redundancies and confusion. Unless I had a record, dialogue is reconstructed.

Last, although I've read mountains of books, studied manic depression for more than twenty years, and worked with too many doctors, I've chosen to write from the heart, from the inside, out. This is not a medical treatise. So for God's sake, don't do what I did and diagnose yourself by reading a freaking book. See a competent doctor.

ABOUT PORTUGUESE NAMES

I've dispensed with the correct spelling and pronunciation of many Portuguese names and phrases, choosing instead to spell phonetically the words of our family's particularly butchered patois. So:

Grandfather, usually spelled *avô,* is spelled Vu, sometimes Vuvu.

Grandmother, usually spelled *avó,* is spelled Vo, sometimes Vovo.

Godfather, usually spelled *padrinho,* is spelled Paneen.

Godmother, usually spelled *madrinha,* is spelled Dina.

When greeting relatives, it's customary to kiss them and ask for a blessing, such as *"Pai, sua bênção"* or *"Mãe, sua bênção,"* which here has been bastardized as "Dad banse" or "Ma banse."

So kill me.

PART I

EARLY ONSET

A CLINICAL TERM USED FOR WHEN MANIC-DEPRESSIVE DISOR-
DER FIRST APPEARS EARLY IN LIFE. FOR A LONG TIME, DOCTORS
BELIEVED CHILDREN COULDN'T SUFFER FROM THE MOOD SWINGS
OF THE ILLNESS. DUMB-ASSES.

1

THE ARMPiT OF MASSACHUSETTS

It was one of the first jokes I learned. My hunch is I picked it up from my wiseass cousin, Barry, when I was about five. I'd walk up to people while they were having dinner around our green Formica kitchen table, the one flecked with glitter, and demand, "Ask me where I live." They'd glance at my parents, then, curious, bend over and oblige.

"And where *do* you live, David?"

I'd lift my left arm like a bodybuilder—bicep flexed, fist curled—in the shape of Cape Cod.

"Here," I'd say, pointing to my armpit. Yelps of laughter followed from those who hadn't heard it before. *Oh, that kid of yours, Ellie,* they'd say to my mother. She'd just flash her what-can-I-say smile and pass bowls of Portuguese rice and platters of fat links of *chouriço,* garlicky pork sausage, with an enormous fork jabbed menacingly into them. With the show over, I'd wriggle back onto my seat or open the door and scream for Paneen, my godfather, to come upstairs and carry me to their apartment so I could watch TV with Barry.

If you looked at a map, my hometown of Fall River, Massachusetts, was pretty much in the geographic armpit of the state. Mount
Hope Bay divided the South Coast: To the east, Fall River and the
tougher city of New Bedford, both swollen with newly arrived Portuguese immigrants; to the west, the more bucolic towns of Somerset
and Swansea. And beyond: rarefied Newport, Rhode Island, with its
mansions, yachts, and Kennedy history. At the time, I found the joke
hilarious, because anything with butt cracks and burps and armpits
was funny. It would be a few more years before it took on a different
meaning.

I grew up in a sliver of the city called Mechanicsville, which was
so inconsequential it was swallowed up by the sprawling and far
more regal-sounding North End. On our block of Brownell Street, we
kids were indistinguishable. We could end up at each other's houses
for supper, and our mothers would look at us for a second, confusion creasing their foreheads, and set more plates, as if they'd suddenly forgotten how many children they had. Our parents were just
as interchangeable. Act up in someone else's yard, and you could be
sure some father would crack you across the ass and think nothing
of it. But if a kid from another block began whaling on one of us, all
our mothers would fly from their porches, haul off the intruder, and
shout down his mother until she and her kid slunk away. It was understood: We were children of the neighborhood. And playing in our
slice of the city, which bled into the rocky Taunton River, we didn't
know people spat out words like *Portagee* and *greenhorn* as a way of
insulting our parents and making them feel small. Hell, we didn't
even know there was anything other than Portuguese, which meant
we didn't know how to be ashamed.

Television showed us that.

I don't remember a time without TV. I was allowed to watch pretty
much nonstop while my mother cooked, made beds, rearranged clos-
ets, hung laundry, and babysat my cousin Barry and me. But at some
point, I noticed there were no families on TV speaking the soft sand-
paper shushing of Portuguese words. Houses weren't crammed with

eight or ten people. No kid was ever forced to eat salt cod or octopus stew that seemed to take on pulsating purple life in the bowl. Fathers weren't carpenters, and mothers certainly weren't fat. TV people had *maids* who were plump, but it was always the mothers who pirouetted out of swinging kitchen doors, their dresses fanning open like morning glories, carrying anything made with Velveeta. We didn't even have a door to our kitchen.

What we did have was whole apartments filled with the aroma of pungent garlic and sweet onions slowly melting in big pans. *"Refogado"*—my maternal grandmother, Vovo Costa, would tell me its name, urging me to repeat it. *Refogado.* Meat so smoky I could hold my fingers to my nose hours later and still smell it. My mother's singing, soft and trilling, as she swayed to the radio while cooking in our narrow kitchen. And after dinner, all eight of us draped over the furniture in my godparents' parlor. On the wall, watery flickers of Abbott and Costello running from Frankenstein, as my grandfather, Vu Costa, hauled out his wheezing projector and played his favorite movie for us, yet again.

The closest thing to my family I ever saw on TV was *The Honeymooners,* because my father had been a bus driver back in the Old Country, where he met my mother while she was on vacation from Fall River, where she was born. He never screamed at her like Ralph Kramden or threatened to send her to the moon. But we did have a family friend, Pesky, who wore T-shirts and vests just like Ed Norton.

While TV shows made it clear we weren't like others, commercials taught me how we could be. Sitting in front of our flickering black-and-white television set with its screen that always reminded me of my Etch A Sketch, I felt relieved knowing that no matter what kind of kid I was—fat, skinny, the kind who climbed on rocks, tough, sissy, even if I had chicken pox—I'd be accepted because all kids loved Armour hot dogs. My parents had quizzed me repeatedly about what to do if a strange man ever opened the door to his car or basement and asked me to get in, but they never told me what would happen. Commercials explained it all to me. The reason old men with doughy faces weren't to be trusted was because they'd eat my Cracker Jack. TV even taught me everything there was to know about my great-est obsession: proper hair care. Run Brylcreem through my crew cut—"a little dab'll do ya," I was told—and it'd shine like our toaster. The Beautiful Crissy doll showed me that if I pulled a girl's hair hard enough, I could make it grow. And if my mother ever decided to color her hair with Miss Clairol, she'd leave us all wondering, because only her hairdresser would know for sure.

In time, I wanted to be blond and blue-eyed and have a last name like Stevens or Nelson. I wanted a one-story house for just my parents and me, with a sunken living room and brick fireplaces and famous paintings hanging over the mantels. And I desperately wanted that swinging kitchen door, the kind with a round window like they have on ships. I wanted so much.

Instead, my parents, grandparents, godparents, cousin Barry, and I lived on top of one another in a brown tenement my grandfather had bought in the 1940s, in one of the largest communities of Portu-guese immigrants in the country. Now, it's not what you're thinking. To just about everyone back then in Fall River, a tenement was a siz-able working-class house made up of three apartments, oftentimes filled, like ours, with different generations of the same family. Sadly, no one calls them tenements nowadays. All those PBS documentaries about Lower East Side squalor ruined it for us.

A long yard ran down one side of the house, most of it shaded by our cherry tree, which had a canopy so big it hung over two neigh-bors' fences, giving them all the fruit they could eat in summer. My father's garden tucked in behind the house, where he had a few rows of fat, heavy tomatoes and a big strawberry patch, whose leaves looked as if they were clapping when a breeze blew. Lying in the dirt beneath billowing bedsheets that my godmother, Dina, had set out to dry, I'd shove a strawberry on the end of each finger. Holding them up—ten wriggling, brilliant red hearts against a spotless sky—I'd hum to myself as I plucked them off one by one and popped them in my mouth.

Our apartment, with its lightbulbs, telephone, and gas stove, was a first magical glimpse of America for a parade of relatives, men with nubby teeth that looked like barely popped kernels of corn, and women in secondhand polyester dresses Vu had sent to them in huge wooden crates he nailed together in our cellar. Just some of the huddled masses who had emigrated from the Azores in the early sixties. Nine tiny islands strewn like green marbles on the blue felt of the Atlantic, the Azores are where my family is from.

As lush and achingly beautiful as the islands were, many people there suffered from malnutrition and bone-crushing poverty; at least my family did. When my father immigrated in 1959, the stone house he grew up in—four tiny windows, a dirt floor, and a sleeping loft for all five kids until they married—still had no electricity, telephone, or heating. What little heat they had came from the wall oven where Vo Leite, my father's mother, cooked everything.

But for all its space and sunlight and shiny surfaces, our second-floor apartment felt bruised. My grandfather had grown tired of renting to strangers, so it had stood empty for years until my mother brought my father to America three months after they married. The patterns on the wallpaper had faded in great diagonal swaths. The seams had darkened to the color of honey. I used to put my nose against the wall and inhale. It smelled comforting, like old books.

Looking against the low morning light while playing with my Lincoln Logs, I could see the traffic jams of dimples in the linoleum, the vestige of countless high heels over the decades. The edges had been nibbled away by hungry vacuum cleaners. Sometimes a tongue of linoleum would get sucked up by the Hoover and stutter against the beater.

"Sonofa—" I'd hear my mother mumble, as she smacked the machine off as if it had suddenly insulted her, and I'd watch as she pinned the overturned behemoth with one knee, trying to coax out the linoleum without ripping it. Inevitably, she'd toss up her hands and drop them on her enormous tree-trunk thighs. "Why do I even bother?" she'd ask, waving a pizza-slice shape of flooring at me.

We didn't have a bathtub, just a sink and toilet. It was the same with my grandparents' apartment, a modest addition Vu had built onto the back of the house before I was born. We all took turns bathing in my godparents' pink-and-black bathroom—the only full bath in the house—with its trio of ceramic skunks on the wall, all three sporting blond bobs, just like those women in the Alberto VO5 hairspray commercials.

Now, my parents' bedroom—that was a proper room: big and square, with two large windows. It must have faced south, because it was the brightest spot in the house. It was where I'd loll on Saturday afternoons coloring and where I'd help my mother pull in the laundry from the clothesline. And it was where we recuperated from the mumps, my mother moaning beside me, her face a chipmunk's at acorn time.

The week before, all of us had gathered around my godparents' kitchen table after dinner. The adults were talking, sliding beer bottles back and forth, making small wet circles on the blue Formica table. Dina and Paneen pulled on their Lucky Strikes, screwing up their faces to blow the smoke sidewise, away from my parents and me. Now and then, rolls of warm, caramel laughter rose up and tumbled over themselves in the corners of the ceiling. I was intent on putting back together Barry's wooden Humpty Dumpty toy when the lights sputtered out. Everyone went silent. A match flared, and Paneen followed Dina as she rummaged in the white metal drawers for candles. We sat for several hours in the flickering light, Dina making coffee and occasionally banging a small glass ashtray against the bin to empty it. When the lights finally snapped on, my mother screamed, "What's the matter with you?" They all gawked. I reached out my arms and ran to my father. From what they tell me, my face looked like a helium balloon. In the dark of what was later heralded as the Great Northeast Blackout of 1965, I'd come down with the mumps. A day or two later, so had my mother.

We lay together, I on my belly at the foot of their bed, watching the TV my father had wheeled in from the parlor; she, leaning back on a bunch of pillows, doing some sort of word puzzle. She ran the sickbed like she ran our lives: with precision and rigor. Why waste time watching afternoon television when she could challenge herself with a puzzle? "Good for the noggin," she said, tapping her temple with a pen. *Never* a pencil; my mother was always assured. "Won't go cuckoo doing these." And when the doctor prescribed complete bed rest for me, she took it literally. *No feet on the floor* were her orders. Meals were brought to me; so were toys. When I needed to pee, she held up a glass quart milk bottle, which delighted me no end, and turned her head. When I took longer than she expected, she remarked, "Banana, what are you, a camel?" Do you have any idea how hard it is to pee into a bottle with a five-year-old's equipment when you're convulsing with laughter?

Banana.

It's one of the nicknames she has for me, and it's my favorite. My mother slaps nicknames on everyone, whether they want one or not. You can see her sizing up someone at a first meeting, rooting through their speech and behavior to find the nickname they *should* have, as if she's finally correcting the misdeeds of inattentive parents, oblivious spouses, bastard bullies. And when she bestows that name, which is always done with a whiff of ceremony, she forever owns that version of the person. They are her creations now—with her expectations, dreams, and rules of conduct laid out for them.

She says "Banana" came from my yanking on her dress and pleading for "peabot and blanas," my toddler way of saying peanut-butter-and-banana sandwiches. She's also partial to "Banana Head," *"Tarouco"* (essentially Portuguese slang for "Banana Head"), and "kiddo." My father, for whom English was still exotic and mysterious, has always called me just "Son."

Lost in an episode of *The Soupy Sales Show,* I didn't feel her nudging me with her foot.

"Hey, Banana? TMT." That was family code for "touch my toes."

As we lay there, I ran the back of my fingernails up her soles and over the tops of her feet. Every once in a while, she jumped and dug her heel into my butt because it tickled. "You're doing that on purpose!"

"Uh-uh," I lied, looking her right in the eye. She had taught me well in the Art of the Straight Face.

The only room that doesn't thrum with memories is my bedroom. In my mind, it's always dark, the only light coming from the devotional candle with the glittery image of Jesus, his great, kind heart exploding from his chest. A Venetian blind covered the window on the far wall. Sometimes I'd part the metal slats and, while peering out, absentmindedly lick them. I couldn't help tasting and smelling everything. It made objects more real to me, kind of like creating an inventory of sensations.

I don't recall anything that ever happened in my room. Friends never wanted to play there the way we did in the empty attic apartment, even though the linoleum was a grid of board games: checkers, chess, backgammon, bingo. Yet my cousin Barry's room, one floor below mine and just as dark, was a magnet for activity. We napped there, played War and Go Fish there, were punished there. And when Dina found Barry with his hands down his underwear, rooting around in his butt crack, she dragged him there, took a flashlight, and peered into his spread cheeks for tapeworms. Apparently, not even parasites found my bedroom hospitable.

While our rooms on Brownell Street were bereft of anything approaching beauty, they were bursting with people who looked like movie stars. My father, with his ruddy cheeks, warm eyes, and shock of light brown hair pushed back off his forehead, had the Jack Kennedy look before Jack made it popular. And my mother, after she became thin for the first time, could have been a stand-in for Ava Gardner, especially when she tilted her head back and let loose one of her big, explosive laughs. Paneen was all Marlon Brando, darkly handsome with a hard, lean body. He worked road construction, and on weekends raced stock cars over at Seekonk Speedway. He was fond of walking around the house in just his jeans, with the top button popped open. A smoke line of hair from somewhere deep inside those jeans curled up to his navel, riveting me. Even Vu and Vo, with their Old World demeanor, made a good-looking pair. Only Dina, with her hangdog face and housecoats, was out of place.

I couldn't connect all the dots back then in that kid head of mine, but I knew that out of everyone in our Cavalcade of Stars, something special, something amazing, was going to happen to *me*. I had no idea what or how, so I turned to what I did best: waiting. I always got what I wanted, if I waited long enough. Standing patiently in the billows of the sheer drapes, watching the street corner, always brought my father back from work, squinting against the setting sun as he waved up to me. No matter how much she tried to ignore me, my silently looking up at Vo like a *pobrinho*—poor little thing—always made her laugh and lunch appear. And sitting in the dip of the worn wooden steps of the side porch, crying and waiting for my mother to return—from where? someplace called Errands—always led her home to me.

This time I waited for photographers to discover me. On the side porch I posed, for a while sitting erect and cross-legged with Tiny, Vu and Vo's Chihuahua, in my lap. Then slouching, with my legs stretched out in front of me. Sometimes I'd stand against the wall, my hands in my pockets, waiting for the inevitable pop of flashbulbs.

"There he is!" one of the photographers would shout, pointing at me, as they rushed the yard. And I'd tilt my head and grin, not the gummy smile of my relatives—*dentes de cavalo,* my mother called them, horse teeth—but rather her famous Courtesy-Booth Girl smile, the one she'd perfected for work at Fernandes Supermarket. And then I, too, would be far away from that big armpit and on TV with my friends Annette and Cubby and Jimmie, as the youngest member of *The Mickey Mouse Club.*

2

SiSTERS OF THE SPATULA

My church pockabook" is what my mother called it. Her shiny
black patent-leather purse she used only on Sundays. I loved
that purse. It hung from the crook of her arm, level with my
head. I used to imagine it was my own personal TV screen, and I'd
yammer to myself all the way to St. Michael's and back.

"What are you doing?" she'd ask.

"Playing priest on TV," I'd say, pointing to my face reflected in
the glossy blackness as if it were the most obvious thing in the world.

"Well, knock it off, Banana, that's blasphemous." At church my
father would often have to separate us in the pew.

The way we all tell this story, burnishing it each time to make
it shine ever brighter, on the day before I started kindergarten, my
mother was ironing my brand-new clothes, including the T-shirts and
underwear. "No kid of mine is going to school in slouchy underpants
that look like he has a load in them," she said, pointing the iron at
me. The excitement and confusion of the day must have caused me to
flip out, because suddenly she clutched her breasts together, looked

toward the ceiling, and let out an exasperated *"Ay!"*—something she did whenever she was riled up, which back then was often. She ordered me to fish her pockabook out of her closet and find her change purse amid the wadded-up Kleenex, the Sucrets cough drops that I spat out when she wasn't looking, and her rosary.

"Here," she said, digging out some quarters and slapping them in my hand, "go buy us some donuts."

School might have been darkly unknowable, but donuts I understood.

According to the Sisters of the Spatula, my name for the flock of women who ruled my childhood, donuts were lice control—anytime they wanted us kids out of their hair, they'd dole out money and tell us to go to the Terminal Bakery around the corner on Davol Street, buy some donuts, and make sure to get lost on the way back.

The mothers of our neighborhood—mine, Dina, Joanne Martin from across the street, the loud woman from next door who wore nothing but housecoats and everyday hollered over the fence for her kids, and my mother's best friend, Jackie (who technically didn't live in our neighborhood, but had the same smoker's rasp and smart-ass sense of humor)—all parented with a kind of benign neglect and mock cruelty. Dina's nickname for me was "Ugly," and I ate it up. Anytime we kids bugged them, especially on hot afternoons when they were crowded around Dina's table, fanning themselves with a section of the *Herald News* or a stray electric bill, one of them would look at us with the most serious of expressions and yell, "Will you *please* go play in traffic?" Only then would we meep with delight and run outside, looking back to see them cracking themselves up. It was our way, and we didn't feel loved without it.

I took the change, tore down the stairs and out the side door. I started goofing off, singing and hopping on and off the curb like I saw the kids do in *The Sound of Music*. For my big finish, I flung my hands in the air, accidentally sending the change sailing into our neighbor's hedge. Mortified by the thought of what would happen if I returned home empty-handed, I slithered on my belly beneath the bushes, ripping out handfuls of shiny green weeds, until deep inside I found the quarters.

Long, sleek cases lined three sides of the enormous Terminal Bakery, all filled with the kind of Technicolor pastries that showed up at neighbors' houses after major life events: births, deaths, weddings, divorces, parole. Or on Dina's table on Sundays, where she, Paneen, and Barry licked sugar from their fingers, and my mother swiveled my head away from the open door as we filed righteously past on our way to church. These weren't the flat Portuguese donuts called *malassadas,* or the eggy, sweet bread known as *massa souvada*. No, these were real sweets, like the kind on TV. Crullers and jelly donuts that dandruffed my clip-on tie and the Charlie McCarthy–size version of my father's suit. Éclairs so big it was impossible to suck out all the cream before being seduced by the chocolate icing. Cookies practically the size of my head.

I picked out a couple of donuts, paid for them, and raced back. My mother had hung up my clothes, and we sat at our green table, tearing into the bag. As I regaled her with my story of the Lost Coins, she covered her mouth with the back of her hand, laughing. The dirt and grass stains on my clothes were forgiven by her appreciation of my performance, and when we were done she hid any evidence before my father came in from the garden.

S weetheart, time for your first day at schoo-ool," my mother cooed, rocking me awake. I rolled toward her, eyes closed, trying not to let sleep leak out. And then it started, that long, piercing air-raid alarm that begins high and ends impossibly higher: "MAAAAANNNNNY!" From the kitchen floated the low rumblings of my father as he tried to calm her. When he came into my room, they just stood there, blinking at me.

As she peeled off my pajamas with just her fingertips and slathered me in calamine lotion, she explained I must have yanked up piles of something called poison ivy from under Mr. Jeff's hedges looking for the change. Once I was dry, she hiked me into a pair of pants, like a pillow into a pillowcase, and dressed me in a long-sleeved shirt, instructing me to keep the sleeves down no matter how hot it got. She also put a bow tie on me for good measure. Maybe she thought the tie would seal in the rash.

At Carroll School, my mother went up to the waiting teacher and introduced me. I extended my hand, as my father and I had practiced, but my mother batted it away and rolled her eyes. She leaned in and whispered something, and the teacher squinted down at me, a tiny O forming on her lips, and nodded. With that, my mother knelt down, gathered me in her arms, and, after failing to find a pustule-free zone on my face to kiss, planted one on the top of my head.

"Everyone, can I have your attention, please," the teacher said, clapping her hands at the class. "This is another student, David. Can you say hello?"

"Hello, David," they droned.

Then she added: "Whatever you do, *do not touch him*. He has poison ivy."

For the rest of that day, I was marooned at my desk while everyone else got to push theirs together into little islands of learning, jabbering with one another. "But look, my sleeves are *down*," I'd say to my teacher whenever she made wide circles around me. All I got was a pitying look and a shake of her head. By story time I'd given up, and as they all tried to clamber into her lap, I spent my time smelling my new crayons, wondering why my orange Crayola didn't smell like an orange.

The next morning, my mother awoke me again. *I have to go back?* This wasn't a one-off, like a bad birthday party or a visit to my great-aunt Tia Escolastica?

"Look," she said.

"At what?"

"Me!" She pulled me into the light of the kitchen. Her arms and face were covered with poison-ivy rash. She then jutted out her lower lip. The bumps were creeping their way into the lining of her mouth.

"Maybe God didn't want us to eat those donuts?" I offered. She cocked her head as if to say, *Maybe the kid's got a point.* She laughed and reached out to hug me, but thought better of it.

Food. It was one of the ways we bonded. But this shared passion was something collusive and secretive—just between us. Let me illustrate: My mother was never a baker. She wasn't about to let some damn recipe, with its scant teaspoons and delicate dustings, boss her around in the kitchen. My mother doesn't understand scant. Instead, several times a week she'd buy a Table Talk pie that came in those red-and-white packages, because my dad liked a little something sweet after dinner. Those pies were some of the only American foods I was allowed, for which I never failed to thank Jesus and his bursting heart every night after prayer time.

My mother was a rapacious eater, and her joy of food was infectious. Yet each night she'd serve my father, me, and herself a modest one-twelfth of a pineapple or apple or blueberry pie, and my father would smile and pat her arm. What he didn't know was that the following afternoon, she and I would often polish off the remaining three-fourths of the day-old pie, plus a quarter of an identical one she'd bought that morning, so that it would look to my father like his wife was a model of restraint.

When he was out one night, my mother and I lounged on the nubby red couch, watching TV. "Wait right here," she said, squinching up her face as if to say, *This is gonna be good.* I squirmed in anticipation. A few minutes later, she tiptoed back into the room, making believe she was trying to hide from my grandparents downstairs. In her hands was a plate filled with Sunbeam bread, toasted, buttered, and sprinkled with sugar and cinnamon. I adored her completely at that moment. When the toast disappeared, she made more. And then more, and still more. We scarfed down the entire loaf, and I have no idea how much butter, before my father came home. When he did, the empty bag was safely hidden in the bottom of the garbage, where my mother had plunged it. The plate had been washed and put away, and we sat there practicing the Art of the Straight Face.

Just for kicks, my godmother liked to chap my mother's ass by seducing me with her food. It was a battle of wills with those two. "Hey, Ugly!" she'd shout up the stairs. "I just made some French stuffing." Dina's stuffing, a classic French-Canadian dish, which never saw the inside of a turkey, was whipped potatoes studded with a combination of beef, pork, and chopped cooked onions, and seasoned with nutmeg. I loved it. It was nothing like Vo's Portuguese stuffing—a rich muddle of stale bread that had been soaked in water, squeezed dry, and then mixed with sautéed onions and garlic, tons of *chouriço*, and parsley, all turned a burnt ochre by her heavy hand with paprika. "Okay, then," she'd taunt. "Maybe I'll see if Barry wants it instead." I'd look at my mother pleadingly until she relented, then I'd scamper down to their apartment. Dina would wait until I was seated at the table, then heap a mound into one of her white milk-glass bowls with the little bumps on the outside. I'd demolish it while she looked on dreamily, a Lucky Strike cocked in one hand, a cup of coffee garlanded with half-moons of red lipstick in the other.

"Hey, Ellie! I think your kid's half French!" she'd bellow, victorious, to the ceiling, scraping my curls out of my eyes.

"That'll be news to Manny," my mother yelled back, adding a stomp of her foot for emphasis.

While eating defined my relationships with my mother and Dina, cooking is what I shared with my Vovo Costa. Often when she was preparing dinner, she'd scrape a kitchen chair over to the stove and put one of my grandfather's shirts on me backward, like a smock. I'd climb up, and she'd hand me a spoon to stir. One day it'd be a pot of rice, the next beef stew, or maybe onions in a skillet. Once on a stifling summer afternoon, she was poking at *chouriço* in the cast-iron fry pan with a big metal fork. On the linoleum-covered counter was a jar filled with table wine. She nodded, and I splashed some into the pan, causing little clouds to rise up. The brown radio with buttons that looked like big, tan caramels played her favorite Azorean program. She sang along in her thin, reedy voice to the plaintive songs of the Old Country as she fussed, the loose skin under her arm swinging like a hammock. Every once in a while she couldn't resist and gathered me in her arms and covered the crown of my head with kisses, making those big, dramatic smacking noises that made me giggle and butt my head against her chin like a cat, asking for more. Nestled there, I'd breathe in her scent: baby powder and Jean Naté.

When the sausage was cooked, she slid the pan off the burner to cool. She pointed to a heavy carved chair on the other side of the room and said, "Help me pick this up," in Portglish, our personal patois, a mash-up of English and Portuguese I was innocent enough to assume only we understood. I lifted the front end; she heaved up the back. We weaved across the one room that was their kitchen, dining room, and parlor. The chair listed left and right until Vo chose a spot by the window, in the shade of our cherry tree.

I stood behind and fanned her with a magazine as she set to work making fava-bean soup. It's a simple dish, a peasant dish, really, that I liked. Fava beans and chunks of *chouriço* were simmered in a broth filled with garlic and onions. The *chouriço* would stain the liquid orange. Sometimes she'd put green peppers in the pot, but I preferred it plain.

She lugged over a crate of fava beans my grandfather had bought at one of the local farms and kicked a big, white enamel bowl into place between her feet. Even though she sat there in just a slip, with her stockings rolled down her huge pink legs, she looked like an empress to me. The work began. Thick, fibrous pods were slit open with one quick zip of her fingernail. A flick of her thumb sent the beans inside plonking down into the bowl, over and over, until the crate was empty. When she was finished, she placed the white bowl in the middle of the kitchen table and opened the door.

"Elvira!" she hollered up the stairs, which in Portuguese sounded like El-*vee*-da. *"Vem aqui!"* Come here!

My mother shuffled around, then closed the door and clomped down. We sat around the table in the sweltering heat, pinching the favas from their soft, satiny inner skins. My mother and grandmother used small knives to nick the coverings and squeeze out the brilliant green beans, while I was allowed only to pick at them with my fingernails.

"Hey, kiddo." My mother pointed to the growing pile of emerald nuggets in front of her. "This is what you call 'piecemeal.'" What I heard was *peace meal*. After that, any time they served fava-bean soup, I assumed it was their way of calling for a time-out, like a referee sending our three families back into their corners. All the usual scrapes of the day forgotten as we came together at the table.

3

WHAT BECOMES A LEGEND MOST

My mother is a bloodhound for Jesus. She can sniff out sin before it happens, the way some people smell burnt toast before a seizure. Legend goes I was about six years old and sitting on a kitchen chair, banging my shoes on its chrome legs like clappers on a bell. For more than an hour my mother and I had been at a standoff over the cold bowl of Portuguese kale soup sitting in front of me. I had my head down, avoiding her gaze. I knew she could tell I'd been silently breaking the commandment about honoring your parents, because I'd been wishing every horrible, mean, hateful thing I could dream up would happen to her. My face didn't slide off into my bowl, so I took that as a sign from God that I wasn't going straight to hell.

She slid her hand into my field of vision and rapped her index finger on the table. *Tac, tac, tac.* I ignored it, so she inched it closer and rapped harder. *TAC, TAC, TAC.* I looked over at my grandmother, who had begun to worry the last bits of her Portuguese bread into little white rosary beads.

TAC! TAC! TAC!

"Whaaaaaaaaaat?"

"Are you going to eat or not?"

I stared at her.

"Well?"

"Elvira . . . ," my father said, low. A junkyard dog trying to warn off an intruder.

It could have been the slimy texture of the greens. Or maybe I overheard someone say something about Portagee food in a way that made it sound not much better than eating swill. Whatever the cause, I turned my nose up at it. I longed to eat things like hamburgers on buns that looked like tan mittens, and chocolate cake with swirls of Betty Crocker chocolate frosting, a bottle of milk alongside. My last name *means* "milk" in Portuguese; it seemed my birthright. Chocolate layer cake with a glass of milk so cold it makes your throat hurt is so iconically American that it's even called "American-style cake." I wanted to be American by consumption.

I could outlast my mother. I knew it, and so did she. I'd done it before, with stalemates in just about every store we shopped at and with staring matches behind my father's back in church, as she tried to get me to stop yammering as I pretended to read aloud the prayers in the missal.

"For the last time: Eat your soup."

I looked at her and prayed for a lightning bolt to pin her to the floor.

"*Querido, coma,*" said my grandmother, concerned. Sweetheart, eat.

"Momma, if he doesn't want to eat, he doesn't have to," she said to my grandmother, then turned to me. "Right, baby?" Her voice was suddenly filled with the warmth of my favorite TV moms. She yanked my bowl away. I had thrust both fists out to my father, as a sign of yet another victory, when I felt a thunk on my head. Cold broth beaded on my eyelashes. Potatoes plopped into my lap, and slippery greens hugged my face as they slid down and over my cheeks.

My father looked like a goldfish that had fallen on the floor, all goggled eyes, his mouth bobbing open and closed. My grandmother stopped midbead.

I was stunned. The first convulsions of a howl shuddered in my belly. I looked at my mother. One hand was on her forehead, the other on her hip. She was clearly the most shocked of us all. Then a caterpillar of a smile started to wriggle across her face. I stood up and looked pointedly at all three of them.

"I think I'll go to my room now," I said. I turned, bowl balanced on my head, and walked across the kitchen to my room. Behind closed doors, I clamped my hand over my mouth to prevent my sniggers from curling themselves under the door and into the kitchen. But there was no need, because they never would've heard it over their own laughter.

"Good night, Son," my father said later that evening, tucking me into bed, my hair still damp from my bath. My mother came in, as she always did, and sat on my bed as I said my prayers. When I was done, she leaned over and kissed me. He, too.

"Ma banse. Dad banse."

"God bless you," they said in unison.

Just before she turned out the light, she said, "We okay?" I nodded vigorously. And we were. It's our way.

In the dark of my room, I tuned into the television show in my head, the program already in progress.

"Yup, right on my head!" I say as I sit in the guest chair on *The Mike Douglas Show,* my legs too short to reach the floor. Mike's snorting so hard he can hardly speak. "I didn't give in, though. Not me!"

"Is this kid something?" he says, clapping, motioning the audience to join in. They erupt into a riot of applause.

He tells me to move over a seat to make room for Totie Fields. She thunders on like a sumo wrestler. I put my hand out to greet her, but she grabs me and buries me in her chest: "You're so freaking adorable!" After she squeezes herself into her chair, she says, "Let me tell ya something, kid. If they ever make a movie of your life, I gotta play that mother of yours. She's a real spark plug, that one."

Spark plug. Firecracker. Loose cannon. You name it, she's been called them all. Some Azoreans have a word for it: *veneta*. It's hard to translate exactly because it's slang, but it's this indomitable force of nature that you damn well want on your side. It's a capricious temper, an irrational obsession, a fierce determination that uncoils through some families and detonates every so often. Some members have it; others don't. My mother does. So do I. My father, not so much. (Let me take that back. Aggravate him long enough, or threaten any of us, and he could come out swinging, but his *veneta* was always provoked, unlike my mother's and mine, which were at best unpredictable.) How I loved her *veneta,* when its crosshairs weren't trained on me.

With just a look, she could wither cashiers to a stump and cow bank presidents. It was a superpower, like being able to command the wind or bend forks with your mind. There was that time we were driving home on the highway in the old tan Pontiac, and some guy cut in front of us. "You sonofa—!" she screamed at taillights that were getting smaller by the second. She gunned the car and weaved in and out of evening traffic until she caught up to him, and then she turned the wheel hard. There was a chorus of squealing brakes behind us. "How does it feel, you sucker?!" she said into the rearview mirror. We were delirious with victory. And when he came up alongside us and leaned on his horn, she just waved him off like a queen and took the next exit home.

Veneta was often whipped out of her holster in the name of child-rearing. One afternoon I ran into the house with my first spelling quiz, shaking it over my head like a pom-pom.

"Look, Ma!" I said proudly. She laughed as she smoothed the paper against the table. I looked at her face, then down at the quiz filled with my oversize scrawl, then back up to her, just waiting for it.

"You got a forty."

"I *know*!" I replied. "A *forrrrrteeee*!" I whispered, drawing out the word.

"Well, Banana, that's failing." I could feel low, cold clouds swirling around her.

"Failing?" I searched her eyes for a hint of a joke. There was none. *Failing?* Mrs. Conforti, my first-grade teacher, hadn't explained that my grade was forty out of a hundred—a number my father was still helping me count to.

"Go," she said, nudging her chin toward my room. I knew better than to argue. After dinner I watched the circle of light from my Jesus candle flicker on the ceiling and heard my parents shouting. "Well, not my kid, Manny," she said. "Not my kid."

The next morning when I got to the table, a small box was sitting on my plate.

"Open it up," my mother said, her voice all honey again. I looked at my father, then back at her. I didn't like surprises. I pulled off the top. Inside was a pile of what looked like large confetti cut from manila folders. On each was a block letter in my mother's handwriting. "We're going to sit here every day after school until you spell like a champ," she said, banging her finger on the table for emphasis—*tac, tac, tac*. And every day was a test of will—with me refusing, her demanding. It wasn't fun, it wasn't easy, and it sure as hell wasn't what I wanted to be doing with my afternoons. Bottom line: I'm one damn good speller.

Sometimes, her *veneta* was an impulsive ballsiness. The day Paneen was giving rides on his motorcycle, for example, she suddenly grabbed the hem of her dress, wadded it up in front of her, and hooked one leg over the back of the seat. "Ellie! Get your ass off of that thing!" Joanne brayed in her smoker's voice, her cigarette jabbing in my mother's direction. Mercifully, her reply was drowned out by the muffler. The neighborhood huddled on the sidewalk and watched them go the few blocks down Brownell to the river, turn around, and pause. All of us were silent, just waiting to see what would happen. The bike lurched, and a ripping sound followed, like thunder after lightning. They flew up the street, my mother honking with laughter, her head tossed back, her mouth opened so wide, I swear I could see her fillings.

4

i'M NOT GOiNG TO BE iGNORED

U p and down Brownell Street, my mother's whistle was famous. Even people who never met her knew who she was. I could be playing five blocks from home, and when she let loose, it was like the noon siren. The other kids would lift their heads and freeze, a bunch of startled chipmunks. Then they'd all turn to me. That's when some mother would put it together. "Hey, you the Whistle Lady's kid?" she'd ask. I'd nod, secretly thrilled by our celebrity. The farther away from home, the more pitying my friends' expressions. They knew I had just minutes to make it back. If she whistled again, I was tempting fate. A third? Well, let's just say I wasn't stupid enough to find out.

Her whistle was her signature. When she went full throttle at the fireworks or at Seekonk Speedway, cheering my godfather as he climbed into his car, everyone around her would turn and stare, impressed. Even Paneen would stop and swivel toward the sound. *That's my mother,* I'd think. She'd give them all a wink and do it again.

But for me, her whistle was an invisible tether. If I was in earshot, no matter how far away, I was never lost.

One afternoon, she navigated the big boat that was our Buick into a parking spot at the Truesdale Hospital up in the Highlands and turned off the ignition. The building, a squat yellow-brick affair, had the dejected, slumped look of an orphanage.

"Who's sick?" I asked.

"No one." She rolled down the driver's window, put her two pinkie fingers into her mouth, and blew. *Whirrr-iiiiit! Whirrrrrrrrrrr-iiiiiiiiiit!* She looked at me and winked. Then once more, even louder.

She pointed to the top of the building. Standing at a third-floor window was Dina. She was cradling something and waving. She made big, exaggerated pointing motions to the bundle in her arms.

"What's she holding?"

She turned to me as if to make sure there wasn't an axe sticking out of my head. "Your new cousin, Banana."

"What's its name?"

"It's not an *it*, it's a *him*. His name is Wayne, but I think I'm going to call him 'Chipper,'" she said, examining her rings. "I've always liked the name Chipper. What do you think?"

"But that's not his name."

"Well, it is now." And just like that, she never called him Wayne again.

"Can we go see them?"

"Kids can't go in the maternity ward."

"Why?"

"You could have the flu or the plague or something, and you could kill him," she said. "And you wouldn't want that, would you?"

I had to think.

For as long as I could remember, I'd managed to keep the spotlight of our family trained squarely on me. It was simple economics, really: I made them laugh, and they praised me—or, in the case of

Dina's brother Norman, paid me. Whenever he was particularly amused by my antics, he'd pull quarters from behind my ears and let me pocket them. I felt seen and heard.

I don't know how hilarious I actually was, but with my mother in the audience, it didn't matter. She had an infectious laugh that began as barely audible squeals and built to convulsing guffaws and, finally, loud, percussive screams. She was always pulling off her cat's-eye glasses, the ones with the rhinestones, to wipe her eyes with the nearest dish rag. Her laugh had power—to lift a room, to make the people in it forget about everything for a moment. As long as I had her, I was a riot.

After Wayne made his entrance on the family stage, everything changed. Overnight, no one cared about my perfectly executed pratfalls or impressive presentations of my grandfather's favorite saying about determination—*Um gafanhoto foi no buraquinho e trouxe para fora de um grão de trigo.* ("A grasshopper went into a small hole and came out with a grain of wheat." It's more poetic in Portuguese, trust me on this.) Instead, I was met with a quick nod of the head and a distracted "Uh-huh," as everyone leaned in to coo at the swaddle in Dina's arms.

Trying harder was my only option. I rehearsed and rehearsed Tommy James and the Shondells' song "Hanky Panky," choreographing the number with two of the neighborhood girls as backup singers. We practiced the dances we saw on Saturday afternoon TV—the Monkey, the Frug, and the Watusi. Their arms oscillated double-time, legs kicked, asses wriggled.

"YOU'RE NOT DOING IT RIGHT!" I screamed, as their faces grew big with saucer eyes, trying not to cry.

When family, neighbors, and Paneen's friends—tough-looking men with knots of muscles wrestling under their T-shirts, and their skinny wives with lipstick the color of pink cake frosting—arrived carrying gigantic wrapped presents for Wayne, I ran to the front of the porch, sending the girls to the back.

I started: "My baby does the hanky panky!"

"Yeah, my baby does the hanky panky!" The girls repeated.

As I sang, I walked down the stairs, arms out, touching each step with my toe first like I'd seen on TV. They all just waved and hurried past, the women's high heels clicking Morse code on the pavement—"S-o-r-r-y, n-o-t t-o-d-a-y, D-a-v-i-d."

From then on, the house became suffocating. What had begun as just Barry and me, and then Wayne, crowded to include six more cousins on the Costa side. At the same time, I discovered that I had not only another pair of grandparents, Vu and Vo Leite, but a whole *other* set of cousins who lived near Boston. Every time a newly emigrated aunt or uncle visited, there was another damn kid in tow. By the end of the Great Exodus out of the Azores, I had a starting lineup of ten cousins.

The worst, though? TJ and Jeffery from Michigan. They belonged to my mother's brother Uncle Tony and his wife, Auntie Vi.

While I was lying on the parlor rug watching TV, someone kicked my shoe. I rolled over on my back. Both of them were standing over me. It must have been time for their summer visit, which I dreaded. We stared at each other for a long time.

"Hey," TJ said finally. Several years older than Jeff, who was my age, TJ was the leader. And the bully.

"Hey."

He made a scraping sound in the back of his throat. A small ball of spit formed on his lips and grew bigger, until it dangled like a pendulum over my face. Jeffery elbowed him to stop. I rolled out of the way in time, but it was TJ's way of making sure I knew they were back and he was in charge.

With them here, everything shifted. It felt like the apartment was squinting against the glare of the light, throwing everything into shadows as dark as my bedroom. The air sounded hollow. The more they wedged themselves between Barry and me, the more something swarmed inside. He'd already quit me for Brother, a smudge of a boy his own age with a huge bowling-ball head who lived on the other side of us. But when TJ and Jeffery descended, I was completely ignored, even at home. On top of it, they were all-boy. Where was the fun in mooning traffic on Davol Street, or getting into fistfights with the thugs over on Lindsey Street, or holding cats by their legs and dropping them from the porch to see if they landed on their feet?

What made it worse was both of them, especially TJ, possessed a radiating charm that protected them no matter what they did. The turds. And even though all three of them got into more trouble than Barry and I ever did, TJ and Jeffery were always spared The Strap—a beast with five long fingers that my grandfather had cut out of leather and could turn Barry's or my ass into two pink grapefruits with just a few wallops. Auntie Vi wasn't Portuguese, and that meant she was "progressive," as my mother called her, and didn't believe in doing things the old-fashioned way, which to my grandfather meant anything biblical.

I withdrew and grew sullen. Even Barry found it hard to rouse me after TJ and Jeffery had gone. Finally he dragged me outside, and we began wrestling near the mulberry bush my father had planted his first year in America, a sign of hope for the family and the future. As we steamrolled back and forth over each other, reason unlatched and fell away. Consequences didn't exist; Barry's size, twice mine, didn't register. Something ferocious unfurled to its full dimension, and I was suddenly feral. He had me pinned, straddling my chest, his knees digging into my upper arms. I bucked and fought harder, which made him laugh. It was because of that moment, his small lapse in attention, that I was able to hurtle myself at him.

I bit him on his chest. I bit harder, still harder, until I tasted the rustiness of blood. Barry started slapping me on the side of my head and then punching me, but I didn't let go. The pain felt good. It was my way of proving to him how much I loved him. I loved him enough to let myself be hurt because he was turning away from me. Would TJ and Jeffery let him do that? He yelled for Dina. I heard her running out of the house, the screen door slapping closed. She tried to position herself between Barry's fists and my head. She pulled me off. I hollered something long, hard, and guttural, then ran upstairs crying. My mother looked at me, terrified, and the wooden spoon in her hand dropped.

That's when she began screaming. "What the hell is wrong with you?" She grabbed my mouth and pried it open with her thumbs, looking inside for lost teeth or a missing tongue. I was sobbing too much to tell her.

Still wild with hurt, I jerked myself away and flung open our apartment door. "You fucking bastard!" I screamed, repeating the words Barry had hurled at me. I didn't know what they meant, but they stung and felt good in my mouth, like Red Hots. I ran down the stairs. "You're not my cousin anymore!" My grandfather poked his head out of his apartment and was about to lunge for me, but my mother dragged me back upstairs. In the parlor, I put my mouth on the carpet just above where I heard Dina yelling at Barry, and I continued screaming. I was heaving so heavily I began gagging on the dust from the rug.

My mother yanked me up on the couch and held my head in her hands, searching my face as if she didn't recognize me. I burrowed into her, and she held me hard, even when I tried to wriggle free, which I liked. In time, exhaustion claimed me. She led me, limp, to my room, and for once I was happy it was dark. I could hide in the dark. I looked at my Jesus candle and cried. Lying beside me, my mother ran her cool fingers through my hair, kissing my forehead until I fell asleep.

5

MOViNG ON UP

Pride radiated from my father like an aura as he stood at the edge of the road waiting for us. He wore his blue work uniform, with its knife-sharp creases and the white patch over his heart that spelled "Manny" in red cursive stitching. When we pulled onto the chewed-up ground of our new lot, he trotted to the car and opened the door for my mother, who was clutching an unopened bottle of wine. After a few steps she pitched back, losing her balance. "Manny!" she yelped, and grabbed harder on to the crook of his arm. They laughed as her high heels kept sinking deeper into the soft earth.

"Have everything, Son?" he asked over his shoulder. I held up a cross, a dollar bill, and a loaf of bread. He nodded toward the loaf: "No funny business, right?"

He was referring to the time Vu Costa and I had gone to a Portuguese bakery for a loaf of hot, crusty bread. Afterward, Vu swung by the market, the one with sawdust on the floor, big bins of dried

beans that felt like jewels running through my fingers, and planks of
bacalhau (salt cod), with its suffocating smell.

"*Queres vir comigo?*" Vu asked. Do you want to come with me?
I shook my head. The car was filled with a seductive yeasty scent.
While he shopped, I poked my finger through the bottom of the
loaf, pinched out a puff of cottony, warm bread, and popped it in my
mouth. Mistake. Widening the hole, I plucked out more, and more. I
pulled out as much as my stubby fingers could reach. At dinner that
night, when my father broke into the loaf, it cracked like an egg,
most of its guts missing. Me and Flickering Jesus had a lot to talk
about that night.

We made our way around piles of lumber and upended tree
stumps and over rocks to the corner of the wooden form, which was
filled with the cement that would hold up our living room. The ma-
sons climbed down from their trucks and leaned against the huge
wheels to smoke. When my mother looked back, her head low like
a bull's so they could see her eyes over her clip-on sunglasses, they
ditched the cigarettes, then cupped their hands in front of them. She
nodded her approval.

Holding on to my father to steady herself, she crouched down and
pressed the bread, bottle of wine, dollar bill, and cross into the wet
concrete. We clasped hands and lowered our heads. As my father said
something about God allowing our new house always to be filled
with food, drink, prosperity, and faith, his voice kept hitching, causing him to stop for a moment and clear his throat. Me, I squinted my
eyes and stared at the dollar, sending invisible rays into it so that it
would multiply and become a buried treasure.

When we were done, my father turned from the men and pulled
out a handkerchief, then wiped his eyes and mouth. My mother
leaned in, her fingers threaded through one of his belt loops. "You're
a good man, Manny Brown," I heard her whisper. That was her
nickname for him. Manny Brown. He nodded and kissed her, then
motioned for the men to finish pouring the cement and bury our offering.

A carpenter for Laflamme Brothers, my father built our house on Sharps Lot Road, in Swansea—on the other side of Mount Hope Bay—by himself. He did it in less than six months, working at nights and on weekends, all so I'd be able to start first grade in my new school, in our new town. The house, a modest ranch, was four miles but a lifetime away from Brownell Street. It was in the middle of the country, surrounded by farms and endless acres of woods, where there were no tenements or fractured sidewalks or women in worn housecoats screaming over fences.

We had to move, because in several years our old house was to be reclaimed by eminent domain and demolished to lay Route 79, a shortcut through the city to Boston. Vu sold my parents two half-acre parcels on the edge of a swath of land that ran the length of the street and deep into the woods. Over the years, Vu had slowly bought up land throughout Swansea and Somerset as investments, but after he'd seen the kind of craftsman my father turned out to be, he'd hoped they would develop it together. The two plots—one for us, one for me when I married and had children—was all my father was willing to take. My guess is he didn't want to be indebted. Even though my father was too big for The Strap, Vu had other ways to punish.

Throughout the summer and autumn of 1966, as my father erected the shell of the house—first as ribs of a giant living creature, then as skins of plywood, plaster, and wallpaper—I wandered through the rooms, running my hands along the walls, across faux-marble Formica countertops, around shiny doorknobs, over shellacked moldings, as if they were Braille telling me of the new exalted life that awaited. This was nothing like our tenement. Everything was new, and in the air hung the sweet smell of sawdust, the smell of progress and promise, which I have forever associated with my father. And we would live alone.

By November, we had a gigantic, gleaming kitchen; a dining room; three bedrooms; a living room; and our own bathroom, with a tub and a shower and a shiny faucet that looked like the stick shift in one of Paneen's stock cars. Downstairs my mother led me around the bright, freshly poured concrete basement. "Over here," she said, unfurling her hand toward the area just left of the stairs, "will be my kitchen." Every self-respecting Portuguese mother has a working kitchen in her basement, so the show kitchen upstairs never gets dirty. It's the cooking equivalent of plastic slipcovers. "And over there will be Daddy's workshop, and in the other corner will be the washer and dryer."

"Where's *my* space?" I whined.

"Where would you like it to be?" she asked, sitting down on the stairs and pulling me between her legs, one step below. I leaned back against her chest and placed my elbows on her thighs as I surveyed my new kingdom.

"There," I said, pointing to the right.

"And there it will be." She kissed the top of my head and led me up the still banister-less stairs.

My bedroom was as big as my ambition. Long windows that were too high for me to look out of flanked two walls, but I remember my father saying something about the southern light being good for me, and that's why he put me in the back of the house. My room would never be dark again. Earlier in the week, my father had finished putting up the wallpaper—an antique-cars pattern my mother had let me pick out of a giant storybook of designs. Alone in my empty room, I took a pencil and wrote on the arc of some of the black tires in slivery letters that could only be seen if they caught the glare from my father's work light. *This is my room. This is my room. This is my room.* I wanted the walls to absorb me. I wanted to belong to this home, this pristine beginning.

Our new life was delivered unassembled and wrapped in plastic. The furniture was upholstered in champagne, tan, and a staggering number of beiges (my mother's favorite color), plus mustards, browns, oranges, and umbers—raw and burnt. Big men with shirtsleeves rolled up over their muscles and tattoos carried a low couch, a club chair, and an upholstered rocker with a base that looked like something out of *The Jetsons* into the living room. The coffee table was even lower and almost twice as long as I was tall; I lay on it to check. "Scandinavian design," the man at Stafford Furniture had boasted to my parents. When the moving men weren't looking, I stuck my nose in the carpets and breathed in their synthetic smell— validation of our newly minted status.

We didn't have a kitchen table. Instead, my father built a jazzy snack bar, like the kind at Al Mac's Diner. He and I would sit on one side, my mother on the other, the side toward the kitchen, and for years I'd imagine I was a bored movie star sitting at some restaurant, waiting for my fried eggs or French toast before I began filming for the day.

A white ranch with brown shutters and new plantings in the front yard looked like the kind of house people on TV and in magazines lived in. And Sunday suppers in that kind of house meant pot roast or tuna-noodle casserole or chicken à la king (or, if someone had been a very, very good boy, Manwiches). The families in those houses weren't eating *carne assada* or salt cod—that I was sure about. And, I pleaded with God, neither were my neighbors. To make sure, I jumped on my new bike, the one with the banana seat and high-rise handlebars, and rode up and down the street, sussing out the names on the mailboxes. Freeborn. Goode. Jennings. Chase. *Sweet*. Only Miranda, an old farmer whose skin matched my mother's burnt umber drapes, was Portuguese. He and his wife didn't have any kids my age, so I could ignore them. "We live in the suburbs now," my mother told me, standing on a chair to hang a sunburst clock in the dining room. I looked up the word in my dictionary. I was pleased.

Even though we weren't far from our old Portuguese neighborhood and its markets, my mother loosened her grip on our food. She began shopping at supermarkets that had entire aisles devoted to crackers and cheese-in-a-can, snack bars with waitresses who stuck pencils in their hair, and bakeries that sold donuts and crullers and Fourth of July cakes.

"Hey, Banana, c'mere and help me!" she'd shout every Friday afternoon. I'd tear down the hallway and carry grocery bags in from her car, digging through them to look for booty. As soon as I'd pull out a box of chocolate Pop-Tarts, Chicken in a Biskit crackers, Hostess cupcakes, or Pepperidge Farm apple turnovers, my mother would yank it out of my hand and hold it way over my head.

"No," she'd say as I jumped up. "Not until after supper." And then began our pre-dinner dance.

"Please?"

"No." Her lips overemphasizing the word as if I were deaf.

"But you don't understand, I'm starving."

"Then have some fruit." Now it was my turn to see if *she* had an axe sticking out of the back of her head.

In time, oatmeal and some kind of horrid hot white mush were swapped for cold cereal for breakfast. I propped a box of Cap'n Crunch or Apple Jacks or Cocoa Puffs in front of me and read the package again and again and never got bored. Through it all, my favorite breakfast was still peanut butter and banana on toast. Waiting for me every morning, when I pulled out the beige pleather stool from the snack bar, was a banana with my mom's ornate cursive on it. Depending on what was happening that day, she'd written, "Do well on your test!" or "Don't forget to take out the trash!" or "Happy birthday!" (My mother believes in the power of exclamation marks.) Regardless of the message of the day, it always said, "We love you!" on one end, and "God bless!" on the other. To make the breakfast, she'd smear Skippy peanut butter on hot slices of toast, carefully cut the banana crosswise, position both halves on one slice, and cover them with a second.

"Ready?" she'd ask, sliding the sandwich across the counter to me. I'd nod, then smoosh it with my palm. I couldn't eat it if it wasn't smashed.

But for years, whenever my father's family invaded from Boston for Sunday lunch—what we called "dinner"—everything slipped back, and our yard turned into an old-fashioned Portuguese *festa*. Aunts opened the trunks of their cars and enlisted husbands and kids to carry pots, pans, Tupperware, bags, and boxes. *"Toma cuidado!"* they screamed. *"Ay, 'pa! Toma cuidado!"* as small kids half the size of the pots they carried lurched their way to the grape arbor my father had built in the backyard. Underneath, two or three tables were pushed together, mismatched plastic tablecloths billowed smooth over them. My mother, Vo Costa and Vo Leite, and my four Boston aunts tried to outdo one another. My mother opened with her kale soup, which I passed on for obvious reasons; Aunt Irene countered with her livid purple octopus stew, suction cups and all, which I also passed on, for even more obvious reasons. Vo Costa put her pink chicken soup up for contention. No one knows what made it pink—paprika, a blush of wine, the reflection from the pink flowers on the bowl? It was bursting with shredded chicken, hunks of potatoes, and rice that looked like Xs, the grains having split from soaking up so much broth. It was so good, my cousin Mark had eaten thirteen bowls one Sunday. It was my favorite, too, and Vo knew it. *"Coma mais, querido,"* she said. Eat more, sweetheart. And as I held up my bowl for seconds like Oliver Twist, I looked over at my mother, her *veneta* idling.

Next, the women carried platters piled with boiled salt cod and roast pork, chicken, and beef that had been rubbed with *pimenta moída*, a salty, mildly hot pepper paste, through the backyard. Their house slippers slapped against their feet, sounding like yapping dogs as they rushed to beat one another to the table. They'd bend over, bosoms squashing against my head as they placed their dishes in the middle of us all with a loud fanfare. *Chouriço, linguiça,* and *morçela* (the trinity of sausage in our family: pork, spicier pork, and blood, respectively) usually anchored one end of the table. Bowls of rice the color of terra-cotta from the sausage drippings, tender potatoes blushing from the wine they were roasted in, and my mother's famous baked beans held down the other end. Everywhere were baskets of *papo se-*

cos, crusty rolls that looked like two ass cheeks of a baby. Salad was conspicuously missing; my people don't eat salad.

With all twenty-one of us reaching over one another, the women would crouch down beside us kids, the seams of their dresses screaming over the expanse of their thighs, urging us to try their specialties. Beneath the table, Paneen would tip the big green gallon jug of wine into a *Flintstones* jelly glass and pass it down to Barry and me, the two oldest. The conversation floated on the wind—loud and gregarious— sounding like a boxing match to anyone whose last name didn't end in a vowel.

6

SANTA CLAUS iS A HEAVY BREATHER

That filthy thing is not going up in *this* house." My mother stood at the top of the basement stairs, a washrag in hand, blocking my father's way. She was pointing to the box he was hauling up from the basement. "Deluxe Aluminum Christmas Tree Set," it read along its side. It was early December, and we'd been in the house for about a month. The scents of Glade Evergreen and new shower curtain mingled in the air.

"Well, what am I supposed to do with it, Elvira?"

"Throw it out for all I care, Manny Brown."

Although I was as eager as my mother to ditch any evidence of our previous life—for different reasons: she, cleanliness, I, class—I was oddly nostalgic for that old tree. I knew some kids in school whose families wore matching reindeer sweaters while threading strands of cranberries and popcorn to hang on a real tree. But I didn't care. My fake tree had frilly silver spikes for branches, with big silver pom-poms on the ends, that stuck out from a silver-painted pole. A creaking color wheel turned the tree lurid colors. When we had lived on Brownell, I'd wriggle underneath; it was like being inside a giant Christmas snow globe. The needles sparkled and fluttered from the heat of the radiator. As the tree turned from green to blue to yellow to red, I imagined days were passing in fast motion, hurtling me closer to the night Santa Claus would visit us.

At the top of the stairs, I pushed past my mother, who was still blocking my father. "Can I have the color wheel?" I asked him. "Please, please, please?"

"Fine," he said, handing it to me, "but I don't want to trip over this thing in the basement."

That weekend, a formidable new seven-foot artificial tree stood in the bow window. My mother had spent all afternoon punctuating it with a million lights and satin balls, "because they're so much prettier than those old glass ones, don't you think?" The secret to a gorgeous tree, she said as she stood back surveying her work, was to plunge lots of lights deep inside to give it depth. Her goal, I eventually figured out, was to leave no green showing—anywhere. *Holidays* is what she called those few naked spots of fake needles, "and holidays are for lazy people!" To fix that, she unplugged the Christmas lights and walked around the tree, inspecting. Every once in a while, she'd shove in a small bit of gold garland to cover a bald spot. When she was done, the tree was as shiny and glittery as our old one, and I loved it.

"Son, put your boots on," my father said when we were done decorating. My mother flicked off the room lights, and we tromped through the snow to the front of the house. The tree took up most of the window and was so bright, I could see the beach mural on the wall behind the couch. To the right of the porch, lit by a spotlight, was a giant picture of a waving Santa my mother had painted on a sheet of plywood. The midget shrubs my father had planted that summer were speckled with outdoor lights, making them look in all that snow like scoops of vanilla ice cream with rainbow jimmies on top.

"And you're *sure* Santa will find us?"

"Banana, you could see this from outer space," my mother said. I looked up the street to see if we were being outshone by anyone. She was probably right.

Every night leading up to Christmas, I'd switch on the color wheel in my room; it was my holiday decoration, along with the Advent calendar taped to my door. From a box in the closet, I'd fish out the microphone from my parents' old reel-to-reel tape recorder. I'd stand with my back to the light and watch my shadow as the wall undulated red, then green, then blue, then yellow. "Ladies and gentlemen . . . Sonny and Cher!" I took a deep breath, turned around, and began swaying, eyes closed, as I mouthed "I Got You Babe," pretending I was starring in my own Christmas TV special.

As my room whirled in fun-house colors, I heard something. I couldn't tell where it was coming from, so I cocked my ear toward the door to hear if it was either of my parents, but they were watching TV. I turned off the wheel, which wheezed to a silence. There it was again. Heavy breathing. Distinct heavy breathing, like the room was gasping for air. I wanted to bolt, but I was supposed to be asleep. Fear began snaking up my spine. *Maybe it's me,* I thought, and I held my breath, but after several seconds I heard it again. I flew into the den.

"What's the matter?" my father asked.

I began crying. "Someone's in my room."

He jumped up and started for the kitchen, where he had a baseball bat behind the door. As I explained I'd heard breathing, he stopped and looked at my mother.

"C'mere, sweetheart." She gathered me into her lap on her Harvest Gold La-Z-Boy. "It's a new house," she said softly. "You're just not used to the sounds, that's all."

I leaned back and searched her face. She was a practical joker. Maybe she'd put something in the room, like a tape recording of her breathing. She liked to do things like that, same as Vu Costa did, to have that *gotcha* moment—later apologizing through squeaks of laughter. But there were only smiles.

My father put out his hand for me to take it. "Let's go check to-gether, Son." Back in my room, we sat on the bed. I put my head in his lap, listening.

After several minutes: "See? Nothing." He lifted the covers, and I crawled in, unconvinced.

"Dad banse."

"God bless you, Son."

"Don't close the door!"

"I won't."

In the dark, it was just me and Jesus, with his big heart flickering on top of my bureau. When the breathing started again, I put my fingers in my ears and prayed to him something fierce, lips moving nonstop until I fell asleep.

I'm not sure how long after, or how many times, but I heard it again. In my room, the bathroom, the hallway. While I was taking my bath, I'd slide under the water to blot it out. *New-house sounds*, I kept repeating, *new-house sounds*. It could be the furnace or the ra-diators, my father had told me. At night I crept down to the laundry, which is below my room, and waited. The furnace roared to life, but it wasn't the same sound. There was pinging and gurgling, but no breathing.

Years later, I jabbed a tack through these experiences and pinned them to the middle of some bulletin board in my head, pointing to them as the beginning of unusual behaviors. My Ground Zero of Lu-nacy. But I was wrong. The timeline of strange behaviors stretched back even earlier—to three or four, maybe. The way my mother and godmother described it, the clock on *Captain Kangaroo*, with its ogling eyes and chomping mouth, always sent me toddling into their thighs, screaming, "Cloxsh! Cloxsh!" I was inconsolable. Once, they said, a distant relation whom I didn't recognize visited Vu and Vo on Brownell Street, and I was so spooked, I clawed up my father to burrow in his arms. When the man didn't leave, I let loose a shrill blast so unremitting, he slunk out the door backward, apologizing. Later, when I was five or six, angry traffic jams, especially on days so blindingly hot the chrome around the windows left welts on my arms, had me cowering in the footwell behind my father as he drove, pleading for him to get us home. *He's a sensitive kid,* I heard often. *He'll grow out of it,* they all told each other. *Give him time.*

Yes, time is all I need, I told myself. *Time.*

7

TREAD LiGHTLY, MR. GOODE

Mr. Goode, our neighbor down the street, was sprawled, legs apart, on a low lawn chair in his backyard. He kept glancing at the screen door of the kitchen, where Mrs. Goode was making dinner, and then back at me. Dommie Goode and I were playing yard darts or something. Mr. Goode didn't think much of his son; you could see that. Dommie was small for his age. We were both about ten, but I was at least a head taller. Whenever any of us kids played in their yard, which we all hated, Mr. Goode would call Dommie an "idiot," or "stupid," or "pathetic." Dommie would mutter, "Sorry," and try to catch better or throw harder or run without falling.

"Don't listen to your father, Dommie," Mrs. Goode would shout from the window. Mrs. Goode never came out of the house. "You're doing just fine."

Mr. Goode was fiddling with the handle of a broken Wiffle bat; the other part had been flung into the weeds, forgotten. When Dommie wasn't looking, he held the bat handle at his crotch and waggled

it at me and smiled, jerking his head toward the slanted metal bulk-
head that led into the basement.

My face burned, and I ran to the other side of the yard. At the
same time, something inside wanted me to glance back, to see if he
was looking. I liked the attention. Every time I did look over, he'd
waggle the bat and nudge his chin toward the basement door. How a
ten-year-old knows things like this is beyond me now, but back then I
knew exactly what he wanted. I was terrified and disgusted. But I was
also curious, intrigued.

"Dommie, time for dinner. Say goodbye."

"Bye," I said to Dommie as he skulked up the porch stairs, and
I began walking home. When I passed Mr. Goode, he grabbed my
arm and pulled me close to his mouth. His lips were on my ear. "It's
eight inches," he whispered. Another waggle. I froze. He took my
hesitation as consent and led me by the hand behind the house, away
from the kitchen window. "I have a present for you, Dave," he added.
"Come on, come to the basement." I waffled. "Please? You'll like it. I
promise." I drew closer.

He lifted one of the metal doors, and I followed him down and
into a dark corner of the mildewy cellar. My heart was pounding
and I almost ran, but he seemed to know something about me, and I
wanted to know what that was.

"I'll be right back." He took the stairs two at a time, and I heard
him tell Mrs. Goode he had to get something in the basement. When
he came back, I felt a heavy sense of disappointment. He had nothing
for me.

Then he fished himself out of his pants, and I couldn't look away.
I had to see. I felt no shame at that moment, just electric curiosity.
His was different from mine. It was hard and purple and big, but one
thing was for sure: It was nowhere near the size of the handle of that
baseball bat.

"Do you want to touch it?"

"No!" I clutched. But I did, so much. I remembered Paneen and
the smoke curls of hair coming out of his jeans. Mr. Goode had the

same thing, and I finally understood where those curls started, and what they were lapping at.

"Well, look what I've got!" His voice was warm brandy. He pulled a magazine out from the back of his pants and flipped it open. Inside were naked boys and girls, not much older than me, playing shuffleboard. Suddenly I felt as if I'd been slapped in the back of my head by my mother. *This is wrong. This is very wrong.*

"G'head," he pleaded. "Touch it."

Somehow I understood that even though he was much bigger and older than me, I was in control. He wanted something from *me*. He needed *me*. And I *knew* that he would never hurt me because of the trouble I could get him into.

"I really want to touch it, Mr. Goode," I said with the Art of the Straight Face. "I just have to see if my father's van is in the driveway, because if it is I have to go and have dinner."

"Hurry, go check."

At the top of the stairs, I turned around. He was covering himself with the magazine, his pants ringing his ankles. He looked in pain, almost like he was ready to cry. "I'll be right back, I promise." Once I cleared the corner of the house, I ran home as fast as I could. My father wasn't there yet, but that wasn't why I bolted. I ran because I wanted to stay.

I went back to their house only one more time. Mr. Goode had a friend over, and they were sitting at the kitchen table. Between them was a forest of empty beer bottles.

"He's out with Mrs. Goode," he said when I asked after Dommie. "Do you want to wait and come watch TV with us in the bedroom?" The other man smiled at me, but his red eyes seemed to focus on the cabinets behind me.

"Mr. Goode, my father wants me to tell you that you better tread lightly," I lied to him. *Tread lightly* was a phrase my mother used, and it always made people back off. It was as if a window shade had juddered up in front of his face. His eyes grew wide, and his smirk melted. He stood up and walked to the door.

"Get out," he said, holding the door open for me.

"When is . . ."

"GET OUT!"

When I reached the door, I turned around to see the other man standing and unsteadily stuffing his cigarettes and matches in his pocket. He stumbled out the front door and skidded out of the driveway in his car, shooting gravel and dirt everywhere, before I even reached the street.

I never told my parents. How could I? I was titillated and intrigued. I wanted to see everything, to touch everything. Plus, I was hounded by guilt. I knew that what I did was wrong, a sin I was supposed to confess to Father Fraga, who would know exactly who I was even though the confessional was supposed to be anonymous. No, I couldn't admit this to him or anyone. Ever. If I'd told my father, he would have killed Mr. Goode right there. Smashed his skull with the baseball bat he kept behind the kitchen door.

8

i'M MELTiNG

Tongues of fire lick up the woman's skirt, insistent and vulgar. In no time the flames jump to her blouse and devour the filigree ringing her neckline, engulfing her face in a great and sudden whoosh. Her skin cracks and blisters. I watch, immobile, as burnt patches slough off, falling from her jaw, melted. I search for a way out, but I'm blocked. An intense heat suddenly combusts in the middle of my chest and spreads to my face, arms, and legs. As my heart hammers, I begin seeing pulsing white spots in the dark, keeping time. A metallic taste corkscrews its way up my esophagus and explodes in my mouth. *I have to get out of here.* I'm panting for air. Looking over again, I watch the woman's cheekbones, minutes before so lovely and round, collapse into themselves. She's swallowed up now. Just then, her eyes loll out of their sockets. Her head, blackened, falls onto her chest.

Tripping over bodies, I run.

"Where are you going?" Brian Davis whispered as I pushed past him and his brother, Jeff.

Think fast. Think calm. "The bathroom."

Brian, who was also in sixth grade, had invited me that week to go to the movies on Saturday. At the time, it had seemed like a good idea. That is, before I realized it was a horror flick—projected in resplendent 3-D.

I heaved open the doors. The afternoon light slammed into my eyes. The lobby smelled of popcorn and rancid butter. Behind the counter a pimply-faced teenager hunched over a book. She looked up, indifferent by my sudden and frantic appearance in the middle of the movie.

I blinked at her as she waited for me to say something. "Pay phone?"

She pointed to the stairs. I turned and faced the promotional poster. "House of Wax" dripped across the bottom in big red and orange letters. "3-D" was even larger at the top. I ripped the cardboard glasses from my face and stuffed them into my pocket.

"Ma?" I said into the pay phone.

"What's the matter?" It was her panicky voice. "Why aren't you in the movie?"

"Uh, nothing," I stumbled. "I . . . just, wanted to say hi."

"Well, hi. Now get back in the movie." And she hung up.

To stall for time, I scanned the candy counter with a deep seriousness, the same kind of look I've seen hanging on my father's face when he buys a car or tries to talk cemetery plots with my mother. *I look weird. I know I look weird. She can tell I look weird.* Rows of shiny boxes of Raisinets, Milk Duds, Snow Caps, and Red Hots. Any other day and I could've knocked back one, maybe two, easy. I couldn't have been less hungry. Instead I ordered an orange soda and sipped it slowly. I felt conspicuous, exposed.

Small talk. "How long have you worked here?" I asked, or something like that, but didn't hear the answer. Although I was looking at the girl, nodding at the right places to mimic conversation, the movie looped, flickering somewhere in the space between us: bodies burn-

ing, eyes falling out, skin sluicing, and the heat reignited in my chest.
What *is* that? I dug the heel of my hand in hard and rubbed, as if it
were indigestion. No relief. *Is this a heart attack? Can kids have heart
attacks?* Then catapulted again, this time through the front doors.
Pacing in tight tormented circles on the sidewalk, trying to calm myself, did nothing.

Five minutes. Eight minutes. Ten minutes. Any longer and I risked
being mercilessly teased, so I headed back inside. Slipping on the paper glasses, I slouched down in my seat and closed my eyes for the
rest of the movie, but the images didn't stop.

As the show let out, Mrs. Davis was sitting out front in her idling
car. When she saw us, she leaned over the seat and popped open the
back passenger door.

"Hurry up before I get a ticket."

I let Brian and Jeff pile in first. I needed to be near the door; it felt
safe. As we headed down Pleasant Street, I couldn't shake the feeling of being outside of myself, floating. Time pulled and stretched
but never budged. The movements of the others slowed to blurred
smudges. My eyelids closed and opened over what felt like minutes.
Sound folded in on itself, muffled.

". . . Dave? . . . Dave?" someone called. It was Mrs. Davis; at least
I think it was. My head seemed to take hours to crane up to look into
the rearview mirror. She was looking back at me. *What is she saying?*
I shook my head, and the world righted itself for a moment. "Did you
like the movie?"

I nodded.

At the mention of the movie, my guts turned into snakes, knotting themselves just below my rib cage. If I could have plunged my
fist into my belly, like those psychic surgeons I'd heard about in Mex-
ico, and ripped them out, I would have. Anything to stop it. I was
terrified that if I didn't clench, I would shit and piss myself right there
in the backseat. Outside the window, people, buildings, cars whizzed
by in soft focus, bleeding, melting. *Melting.* I saw the faces again. The

snakes lurched. I grabbed the door handle. *What? And fling yourself into the street?* I didn't want out of the car; I wanted out of me. To squeeze through my pores and no longer inhabit skin.

Mrs. Davis sailed up Sharps Lot Road and looped into our horse-shoe driveway. "See ya Monday," I said, trying to act as normal as I could, but it sounded like an actor reading a line.

"How was the movie?" my mother asked.

"Fine." I walked through the kitchen, without my usual lifting of pot lids to see what was for dinner. I didn't want her to see me, because she'd be able to tell something was wrong.

"Just 'fine'?"

"Yeah," I said, continuing down the hall.

"Come back here, mister." I took a deep breath and turned around. "What?"

"Are you okay?" She squinted, looking for clues.

"Yeah."

"Are you sure?"

"YES!"

"Well, if you're so okay, why did you call me from the movies?"

"I told you, I just wanted to say hi." She didn't believe me.

At dinner I pushed my food around my plate. My parents talked, but they sounded a million miles away as I scanned my body for any of those electrical shorts still sparking inside. *What was that, any-way? Some kind of reaction? But to what?* When they were done eating, my mother looked at my still-full plate. She grabbed it, whacked it against the trash bin so the food would slide off, and then plunged it into the sink full of water, saying nothing.

Afterward, I lay on the floor in front of the TV. Rusty, a stray dog we had adopted, always seemed to sense when I was in pain. He licked my face, then grunted himself down along my back. He felt good and safe and sure. Edith Bunker flickered on the screen. People laughed; I didn't see why. Next was Sandy Duncan. Nothing. By the time Mary Tyler Moore aired, something had begun ebbing, pulling with it those crazy detonations and that frightening sense of disconnection, and I grew sleepy. *I will be okay. I will be okay.* When I started awake, my parents were dead away in their La-Z-Boys, and my insides were under siege again. "It," whatever it was, was happening again, and a scream rocketed up from somewhere behind my belly button.

"Ma!"

She shot up, cross-eyed and half-conscious. "What's . . . what's . . . the matter?"

"I don't know. Something's happening to me."

"Are you hurt? What's the matter? WHAT'S THE MATTER?!" Her voice grew shrill with panic, which only scared me more and woke my father.

I explained how there was this explosion of heat in my chest, how I'd had to run out of the theater, that I never saw the rest of the movie, even though I told Brian I did, and that it was happening again, now, here, on the floor, right this very minute.

"Do you need to go to the emergency room?" She patted my body, as if she could find the source of my pain.

"I don't know." I looked at my father. "Maybe?"

"Elvira . . . ," he said, trying to defuse the situation.

"It could be a heart attack, you don't know, Manny."

I knew it. I knew I was having a heart attack.

"Son, come on, let's go to bed," my father said, leading me to my room. "I promise you'll feel better in the morning."

I suddenly ached for the glow of my Jesus candle, but I was eleven, and I'd nixed it years before. "Ma, can you put a night-light in here?"

"Of course, sweetheart." She waved my father to get the one from the kitchen. She sat on the bed and rubbed my chest. "Does it hurt now?" I didn't know how to explain that it wasn't pain I was feeling. It was something far worse.

As they were about to leave, I asked my father to sleep with me. He looked at my mother. I could tell he was evaluating the seriousness of the situation. "Please, Daddy, I'm scared."

"Okay, Son."

Only sleep didn't come. I lay there watching my father's chest rise and fall. When I felt the fear ratcheting up, I placed my hand on his rib cage and tried to breathe like him. He looked so peaceful, so at rest, I thought I could feel that way, too, if I could only mimic him. The next night was the same, and the one after that.

Dave's afraid of a movie," Brian Davis said at our lunch table at school, his voice worming into my fear.

"I am *not!*"

"Yes, you are. Your mother called my mother and told her." That was it. At the mention of mothers, taunts rippled around the table. The kids on the far end stood up and leaned in, trying to get in on the action. They wagged their heads at me, making baby talk and pretending to cry. I grabbed my plate, a hard plastic thing covered in institutional-smelling food, and chucked it as hard as I could. It missed everyone and went scudding across the cafeteria floor. I picked up my tray and was about to whale on someone when Mr. Souza, who had been my fourth-grade teacher, grabbed me under my arms and yanked me out of the folding metal table. I struggled against him, kicking the table and anyone I could reach. The room fell quiet.

"Go to hell, you bastards!" echoed off the walls.

Everyone watched, mouths hanging, as Mr. Souza dragged me behind him like a broken kite, crashing through the cafeteria doors, and deposited me onto the lobby's wide stairs. His mammoth jaw was jammed to the side, like it always was when he was angry. I explained to him through sobs what had happened, and his face softened. "It's okay," he said. He motioned with his head. "Go on, go out to recess."

No one bothered me the rest of the day. Even Billy Meechan, who tormented me endlessly, and had once tackled me so hard on the asphalt that one of the teachers had to rush me to the nurse for huge gashes in my elbow and knee, left me alone. I spent recess by myself, watching from the edge of the playground, near the woods. Knots of kids swelled and shrank as they ran shrieking across the yard. Big

red rubber balls ricocheted off heads, backs, legs, as some sixth graders played dodgeball. Choruses of the syncopated "Miss Mary Mack,
Mack, Mack, all dressed in black, black, black" flitted in the wind. I
stood there wringing my hands and begging God to fix me.

I've got a surprise for you!" my mother said after school a few weeks
later.

"We're not going to a movie, are we?" It was more a verbal projec-
tile than a question. I'd overheard my father saying the best way for
me to get past this was to see *House of Wax* again and again until it
carried no emotional charge.

"No. We're going to lunch." I must have looked at her cockeyed,
because she put her hand on her hip. *"Lunch,"* she repeated. "You
know, what you eat in the afternoon, Banana?"

"I know what lunch means, Ma." My confusion was over the fact
that until that moment, my family had never gone to a sit-down restaurant together. My father liked only Portuguese food, and there
was no reason to go to a Portuguese restaurant when, as he liked to
say, "I have the best Portuguese *cozinheira* right here." And with that
he'd usually wrangle her in a hug, and she'd laugh, then sashay out of
his grip, slapping his hands in mock protest saying, "Manny, stop it!"

She pulled up to China Village, in nearby Somerset. Inside, she
clasped her purse to her chest and peered through the elaborately
carved gold and red filigree. Not a soul eating. Crossing that archway
meant being caught up in a different culture, one that used chopsticks and smelled divinely of fried foods. No matter how bad I felt, I
wasn't about to pass that up. I stepped into the room so that the lone
waitress could see us before my mother lost her nerve.

Up until then, the only Chinese food I'd ever eaten was chow-
mein sandwiches Dina had picked up at the joint on Brightman
Street. They were pillowy hamburger buns filled with noodles (not
the long, supple ones I had years later, but short, crisp twigs) that
were mixed into a brown, snotty-looking sauce studded with hunks

of celery and onion and specks of ground pork or, if someone was willing to spring for it, shrimp. Barry and I would howl as we dug into the sack, because they were so hot. Even the sandwich wrappers were damp and shapeless because of the steam. I could pack away two, easily.

My mother and I slid into a red booth at the rear wall of the restaurant. She kept tugging her coat closed and smoothing the side of her hair.

The bored waitress handed us scuffed plastic-covered menus. My mother let me get a pupu platter, even though neither of us was sure what it was. I tittered at the name when I ordered it. "And can I have chopsticks?" A short time later, the waitress returned with what looked like a lazy Susan and two plates. My mother started to protest, but gave in and let the waitress slide a plate in front of her. I spun the platter like a roulette wheel, waiting for luck to tell me what fried wonder to eat first. I stabbed a crispy wonton with a chopstick and dunked it in something called duck sauce. It was sweet and fruity, but mostly sweet, and the wonton crackled, then gave way to a soft belly of some kind of marvelous meat.

"Son," she said, leaning in.

"Uh-huh?" I skewered another batter-coated, deep-fried bite.

"Do you think you can tell me what's going on?"

"I don't know," I said, reaching for another. "I'm just scared all the time."

"Scared of what, though?"

"Everything."

"What do you mean, *everything*?" A little *veneta* began etching her voice.

I confessed to her that I had stopped watching the news. Everything from Richard Nixon, with his enormous hound-dog face, to the eviscerating gunfire of the Vietnam War terrified me. As far as books, I refused to read anything unless it was for school.

"Music, though, is the worst." I told her how the sounds could drag me under, as if the notes were weights attached to my feet. I couldn't listen to the dirgelike "A Horse with No Name," or Roberta Flack's mournful "The First Time Ever I Saw Your Face," two songs that looped endlessly that spring, without setting off a magazine round of panic. She listened quietly, shredding her paper napkin. Every once in a while she nodded, or lifted her head to speak, then stopped herself.

We sat for a long time in silence, until I pushed my plate away.

"Do you want to take this home?" My mother pointed to the mostly uneaten platter. I shook my head. She said something about my eyes being bigger than my belly.

"Can I have these, though?" I asked, holding up the chopsticks. She nodded, then motioned for the waitress and pulled out her wallet.

While my mother's attempt at a solution was communication, my father's attempts were all action, and since that required manual labor and didn't include food, I was predisposed not to like them. On Saturdays and on the occasional weeknight, he took me along on some of the carpentry jobs he did on the side: building new bathrooms, refinishing basements, adding decks that overlooked pools. I stood alongside him, a lump of flesh, handing him nails, fetching tools, holding two-by-fours steady while he sawed. He tried to engage me by making me think logically—at my best, something I wasn't very good at—and then think logically *backward*. From the finished project to the last step to the step before that, and so on, until finally we backed into that singular step that would begin this chain reaction, so that I could understand what needed to be done first.

"Imagine it's like a movie going in reverse," he said, encouraging me. Pointing to a sink still in its crate, or a wall of studs, or a sliding glass door with a six-foot drop on the other side where stairs should be: "What's the *first* thing we need to do here?"

"I don't know."

"Think!" He said it as if by his simply ordering me, the neurons in my brain would suddenly clasp tendrils on command, making a chain of impulses that would thread itself through my head, into my mouth, along my tongue, and out would come the answer.

"I don't know!" I shouted.

"*Ay, paciência,*" he hissed under his breath. Translation: Give me patience. It's not that my father wasn't patient with me; he was. More so than my mother, actually. He was just unable to understand how a life could come to a slamming halt, drained of all enthusiasm and color; I was the walking dead, muscle and skin hanging on bones but no longer with a recognizable personality or purpose. What made it worse for him was he was ripped up inside because he, the one man who was supposed to protect me from harm, couldn't.

"Can I wait in the van?" I said flatly. He jerked his head in the direction of the street as if to say, *Go.*

Sitting there, I watched fat raindrops splotch the windshield. They created, for just a moment, glassy-eye reflections of streetlamps, red taillights, lampposts, before bleeding down the window. Every once in a while, I turned on the ignition so the wipers would smear them away, but more rushed to take their places. There was something so incalculably sad about those winking, starbursted raindrops. Their rhythm thudding on the van's roof was chilling. It heightened, orchestrally, my sense of isolation. I was alone. My mother couldn't help me; my father was at a loss.

Eventually, my parents called Dr. Herring, our family physician. I didn't like him much. He treated everything as minor. Everything, that is, except my weight. Until then, I'd always considered myself a three-piece Kentucky Fried Chicken dinner away from husky (which to Portuguese mothers, grandmothers, and aunts translated as "too thin"). Dr. Herring, on the other hand, preferred to describe me as standing on the threshold of fat. He liked to point to a weight/height chart on the wall that had a rainbow curving from the lower left to the upper right. "Normal" cut a swath of cheery green through the middle. Above, in yellow, was "overweight," and above that, in ambulance red, was "obese." Every time I stepped on the scale, he'd plot my weight and height and tap the intersection—which always fell just north into yellow—then make little *tsk* sounds, as if his tongue were wearing tap shoes. This time, though, he nodded his surprise. I'd dropped several pounds from having lost my appetite.

After I explained to him what had happened, he leaned against the metal cabinet in his office and shook his head in exasperation.

"These movies," he said to my father. "I've gotten more calls about *Mark of the Devil* in the past few weeks than any movie in years." *Mark of the Devil* was playing about the same time as *House of Wax*. Barry had seen it and loved to terrify me by describing how they ripped out a woman's tongue with a pair of pliers.

"But it's been more than a month," I said. "It hasn't stopped. I'm scared all the time."

He looked at me a long while, then up to my father, and sighed. "Well, I can prescribe a tranquilizer, if you want."

"A *tranquilizer?*" my father asked, making some sort of a defensive move toward me.

I didn't understand their exchange at the time, because I didn't know Dr. Herring and my father had a long, hard history with tranquilizers. It had started a few years after my father came to this country. He felt restless, so he went to a doctor who, after hearing him out, looked him in the eye and said, "Manny, your problem is you can't handle the pace of America." Believing in the power and authority of medicine, especially in his new country, he accepted the doctor's diagnosis and the prescription he handed him for phenobarbital. In time, though, he started suffering from a jackhammering heart and skipping beats. "You're just too nervous, Manny"—and more medication was prescribed. This time, Librium. When he found he couldn't go to work without the security of them stashed in his lunch box, my father finally went to Dr. Herring, who kept him on the drugs for two more years but advised that he give up caffeine. By the end, my father says, he was so crippled with heart problems and nervousness that one day he grabbed the bottles of pills, walked out behind the house he was building, and, howling like a wounded animal, flung them into the woods. It took more than a year, but his heart found peace. Few, including Dr. Herring, believed the tranquilizers were his problem. My father knew different.

What I *did* understand, sitting in Dr. Herring's office, was that tranquilizers were pills Hollywood actresses and mothers with too many children took. Dina and the Sisterhood had talked about it. Judy Garland, they said, took them, and she was dead.

"I'm only eleven," I said. He shrugged as if to say, *So?*

"Come on, Son." My father cupped his arm around my shoulder, and we walked out. I was unfixable. For the first time in my life, I wished I was dead.

And then, it was over. Gone. Unlike its beginning, which is cauterized into my memory, the end escapes me. It was just there, a present left outside the front door that I was no longer frightened to walk through. I think because I didn't have to analyze it—turn it over and over in my head like an artifact to be examined, understood, and cataloged—I didn't hear its departure, didn't sense its absence. All I remember is, suddenly, glinting summer days. A scavenger hunt for some kid's birthday party. Standing around a rusty barrel at night, the flames inside licking at our marshmallows, all of us shrieking with laughter when they caught fire and began charring and melting on our twigs. The bitter taste of burnt, molten sweetness.

PART II

RAPid CYCLiNG

A TERM USED FOR PATIENTS WHO TRANSITION FROM DEPRES-
SION TO MANIA AND BACK AGAIN. SOME CYCLE OVER A PERIOD
OF MONTHS, OTHERS OVER A PERIOD OF DAYS; STILL OTHERS
YO-YO SEVERAL TIMES THROUGHOUT A SINGLE DAY. SEATBELT NOT
INCLUDED.

9

iF YOU DON'T STOP iT, YOU'LL GO BLiND

The first time I was called a faggot, I was in seventh grade. I was running around screaming with some of the girls on the front lawn at Joseph Case Junior High when Billy Meechan pushed me against the bushes, out of the sight of the teachers, and drilled his forefinger into my chest.

"You know what you are, Leite?" I leaned back farther to relieve the pain and shook my head. "You're a *faggot*." He spat out the word, then hiccupped a disgusted laugh. He looked at the two bullies in leather jackets who framed him, and they all walked away.

I had no idea what the word meant. That night behind closed doors, I looked it up in my red clothbound Merriam-Webster dictionary: "a bundle of sticks." Billy Meechan wasn't smart enough to use such erudite language. "Faggot" clearly meant something else, and if his tone was any indication, it wasn't a compliment.

What made it even more anxiety-provoking was that his ambush seemed so arbitrary. Why, out of the entire school, did he choose to shove *me* into a corner? I'd worked hard to blend in. After *House of*

Wax, my mother had asked Barry, who was now sixteen, to take me shopping for clothes at Sawyer's Campus Shop. Over my protests, he had ditched my groovy orange Greg Brady pants and striped poly-ester sweater vests in favor of Levi's bell-bottoms, colored T-shirts, and a Levi's jacket. My mother smiled, but I thought I looked like a blueberry Popsicle. But now that I was swaddled in denim, the effect was immediate. Allison, the daughter of one of Vu and Vo's neigh-bors, who had ignored me all that summer, suddenly began making excuses to stop by their house when I was around. I never told her, because I liked the attention, but I was revolted by her behavior. If all it took was a wardrobe change to win her affections, she was too shallow and common for me. And, as I convinced myself then, my reaction had nothing to do with her being a girl. That was merely a coincidence.

After dinner that night, while my mother was washing dishes, I asked, "Ma, what's a faggot?"

The room immediately grew frosty. She turned to me, her fists jammed into her hips, which by this time were sizable again. "Where did you hear that word?"

"Um, in school."

"Who called you that?" Her voice turned brusque and interroga-tive, like she was going to pressure me until I coughed up names, like a spy being tortured.

"Not *me!*" I lied. "Someone called Greg Martin that."

She softened a bit and turned back to the sink. "Well, it's a terrible and ugly word," she explained, "and I don't want to hear you saying it. Understood?" I shook my head. "Ever." She slapped the wet dishrag that was in her hand against the counter. It was her way of whacking it dry, but whenever she used it as punctuation to her conversation, it meant a tide of *veneta* was rising. Then she stopped: "You know what? I have half a mind to call Mrs. Martin."

"No! Don't do that." I tried to derail the plan that I could see was gathering momentum: "Think of how upset she'd be." She wagged her head side to side, considering, then relented.

"But . . . Ma, what does it *mean?*"

"*Outra vez!?*" she asked, pure disbelief. Again? "MANNY!"

When my father ambled into the kitchen from the breezeway, she took to scouring the big copper-bottom Revere skillet so hard, I worried she'd scrub the copper coating clean off. "David has a question for you," she said, head down, hands a blur. *Jesus, she's making me ask it again.*

"Yes, Son?"

"Forget it."

"Oh-ho-ho, no you *don't*, mister," my mother said, pointing at me. "You asked me, now you go ahead and ask him." And she returned to her pot.

"Daddy . . ." I hesitated, "what's a faggot?" He glanced over at my mother, then back at me. He cleared his throat.

"Well, Son," he exhaled hard. "It means someone . . . who's a homosexual."

That, I understood. And that explained Billy's attitude.

"So it doesn't mean 'a bundle of sticks.' "

My mother stopped scrubbing, relief rippling across her face. "What are you talking about, Banana?" She shook her head and laughed. "Sticks," she said to no one in particular, as she rinsed the skillet under scalding water. "Oh, Lord, where does he get these ideas?"

What I'd neglected to tell them was I'd become preoccupied with my body—"the downstairs parts"—and the bodies of other boys. Gym class did that. All throughout grade school, gym was just a bunch of boys and girls running around the schoolyard playing red rover and kickball and competing in races. We didn't have to change clothes or shower. But suddenly in seventh grade, it was regulation gym shorts, jockstraps, and the naked bodies of boys I'd known all of my life.

I was mesmerized at the differences in our bodies. Some boys, like Arthur Antunes, were powerful, the muscles in their legs and, especially, their asses undulating as they roughhoused with each other.

Antunes had to have been held back at least two times, making him about fifteen, because he towered over us and had fireworks of hair that set off from his crotch, wriggled in a ragged line up his stomach, and exploded across his chest. He took sadistic pleasure in embarrassing anyone who happened to drop his soap. "Look, [insert a random name] is open for business!" he'd shout. Desperate not to be his next victim, I softened my soap in the bathroom sink at home and dug my nails into it to create a grip. There was no way in hell I was going to drop it.

Some boys, like Tommy Shields, were small and nearly hairless. They reminded me of those yapping stray dogs that run around the edges of playgrounds only to get kicked, yet keep coming back, hoping for affection. To survive, these boys sidled up to some of the bigger guys, often playing their flunkies and suffering their abuses. Like the time Carl Mullard pissed all over Tommy in the shower, great yellow arcs splashing across his chest and belly. Tommy laughed it off; it was his only defense. Later I saw him trying to joke with Carl, trailing after him as he left the locker room. A cartoon sidekick, bludgeoned and beaten, but always loyal.

And then there were boys like me who, mercifully, fell in the middle. Big enough to blend in, but physically unremarkable enough to be the target of an occasional bully with his shoves and jibes.

Once "faggot" had been added to the short and unimaginative roster of names I'd been called—"homo" and "queer" pretty much rounded out the list—I noticed it was being volleyed indiscriminately at everyone, as innocently as if they were calling each other a butthole or a "who-a"—our particular way of pronouncing the word *whore*. But ever since that afternoon when Billy Meechan had pitched me into the bushes, I couldn't help feeling like these ubiquitous, mindless slurs were somehow personal and deeply descriptive when hurled at me.

Erections, I was certain, would be my undoing. Almost overnight, they began happening—without warning and without regard for time, place, or company. Anything could set them off: the jouncing of the morning bus, riding my ten-speed bike, slipping on underwear warm from the dryer. And that was nothing compared to their staying power. An entire science class on the emphatically unsexy topic of latitude and longitude could pass, and I'd still be stuck pointing toward magnetic north. I walked through the halls with my books clasped in front of me and prayed Antunes or Mullard wouldn't slap them out of my hands, because as much as they'd never admit it, they knew what it meant. So the shower was always a crapshoot. Not one to press my luck, I made sure to be the first in and out and to face the corner while washing—digging my nails into that soap as hard as possible.

If at school the locker room was the scene of a possible life-shattering humiliation no twelve-year-old could survive, at home—and behind locked doors—it became the stuff of fantasies, throbbing with sexual energy that drove my newly discovered, nearly round-the-clock compulsion. All that was missing was a funky electronic soundtrack.

The summer before seventh grade, with the whole *House of Wax* episode behind me, I hung out with Jimmy and Russell Cantor, who lived around the corner from Vu and Vo Costa in Somerset. Russell was a tall kid, a few years older than us, who had matured early. He had one of those sinewy athletic builds, with broad shoulders and a narrow waist, nothing like my stout, barrel-chested frame. Some of the kids called him a retard because he'd been held back a grade or two and didn't say much when we all hung out together. Sometimes when he was taunted, he'd lash out, lumbering at anyone in his way, forgetting how much stronger he was than the rest of us.

Jimmy and Russell's backyard sloped down to the Taunton River, where an outcropping of rocks tumbled into the water. They were goofing off, motioning to me to join them. I'd never learned to swim, so I was terrified of jumping in over my head. It didn't help that the summer before Russell, who had thought I was teasing him, had pushed me in the back so hard the air expelled in a violent wheeze, like a broken accordion, and I'd pitched headfirst into the water. He

had sat on the rocks, glaring at me, as I blubbed and sputtered, trying
to make my way back to shore.

When Russell saw that I wasn't about to move off the rocks, he
swam over and walked out of the river, water sluicing off his body.
He was wearing fringed jeans shorts as a bathing suit.

"Come on," he said. I shook my head. "I'll help you. I swear." I was
hesitant. I couldn't tell if he remembered the previous summer. He
put his hands up in the air, the way bandits did in movies to prove
they weren't hiding a gun.

He reached out for my hand, and I bumbled off the rocks and
slipped into the water.

"It's okay," he said in a soft voice. "Get up." Holding both of my
hands, he walked backward into the river as I planted each foot firmly
on the bottom. When the water was up to my neck, I shook my head.

"I can't do this." I pulled hard, trying to guide him back to shore.

"Just turn around." I did as I was told and faced the shore. Jimmy
was now on the rocks watching, a smirk on his face.

"Trust me?" I nodded my head. He threaded his left arm under
mine and around my chest. "Lean back." He pulled me close, and I
could feel the warmth coming from his body even in the water. He
pushed off, and I lost contact with the bottom, my last bit of surety
and control. With his free arm he paddled out into the river. Now
and again, I could feel one of his legs slip between mine as it scissored
through the water. I grabbed hard on to his arm with both hands.

When we were out way over our heads, he stopped lurching and
began treading water. "Still alive?" he asked.

"Uh-huh."

"Now, just relax." He let his legs go still, and I felt us float up, me
on top. Lying on him, his stubble rubbing against my temple, I was
struck by that engulfing fish-eye sky; we were too far out for trees
and houses to puncture the circle of my vision.

"Nice, right?"

"Yeah."

We stayed there for I don't know how long. The sun beating on my face and Russell's rhythmic breathing in my ear caused me to slip away, forgetting myself and gravity.

When we reached shore, Jimmy was gone. While Russell and I walked up to the house, I watched as the water from his shorts ran down the back of his thighs, creating rivulets in the hair. We entered the basement through the back door. Russell wrapped a towel around his waist and tossed one to me. I did the same.

"My mom would kill me if we got the couch wet." I didn't see why; it already looked ratty and exhausted, as if the cushions had just given up and deflated. He put his feet on the coffee table—which was covered with a Venn diagram of watermarks from sweaty soda cans and beer bottles over the years—and heaved a deep sigh.

"Feel better?"

I plopped down beside him. "Yes."

"Think you could go out there later and do that on your own?" I had no idea if I could, but I didn't want to. I had felt so transported in his arms, anything else would just be a disappointment.

He sat there with his eyes closed, then out of the blue asked, "Do you know what 'whacking off' means?" I swallowed hard. I had heard the guys at school talk about it, but I didn't really understand the mechanics of it.

"Of course," I lied.

"Have you ever?"

I hadn't because I had no idea how. I figured if I waited long enough, someone at school would say something that would clue me into it, and I'd join the armada of boys who bragged about being able to go at it three or four times a day.

Although I didn't think Russell would tease me, I hesitated.

"Have you?" he asked again.

"No."

"Do you know how?"

I paused for what felt like a million hours. "No."

And just as with swimming, he took it upon himself to teach me. He flipped off his towel, unbuttoned his shorts, and slid them down to his knees. He wasn't wearing underwear. I looked nervously to the door that led upstairs. "Don't worry, no one's home."

"What about Jimmy?" He explained that his bike was gone, so he was probably at his girlfriend's house.

He was already hard and began moving his hand. I watched, hypnotized. He didn't ask me to join in or to help. He was content with simply showing me. I was awed at how his fist pistoned, faster at times and then slower, like he was trying to turn over a stubborn engine. His belly hollowed as he breathed heavier. Some charge seemed to zap through his body: His thighs tightened, calves knotted, toes spread, then curled under hard; his face contorted. Beneath my musty towel and shorts I was listing undeniably toward magnetic north, but even that didn't stop me from freaking out. All I could think of was that girl who'd had a seizure on the bus and fallen off the seat and began flailing on the floor. Suddenly, he let out a deep, guttural moan, like he was hurt. An arc of something white shot up to the middle of his chest, and some puddled in the hollow of his throat.

If that was whacking off, you could count me out.

"Woah!" he heaved deeply. He grabbed the towel and cleaned himself. He lay there for a few minutes, drowsily. Then he lolled his head in my direction. "That's all you have to do to become a member of the Boys' Club." I nodded, still not convinced he was okay. "And think how much better it will be when a girl does it to you."

Huh?

It was as if someone had switched off all the electricity in the air. The thought of doing that with a girl a) had never crossed my mind, and b) grossed me out. I wanted this to be something special between Russell and me, something we'd eventually share, but, apparently, he had other plans.

Back home, in the darkness of my room, it didn't work the first two times. I felt like a peeled carrot. I thought of going back to Russell and asking him what was wrong with me, but seventh grade had started, and I got swept up in the activity of classes. Eventually, on an inconsequential Saturday, I became a card-carrying member of the

Boys' Club. As soon as it was over, though, I felt shrouded in shame and guilt. Unlike Russell, who when he was done had clapped me on the back and made us sandwiches, I turned over and over in my head whether I would have to confess this, this *thing,* to Father Adam at St. John of God. Instead, I decided to confess to my own father.

He was stacking some apple baskets in the garage, and I stood beside him, silent.

"What is it, Son?" *How do I say this?* "Is everything all right?"

"Yeah. It's nothing," and I headed back inside.

"You sure?"

I stopped. "No." I took a deep breath and looked at the smooth cement floor he had poured years ago. "Daddy . . ."

He stood up, concerned now.

"Yes."

"I . . . I touched myself and cream came out."

A very long pause followed. "You didn't just touch yourself, did you?"

Oh, God, he's going to make me talk about it. "No." My head was down.

"No, you didn't." He motioned to the stairs to the breezeway. "Son, sit down." I prepared myself to be punished. "Son, what you did and what happened to you is very natural. It means you've become a man." I nodded, my heart pounding. "But you can't do it too often."

"Why?"

"The more you do it, the weaker you'll become. It takes away your strength."

I felt my stomach squirm. I'd been doing it for several weeks by then. By my calculations, I should be bedridden and drooling by the time I turned thirteen. I promised myself right there that I'd never do it again. But over the next several months, I couldn't help myself. No matter how hard I tried, I'd get all bothered looking at the men's underwear ads in the Bradlees circular, and I'd have to creep off to the bathroom, the only room in the house that locked.

One afternoon, we had gym class with a substitute teacher who

looked like a G.I. Joe action figure. Rather than making us play football or baseball or run laps in the back field, he had us gather in the
boys' side of the gymnasium. In front of us were blue mats, a thick
rope spiraling up to the ceiling, and a horizontal bar whose feet were
held down by weights. When he blew his whistle, he explained, we
were supposed to climb the rope to the tape marker and then jump
down. After that we had to run to the bar and do as many chin-ups
as we could, and then when we were so weak we couldn't budge,
we were to fall to the mats and keep doing sit-ups until we felt like
puking.

While the jocks like Antunes and Mullard elbowed one another
out of the way to be first in line, I hung back. I worried the hem of my
maroon shorts, running my fingers over the gold rectangle on the leg
where my mother had written "LEITE" in big block letters with her
Magic Marker. Boy after boy clambered up the ropes, most with no
problem, then jumped down and trotted over to the bar. When it was
my turn, I wrapped the rope around my leg, like I'd seen those lady
trapeze artists do, and tried to hoist myself up, but no matter how
hard I yanked, I didn't budge from the floor. I stepped back and gave
myself a running start. Nothing helped.

"Forget it," the teacher said. "Go do chin-ups." I jumped up and
hung from the bar. The most I could squeeze out was one. The other
boys, who were on their way to hurling breakfast doing sit-ups, began laughing. The teacher leaned in as I was hanging there like so
much limp laundry and whispered, "That's disgusting."

Trying for just one more, I was reminded of my father. He was
right. I'd grown weak. And now that they knew what I'd been up to,
it'd be all over school by sixth period: David Leite whacked himself
nearly comatose.

10

DRIVEN TO DISTRACTION

Stupid comes in an assortment of sizes, but none dumber than that of a pudgy adolescent boy. For the previous six months or so, ever since summer, I'd appeared to everyone to be fine. Exuberant, even. The terror of *House of Wax* had been reeled in, and from this side of the ordeal I think they all chalked it up to bad timing. A sensitive kid who'd clashed headlong into life a bit too early and suffered a concussion. *Nada mais, nada menos,* they all said—nothing more, nothing less—nodding to each other in that "I told you so" way my family has, as they reached for capon (my father doesn't like turkey), Portuguese stuffing, creamy rose-colored rice, roasted potatoes, and a cork of cranberry sauce my mother had pushed out of a can and set out for Thanksgiving dinner.

What no one knew was the monumental effort I was exerting to *feel* fine. I moved through my days in a tight, prescribed circle with just enough space for the familiar. A narrow spotlight, out of which I refused to step. Anything new or unknown was deeply suspect, and therefore rejected. On the spot. I'd never heard a good enough explanation of what had happened to me the year before, and I didn't see the point in taking chances. So I created a Byzantine set of rules that governed my behavior. Just a few I remember: Funeral homes, cemeteries, and hearses were to be avoided. If we happened to drive by one, I closed my eyes. Any conversation at school having to do with ghosts, murders, war, the occult, being buried alive, or freezing to death was to be walked away from. *Immediately.* In church, the near life-size statue of Jesus on the cross, with its wet, winking enamel blood coursing down its head, hands, and torso, was never to be gazed at or prayed to again. Movies, as I'd told my mother in China Village, were blacklisted. If my parents tuned into the *ABC Movie of the Week,* I suddenly had homework to do. I avoided PBS at night; too many historical programs. The haunted, hollowed faces in concentration camps, the anguish of college students after shootings, the emotional explosions following the assassinations of John and Robert Kennedy, left me rattled. If a TV show didn't have a laugh track, I didn't watch it.

Those were the rules, and as long as I followed them, I was safe.

So then what possessed me to walk back into a movie theater just nine months later, in January 1973, to see *The Poseidon Adventure*? Some unique brand of stupidity? A hormone-addled brain? Adolescent short-term memory loss? All these years later, I think it was *veneta.* I had to prove to myself that I really *was* fine, and that Brian Davis and all those kids at the sixth-grade lunch table, many of whom had gone on to become bottom feeders in junior high, could go straight to hell.

Bad call.

As I sat in my seat, something grotesquely familiar began roiling inside as I watched the ship capsize, people skittering down walls and being crushed by pianos, falling, arms spread, waiting those few horrid seconds for impact on the huge stained-glass ceiling below. It didn't help that Shelley Winters was always bleating, "MANNY!"—her on-screen husband—in that same shrill, frantic way my mother calls for my father when she's nervous. I began having emotions by proxy. Their panic was my panic. Their terror, hysteria, desperation—all mine. The membrane between me and the world had become so permeable that I was helpless to stop myself. I went hurtling back, fiercely. Déjà vu. That metallic taste flooded my mouth again, prickling my tongue. Hot molten lead poured onto my chest, sending waves of heat galloping through my face, arms, and legs. I gripped the arms of the seat, determined not to run but to stand it down this time, when a close-up of a man's burnt face, so reminiscent of the burnt wax dummies, flashed large on the screen. I careened out, out, out of the theater. In the lobby, I felt I was disintegrating, as if bits of me were dropping off with each step: double-jointed thumbs unhinging from my hands. Shoulders dislocating and slipping from their perches. Teeth scattering like jacks on the stained carpet. Nothing left to hold me together. Stuck with no ride home, I took a few shuddering breaths and returned to the theater.

That winter, time spliced. All the good that had happened since summer was edited out, curled and forgotten on the floor. Jump-cut to anxiety, insomnia, inability to concentrate, and loss of appetite, all of which were rested and reporting for duty. If that weren't enough, my mysterious invisible mouth breather was back, too. I could plot the nosedive of my grades before it happened. Between classes, teachers murmured in their hallway clusters, looking my way and shaking their heads at one another. Friends noticed I was preoccupied, distant. "You're being wicked weird," they said. *Wee-id,* is how they pronounced it. *Wee-id.*

I needed a distraction.

Having been abandoned by sleep, I sat up in bed one night, trying to calm myself, inhaling deeply and whispering a mantra from some bullshit Transcendental Meditation workshop a friend had gone to. I looked toward the window on the far wall, the one my father said would always be bright, and saw a demonic face peering at me. I tried blinking it away, but it didn't move. Just stared, lurid and ungodly. I covered my mouth so my parents couldn't hear me cry, because I was terrified I'd be committed to Taunton State, the local psychiatric hospital.

Back on Brownell Street, the Sisters of the Spatula had had a default hair-trigger response whenever any of us seriously pissed them off. It was usually some variation of: "You're going to drive me to Taunton State, [insert name of that sonofabitchin' kid]! Right to Taunton State, in a straitjacket!" To the others, it was a goof. They loved to see how far they could push before their mothers would point two fingers—a lit cigarette cocked between—and start braying. Me, I took it literally. The hospital loomed dark and constant in my thoughts. I was preoccupied with it. Most twelve-year-olds' biggest fears were plebeian: dark cellars, thunderstorms, hell and damnation. Mine, from as early as I can remember, was going insane, sitting side by side with my mother, whom, I was certain, I would have sent there, each of us wiping drool from the other's mouth.

Lose my mind or carry on? No contest. But carrying on was only beneficial if the effects were cumulative, like snow blanketing the pain, whiting out the panic. Every morning, though, something reset, and I had to begin again. Each insight, each comfort, each moment of lightness I'd achieved the day before was wiped out when I awoke at four or five in the morning, listening to the low murmurs of my parents as they had breakfast before my father went to work. I lay there feeling shards of electricity shooting through me. My legs fizzled with so much energy, I had to shuffle them constantly to stop myself from running out to the kitchen and seeing my parents' faces fall as they realized I once again wasn't sleeping. Around seven, I'd get up, a facsimile of myself.

"How'd you sleep, Son?" my mother would ask.

"Fine." I always lied. On the snack bar was my morning banana with its futile wishes: ❤ *Have a Good Day!* ❤ *We Love You!* ❤ *God Bless!!* ❤

During the day I felt like I was peering at the world through the wrong end of a telescope. People looked small and far away, sounds, distorted and muffled. My mind wandered in class, and whenever I was called on, I was startled. I was too busy scanning my body for signs it was happening again. "Hypervigilance," psychiatrists call it.

I didn't have the vocabulary then, but I was acutely aware that if I stopped my internal scans for any rumblings, any blips on the screen, I'd be blindsided. Like that time I was in the second-floor library flipping through an old *Life* magazine, doing research for a project. I turned to an article on World War II and came face-to-face with a picture of a man's severed head propped up on an army tank. He was still wearing his helmet. His skin was charred black and awful, burned down to the bone on his nose and around his mouth, making him look like a snarling dog. I grabbed my bag and took off. The librarian yelled in the hall that I couldn't leave without a pass, but I was out of the building and panting in the parking lot before I realized what she had said.

It was short-sleeve weather, so it must have been May or June, four or five months later. My backpack of school books slumped, unopened, against my father's La-Z-Boy. Near the breezeway door, my Top-Siders sat pigeon-toed where I'd mindlessly stepped out of them. My Baracuta jacket was crumpled next to them. I curled up on the floor in front of the TV, my head tucked into the crook of my elbow so my mother couldn't study my face for signs that it was happening. Rusty, protective, was lying against my back, like he was trying to leach the pain from me. Through the open windows, I could hear the neighborhood kids playing. *Please don't make me go outside,* I begged my mother in my head. I just couldn't do it. Out there unnerved me. Sapphire sky, backyard like a crocheted green quilt, street full of friends. Although the rightful place for an almost-thirteen-year-old, it gave me no relief and reminded me just how troubled I was.

I cranked the dial on the TV, looking for channel two, WGBH. A riptide of anxiety was pulling at me, as it did every time. *Please let me watch it. Please let me watch it. Please let me watch it.* I'd had a bad day. I deserved this.

"You're going to twist that thing right off," my mother said. "Then what?"

"Sorry," I mumbled into my elbow.

Just then the jaunty music from *The French Chef* mingled with the rhythmic *thonk* and hiss of my mother's iron as she pressed my father's underwear. Suddenly the hamster wheel of punitive thoughts in my head slowed.

As I watched TV, mist from mother's spray bottle would every so often arc over the board, and I turned my face to its coolness. Show after show, Julia wrestled with pots, wielded a sword over her famous kick line of fowl, and thwacked pieces of meat the way mothers back then would swat the asses of bratty kids when they misbehaved. This soothed me, ebbed the riptide so I could float, like that time with Russell Cantor. Wide sky; quiet, warm breaths; slow heart. Julia accomplished something very few people could: She helped me forget myself. I felt normal, a concept whose meaning was growing increasingly meaningless.

Sometimes I'd even feel enough like myself to do a rousing imitation of Julia for my mother. I'd stand and plant both fists on my hips, lifting my head like I was about to crow. "Welcome to *The French Chef;* I'm Julia Child," I tooted, my voice rising and plunging. Then I added the only phrase I remembered from French class: *"Comment allez-vous aujourd'hui? Allons à la piscine!"* (How are you today? Let's go to the pool!) She'd fall back against the door and laugh. Her fingers, red from housework, would burrow under her cat's-eye glasses to wipe away tears—as much from relief as delight, I now suspect.

Boeuf Bourguignon. Coq au vin. Quiche Lorraine. French onion soup. I recall her food in the abstract, in the collective, although I have no memory of her making it. I think my mother mistook my fascination with Julia for an interest in cooking, so she bought me *Betty Crocker's New Boys and Girls Cookbook.* Flipping through the pages, I was charmed by the drawings of kids my age making bunny salads from pear halves, using raisins for eyes, almonds for ears, and pom-poms of cottage cheese for tails. There were recipes for cheeseburgers, sloppy joes, Mad Hatter meatballs, and tuna-and-potato-chip casserole. One dish that especially captivated me was cube steaks. Not for the recipe ("sear floured cube steaks in butter"), but for the illustration: a blond boy poking at the steaks in the pan with a fork, and another boy, his head just inches from the other; both smiling. I stared at that drawing so much that the book's binding, now forty-four years old, is broken open to that page.

Inspired by the recipe for simple spaghetti, I decided to wing it and make lasagna as my inaugural supper in our basement kitchen. I clattered around for my mother's square Pyrex baking dish. Ignorant of the existence of mozzarella and ricotta cheese, I made my Italian classic with layers of Prince lasagna sheets, Ragú spaghetti sauce, and thick slices of Cracker Barrel Extra-Sharp Cheddar cheese. To call it a "brick" would be kind, but when I slid it onto the Formica-topped trivet my father had made, you'd have thought we were hosting a White House state dinner. A sudden formality descended over the table. My mother cooed something like, "That's beautiful, Banana!" and my father sat up straighter, beaming. We all choked down a square, and my father even held out his plate for seconds. But in time, the book lost its power to soothe and was swallowed by one of the boxes in our basement. I needed fresh distraction.

"I want to be a writer," I announced one afternoon when I was feeling unusually calm. When I was smaller and spent the weekends at my grandparents, I used to hunch over my grandfather's old clacking Underwood typewriter, with arms that catapulted the letters onto the page. I pretended to write, but what I really loved was the look of letters, the way their shapes revealed their sound. How a *g* reminded me of air gathering in my lungs and threading its sinuous way up my esophagus and out my open mouth. How an *S* looked like a slithering snake, hissing. A *B* was lips puffed with plosive air about to release. Yes, I told them, I wanted to be a writer.

"Here!" my mother said a few days later, tossing a bag on the bed where I was lying.

"What is it?"

"Well, kiddo, you're just going to have to open it to find out." Inside was a Big Chief writing tablet. "You want to be a writer—I figured you needed something to write on."

I said some wiseass thing like, "Why not a typewriter?" which caused a bolt of anger to flash across her face.

"Give an inch, take a yard." She sounded so disgusted. "That's all it is with you, isn't it?"

She wheeled around, then stopped herself. I could feel the colossal energy it took to shake off the fury, rolling her shoulders back and collecting herself. A bird of prey folding its wings into place, refusing to kill. Turning back, she said with a warmth that shamed me: "Why? Because real writers write longhand." I knew I was being an asshole. I'd been an asshole for weeks, and I didn't know how to stop it. Everything was pissing me off. I held my frustration underwater long enough to say, "Thanks, Ma." As she leaned over and kissed me on the forehead, her coat fell open, and I could see her pink Courtesy-Booth Girl jacket underneath and smell her perfume, Chantilly.

Kneeling at my bed, I grabbed a pen. The tablet had the smooth, putty-colored paper we used in math class, the lines a thick sky blue. I began writing, a story about pirates. Halfway down the first paragraph, I tore out the page. My handwriting wasn't right. The letters didn't lean at the same angle—they weren't identical like the letters on my grandfather's typewriter, and if I was going to be a writer, not only was the story going to be perfect, so was my penmanship. I copied the paragraph on a fresh page, this time going slow to make it right. I turned the pad counterclockwise a bit and leaned back: All the letters were parallel. But by the bottom of the first page, I stopped. I knew nothing of pirates, of armadas, of the sea. As a boy, I knew I was *supposed* to like pirates, but I didn't. Actually, I detested them; they were thugs with bad dental hygiene and awful taste in clothes. Feeling defeated, I flung the pad across the room, pages fluttering, and it hit the wall, like a bird slamming into a window and falling to the ground. Dead.

"What happened?" my father asked when I walked out of my room. "I thought you were writing a book?"

"I don't have a story to tell," I said, as I curled on the couch and turned on *Candlepins for Cash*.

Sunday drives through Newport, parties, ice skating on a pond in Somerset. My parents tried everything to rouse me. When I wanted to be an artist, they enrolled me in private classes. When I showed interest in science, they bought me a chemistry set and microscope. My mother started a Saturday bowling league just to get me out of the house. My father encouraged reading, but it was rare that I could wring meaning from the words. And I didn't really like books. I liked the concept of them, but I seldom read them, which most likely contributed to my staggering lack of knowledge about pirates. No Long John Silver, no Captain Hook for me. When I did read, I'd stare absently through the book, my mind wandering. Sometimes my mother, lying next to me on the couch, would toe me in the leg when I forgot to turn pages.

My parents traveled miles for sleepovers. Too often, though, the mental distraction I was hoping for ended in burning humiliation: My friends and their families huddled together in their pajamas, looking on in the middle of the night while I called my father and explained how some stomach virus had suddenly hit. I'd learned that bugs and viruses were the ultimate excuses because, unlike with faked fevers, there was no way of checking their validity. Plus, they had the added advantage of making everyone all too happy to get me the hell out of their house.

Eventually, sleepovers ended, because of a tumult of violent night terrors in which I'd thrash or scream in my sleep—full, alarming sentences that sent friends' parents flying into the bedroom goggle-eyed. At home, the terrors worsened. One night I was standing on the bank of a river, and huge snakes were slicing the water into big typewriter

S's as they approached. I screamed for my mother, but it felt like a fist was jamming the words back down my throat. A man grabbed my arms and yanked me into the river with the snakes. The water roiled as a frenzy of huge jungle jaws closed around my legs, fangs puncturing muscles, snapping tendons, crushing bones. I slugged the man in the head, trying to get away.

"Son! SON!" My father's voice. *What is he doing in the river?* I wanted to tell him to get away, but I was being shaken and pulled. Disoriented. The river began meandering around my bureau. Snakes swam through my aquarium, glowing yellow in the corner. I found myself standing, unaccountably, on my bed. I looked at my father, who was standing in his pouchy underwear below me. Lying to my right was my mother, crying.

Confusion stopped my breath. "What's the matter, Ma?" She explained through stuttering sobs that I had hit her in the head as she was trying to shake me awake.

They tucked me into bed, and I apologized to her again. She shook her head. "It's nothing, sweetheart." She kissed me and told me not to worry. "Okay?" she asked, giving me her Courtesy-Booth Girl smile. From their room, I heard her muffled cries. She must have had her face buried in my father's chest.

In the end, happenstance was the best I could hope for. Maybe Mr. Dunn would say something in science class that would make me laugh—he was fond of stupid puns and jokes—or Mrs. Santon would once again scream, *"Sacre bleu!"* in French class when startled. It made all of us titter because it sounded like "Suck my blur!" And anything with the word *suck* was funny to a room of seventh graders. Or maybe I'd have that dream again, the one where I was Dave, the seventh Brady kid, and I'd awaken happy. At these times, I forgot myself for just a minute, and I reasoned that if I could feel better for a minute, I could feel better for two . . . three . . . maybe ten . . . fifteen . . . thirty, and then even an hour. And eventually, I'd be well again. But night would always erase the chalkboard in my head of all my hard-won tricks, so that in the morning all I could do was start filling it up again, top left to lower right, with happenstance. When I first learned in English class of Sisyphus and his never-ending task, I asked for a hall pass from Mrs. Hopf and slipped into a stall in the boys' room and cried.

Late summer. Rummaging through boxes under the basement stairs, I came upon a blue book with yellow letters: *Boys & Sex*. I could feel my neck swell as my heart beat faster. The book's spine was cracked open to the chapter: "Homosexuality." *Do Mom and Dad think I'm a faggot?*

I read. "All but one of our states have laws which provide jail sentences for adult males who engage in homosexual activity with each other." *Provide.* What a funny word to use in this case. As though they were offering these men something, like all-you-can-eat buffets, a free happy-hour cocktail, complimentary towels at the pool.

Mr. Goode popped into my head.

"Your honor, for our first witness, the prosecution calls Mrs. Adele Goode, a neighbor of David Leite, the accused; and the former wife of Mr. Goode, a pedophile who introduced him into this life of perversion and filth."

And in a later paragraph: ". . . boys who have sex with each other can be ajudged juvenile delinquents and sent to institutions."

Bobby Romeu, a kid a few years older than me, couldn't be a delinquent. Come on, he was in a model-airplane club. He liked to show me his creased picture from a dirty magazine, of a woman with saggy breasts and nipples like Ring Dings. He'd flick his thumb against his zipper as we looked at it. I was disgusted by her, but couldn't stop watching what he was doing with his hand. Then we'd play tag, and he'd wrestle me down where the yard sloped out of sight and lie on top of me, grinding his hips into mine.

"I think the evidence will show that the accused was actually not chased by Mr. Romeu, but rather, using his substantial tricks, the accused lured the poor young man into the shadows to have his way with him."

And all those times I locked myself in the bathroom and paged through the Sears catalog, looking at the men in their underwear.

"In closing, Your Honor, let us not forget that the true sign of a pervert is not just how he degrades other men, which is a horror in itself, but how he thinks and acts when alone in the sanctity of his own home."

So this had been my problem all along? This was going to be my life? First I was going to be shipped off to Taunton State, and then when I turned eighteen, hauled into prison. I deep-sixed the book back into the box. My mother's yearbook from Durfee High School, class of 1956, caught my eye. I opened it. It smelled of must; tiny black dots of mold peppered the pages. I tilted my head left and right, reading all the inscriptions. She was pretty, so young, my mother. Looking at her, I shriveled with shame. She had no idea she would have a son who was broken, a deviant, a boy she and her future husband could never fix.

11

HAPPiNESS BACKWARD

Alone in the house, I was dancing at the stove in my underwear. A big metal spoon as my microphone. A steady curtain of snow falling outside. The hi-fi blasting "The Bitch Is Back." I was screaming the lyrics; it felt good to curse with impunity. It had been a good day so far. Somehow I'd managed to forget myself all morning. Unusual, but I knew better than to consider it anything more than happenstance. Too many times I'd looked upon a few good hours as a start, some engine inside finally turning over, only to be slapped back. A trick of the weather, a lift of the music, nothing more.

I stirred the dried matchstick noodles in the copper-bottomed skillet. Green BBs and tiny orange cubes, hard and unyielding, were growing, softening, as they sucked up the creamy sauce. To my right, an empty box of Tuna Helper. No need to refer to it; I knew the instructions by heart. When the peas and carrots were plump and the noodles soft, I mixed in a can of tuna, scooped all of it onto my plate, and levered myself up in my father's recliner in the breezeway. Our dogs, Duke and Rusty, came over, their heads following the arc of my fork from plate to mouth. *Click.* A game show popped up on the TV, loud cheering as contestants in lame-ass costumes looked into the audience for guidance. I cranked the volume to drown out Elton.

Because our school was overcrowded, we were on double sessions: Upperclassmen went in the mornings; lowerclassmen in the afternoon. Being a ninth grader, I was home alone until noon. Given all that free time, I chose to cook. By now, I'd pretty much broken from Portuguese food. I still had a few favorites I wouldn't pass up: my mother's *carne assada;* her *galinha com molho* (chicken in an oniony wine sauce); beans mixed with links of *chouriço,* a slab of bacon, and, oddly, hot dogs—her nod to American franks and beans. Most of all, though, her stuffed quahogs, which are a New England specialty. These weren't those anemic half-shell jobs filled with nothing but pallid breadcrumbs and a few bits of clams. They were amped-up Portuguese-style.

The dish started with my father. Or at least it did back then, when Mount Hope Bay was bracingly clean and fresh. We'd wade in knee-deep water in Tiverton, Rhode Island—him in a madras bathing suit, me in cut-off jeans. My father was milky white except for his arms, neck, and face. If you squinted, it looked like he was wearing a T-shirt with a smudge of dirt where a few chest hairs clustered. (He, like me, wasn't a particularly good specimen of Portuguese hirsuteness.) He could divine where quahogs were nestled just by ambling along. He'd stop suddenly and put his arm out, to prevent me from walking over the clams, as if that could somehow make them scatter in the sand. Then, using his nearly opposable big toe like a trowel, he'd pivot his leg deeper and deeper into the sand, tongue twisting in unison, until his face blossomed with a smile. If he got it just right, he could grab the clam in his toes and lift it right out of the water, hopping on the other leg as he offered it to me.

Even when we were just walking along the beach in Swansea, my mother tucked low back in the car, wearing her clip-on sunglasses and a kerchief—she was never a fan of the sun or the water—he'd suddenly stop and twist his leg while I squirmed and whispered, "Stop it!"

"Take it!" he'd say, his toes clutching a huge quahog.

"Daddy!" No one else's father was hunting their own food.

"It's not going to bite."

Broiling with embarrassment, I'd snatch it and stick it in my bucket.

To make the dish, my mother would leave Portuguese bread to get stale on the counter for a few days, then break it up and soak the pieces in the liquor spilled from a big pot of steamed quahogs. She'd chop the clam meat and links of *chouriço,* add them to the softened bread along with my father's fermented pepper paste, tomato paste, and her secret blend of seasonings, and beat the mixture until it was perfectly smooth and as red as desert clay, with bits of clams and sausage studding it. The shells that had yawned open while steaming were carefully washed and dried overnight. She would then feed giant spoonfuls of the stuffing into the shells—so much that they couldn't close, leaving an inch gap of exposed stuffing—and wrap them with twine. She'd line up the clams in identical rows in the blue broiler pan with the white speckles, their openings facing up, so that they crusted over in the oven.

When you unraveled one and snapped off one half of the shell, the stuffing was steaming hot and amazingly moist. It tasted of the sea, briny, with just a hint of the sweetness from the chewy clams. The sausage and pepper paste gave it heat and heft. Whenever she presented a platter of them to my father and me, or to guests—and that's what she'd do: present them, with a flourish and the knowledge that she was about to delight us immeasurably—she'd stand back, worrying a dishrag or shredding a paper napkin, waiting for the sighs of pleasure that always followed. "You like them?" she'd ask, relieved, every time, even though they'd never been anything less than spectacular.

When I was full, I clicked off the TV and I put my plate of Tuna

Helper on the floor for the dogs to lick clean, then dumped the skillet in the sink. *Shit*. Written on the banana at my place at the snack bar:

❤ Don't forget to shovel the driveway! ❤

Shit, shit, shit.

Bundled in my blue parka with the matted fake fur ringing the hood, I bent my head low against the whip of the wind and fought the relentless snow. My breath formed tiny spikes of ice on the fur collar, and I chewed on them. As I made my way toward the street, rectangles of wet snow thudding where I tossed them, I twisted my head inside my hood to the left, then right; I was the only person out in the storm. No cars, not even kids playing. Sound was dead, killed by the snow. The sudden sense of isolation, of being so terribly disconnected, *un*connected, was like a punch to my windpipe. I closed my eyes against it. My guts started dropping. *You've been here before*—I took a deep breath—*it will stop.* More deep breaths. But without the distraction of cooking and TV and Elton the Bitch, I was helpless against it. The dread, the blackness rushed in, as if filling a vacuum. *At least the morning was good. I should be grateful for that.* I leaned against the shovel and sobbed. Snot ringed my nostrils and froze there. I looked up and screamed: "Enough! No more, please. No more." And just like every other time I had pleaded with God to make it stop, no relief came. If I wanted help, I had to get it myself. I could feel *veneta* hurtling up from the cradle of my pelvis, and I flung the shovel into the snow, where it disappeared, and walked into the house, tracking slush and mud.

In front of the phone—the beige flat-panel model with the cord that retracted into the wall—I hesitated. I knew that once I did this, I could never take it back, never reverse it. From this point on, my parents would forever see me differently. I grabbed the phone and dialed.

"Fernandes Supermarket, Ellie speaking. How can I help you?" my mother chirped in the phone. I could see her, in her pink smock, phone cradled against her shoulder, organizing coupons, or waving goodbye to a customer.

"If you don't let me see a psychiatrist, I'll kill myself."

She was quiet. No one we knew saw a psychiatrist. Even though it was the early seventies, and housewives were knocking back Valium with their morning coffee while they pulled on Virginia Slims, not one friend of hers partook, or at least admitted to partaking, in modern psychiatry. It simply wasn't done. A rumor rumbled on the periphery of family gatherings that my Aunt Jessie, Uncle Joe's wife, had a sister who was crazy, but my mother made it clear she wasn't related to us, and that it was from Jessie's side of the family that my cousin Kevin inherited his paranoid schizophrenia. I was beginning to wonder.

I knew my mother was silent because of the shame she thought it would bring onto the family. She saw how heads lowered and voices dialed down to whispers when discussing Jessie's sister. Shame prickled our family. It hamstrung our behaviors, our career choices, even our dress. My mother stewed when in fourth and fifth grade I began wearing strings of sunflower-seed love beads. Things weren't much better when I moved on to a metal peace sign the size of a saucer in sixth grade.

"Why do you have to wear that getup?" she asked, shaking her head.

"Because it's cool."

I always found it odd, because the Costa side of my family was crowded with outsize personalities, my mother included, as if we were consciously trying to prove to the world: *We don't give a rat's ass what you think!* But in the end, all of us kids were literally, or later, when we were too big, figuratively yanked back by our wrists, our parents hissing, "What will people think?" But I had made it impossible for her to balk this time. The threat of suicide wasn't a bluff she was willing to call. She loved me too much to let that happen. Plus, the shame that she'd heap upon herself if her only child killed himself would be too much to bear. Through those past two years, I had learned to play my hand well.

"We'll talk about this tonight when your father gets home." And
then she hung up.

With a sweep of her arm, an officious-looking woman ushered
my father and me into a large waiting room in Emma Pendle-
ton Bradley Hospital, in East Providence. It looked like the elegant
living room in a mansion. My father lowered himself into an overstuffed couch and leaned forward, elbows on his knees, and massaged
his forehead.

"Daddy, what's the matter?"

He looked up. "Oh, nothing, Son," he said in a too-cheerful voice.
I felt obligated to lift his worry. I leaned against the fireplace, crossed
my right leg in front of my left, and planted the toe of my shoe in the
carpet.

"Hey, look. I'm Jay Gatsby." He furrowed his brow and cocked his
head, like he was trying to recall the name of a friend from the Old
Country.

"Gatsby. Jay *Gatsby*," I repeated, like it was the most obvious thing
in the world. "From *The Great Gatsby*?" Just a couple of years before,
all three of us had driven down to Newport, because they were filming the movie with Robert Redford and Mia Farrow there. I'd read
the book and begged them to let me audition to be an extra, but
they'd refused.

My father shook his head, confused, and went back to studying
the carpet between his feet.

A young woman came into the room and called my name. My
father jumped up and extended his hand as he walked to her. I was
relieved it was a woman. I didn't want to talk to a man about what I
was feeling.

"Bye, Dad," I said, leaving the room. I felt thrilled, delirious. I was
finally in the hands of professionals, professionals that my parents
had picked out, who would talk to me and find out what was wrong
and make it right.

Before I could begin seeing a psychiatrist, the woman said, I had to take some tests. The first was simple, she promised. All I had to do was look at inkblots and tell her what I saw. She explained that it would help her understand me better. As she held up each image, I pointed out killer bees, described a giant with huge feet trying to step on me, traced the outline of two angry pink jackals with my fingers. I didn't see how looking at these moronic images would in any way help, but she kept on nodding and urging me to find more.

"Anything else?" she asked sweetly after each picture. I tried to find more for her. I liked her. I thought she was the kind of woman I could have coffee with outside of the hospital. I didn't drink coffee, but there was something about her that made me think I could.

I shook my head. "Nope, nothing else."

Next she showed me scenes of people and wanted me to tell her a story about each one. Picture after picture was so depressing. *Jesus.* In one, a young woman was revolted by the pregnant town slut, who was sleeping with the farmhand with the impressively muscular back whom the young woman secretly loved. So she'd grabbed some books and was waiting for the bus so she could go to college in the city, far away from all this. In another, an old woman was looking out the window, failure hanging from her face. *I see why.* Her son, who was dressed in a jacket and tie and was holding his hat, had just told her he was a homosexual and was moving to a big city so he wouldn't embarrass her and his father, I said.

Wait a minute! Where did that *come from? I was tricked.*

"There's no right or wrong answer, David," she said cheerily. I looked back at the picture of the young man. Still a homosexual. Still on his way to a big city.

She put the pictures away and handed me paper and a pencil.

"Next, I want you to draw a person."

"Any person?"

"Anyone."

I grabbed the pencil and hunched over the paper. This was going to be a cinch. I didn't think too many of the kids she saw had taken several years of private art lessons like I had. I drew a woman with soft billows of dark hair, a white dress that was tight through the bodice and flared from the hips. On her feet were white matching pointy pumps.

"I'm done," I told her, sliding the overturned paper across the desk. I was certain she'd turn it over and gasp. *That's* how good of an artist I was.

Instead, what I got was nothing. No gasp, no flutter of a hand over her mouth acknowledging she was in the presence of genius.

"What's the matter?" I asked of her appalling lack of response.

"Nothing." Her smile seemed genuine, but I had an unusually well-honed gift for reading women. Something was up.

"Did I do something wrong?" I ask Dr. Joyce Brothers, as I duck into her cubicle on *Hollywood Squares*.

"No, of course not, David," she says. She lifts her head toward the makeup woman so that she can powder down her oily nose.

"Then why did the doctor hold back?"

"Thank you," she says to the woman when she's done.

"Is it because I drew a lady?"

"Could be. Who was the woman?" I explain that it was my mother. There's a photograph of her sitting on the arm of an overstuffed chair, my father on the other, and in between is my father's dad, Vu Leite. In front of them is Barry, still looking scuffed and beat up, despite wearing his white Communion suit. My mother has swirls of dark hair that softly frame her face. She's wearing a white dress, sleeves to just below the elbow. Chunky buttons crawl up her blouse to a Peter Pan collar. Her shoes: white pointy pumps.

"I loved her white shoes. Does that mean I'm a sissy?"

"Did you ever want to wear them?"

I'm silent.

"David?"

"I tried them on once when I found them in an old box in the basement," I blurt out.

"Did you like it?"

"Actually, no, they hurt."

". . . Interesting."

"So what does it mean?"

"It means you have good taste." She lifts a leg and laughs. On her feet are a pair of white pumps just like my mother's. Paul Lynde looks over and smirks at me.

In my twenties I would once again be asked to look at Rorschach's inkblots, interpret the images of the Thematic Apperception Test, and draw a person. This time they'd be administered by an old doctor wearing a fraying tweed jacket in his home office. I was having a hard time focusing, because bits of his lunch were nesting in his beard and bobbled as he spoke. Nonetheless, in each instance my responses were pretty much the same as when I was fourteen—giants, killer bees, jackals, a gay man who had grossly disappointed his parents, and a woman in a white dress with white high heels. The therapist who'd ordered the tests would explain it was unusual for patients to draw the opposite sex. She said it could indicate gender issues, which I deemed bullshit, once she explained what it meant. I didn't identify as female. I was a guy, I liked being a guy, and I was quite fond of my junk. I explained to her that I'd drawn a woman—who, yes, was my mother—because I had briefly considered becoming a fashion designer in my early teens. That and the fact that dresses are a hell of a lot easier to draw than pants. She recommended we see each other twice a week. Three, if I could afford it.

The young woman at Bradley gathered up my papers and slid them into a folder.

"One last test," she said. She then asked me to spell my first name backward.

"D-i-v-a-d," I replied without stumbling.

She looked up from her pad as if she had misheard. "Spell your last name backward."

"E-t-i-e-l." Just as easily.

And so it went. Spell *mother, father, today,* and so on, backward. I barely stumbled. All I had to do was look off to the left, and I could see the letters unmooring themselves and then drifting into position. She was impressed, I could tell. *Finally.* I felt a shiver of superiority. From her reaction, I deduced that spelling backward was a sign of sound mental health. That I could somehow spell myself backward into happiness. From that point on, I obsessively spelled words in reverse. *The better and faster I do it,* I thought, *the better I'll become.* I'd look at signs or billboards or titles on the TV and spell them backward in my head.

On the way home, my father asked me how everything had gone.

"Okay, I guess." I told him about the tests, and how afterward I'd spoken to a doctor, who asked me all kinds of questions about why I'd come.

"Did he ask about us?" He meant my mother and him.

"Yes." I braced myself for more questions, but he just nodded and kept driving.

Because we were observing meatless Fridays, even though Catholicism had come to mean nothing to me, my father drove us to a little fish-and-chip joint in Somerset. He must've felt guilty, because he allowed me to order whatever I wanted. At the small square table, I pulled apart the batter-covered cod fillet, watching it flake into neat white rows, as if chiseled. I felt deeply comforted, cocooned even.

Recently, I heard a research scientist talk about the act of eating in animals. For them, she said, there is no sense of pleasure or comfort; it's strictly an instinct, hardwired in them for survival. She had a theory that when an animal's tongue is injured, which you'd think would prevent it from eating, and therefore increase its chance of dying, the very *act* of eating actually tamps down the pain, allowing it to feed until it heals. That's what eating had been for me for so long back then: something that tamped down the pain that was threatening my life, my existence, and was nourishing me until I healed. But for years, healing had ducked whenever I grabbed for it. Finally, now, with my first visit to the hospital behind me, I felt sure that health was within reach, was truly mine, and because of that, eating those fish and chips suddenly became something else: celebration. I was overwhelmed with an incandescent hope. I swiped a chunk of fish through tangy tartar sauce and offered it to my father. He scrunched his nose and shook his head. "Come on, Daddy, you love cod." And he did, but only when it was salted and dried, the leathery slabs smelling of unwashed underarms.

"Sure?"

"Yes, Son."

Although neither of us was aware of it at the time, that afternoon a divide that had been slowly cleaving our world in two was complete. I had turned from the closed, humid huddle of our family, and instead chosen the white, fluorescent-lit environment of the hospital, a place filled with strangers who weren't Portuguese, for relief. That day proved I was different and perhaps even wiser than them all, because only *I* understood that my chances lay outside—of the home my father built, of the embrace of my parents.

12

SHRiNK WRAPPED

During the weeks leading up to our return to the hospital, to meet with a doctor about the results of my tests and hear his recommendations, my mother seemed tense, like a fist, clenched and yellow knuckled. My father was quiet, unusually so. I, on the other hand felt expansive, as if a huge millstone had been cut loose from my neck.

"Maybe it's me, but I don't see why you have to go see a psychiatrist," my mother said one night over her Weight Watchers dinner. "You seem absolutely fine."

My father was poking at his plate, something Portuguese, of course. "Elvira," he said, shooting her a look. Translation: *Let it go.* Head bent, I stared at my usual dinner: three hamburgers slathered with ketchup, which didn't put a dent in the seventy pounds of ground beef we got from the half-steer my father had bought that winter.

"I'm just saying—"

"Ma, I just need it, okay?" I said, cutting her off.

What my mother didn't understand was that I didn't feel better because somehow the crushing blackness and anxiety that had dogged me for more than four years had suddenly lifted. No, I felt better because I had done as instructed: I'd dumped everything in the lap of that sweet, coffee-drinking young woman, answered every question truthfully, balked at nothing. In exchange, I was no longer responsible for figuring things out. There was a team, I was told, of psychiatrists, psychologists, and educators consulting each other and figuring out what was wrong with me.

In short, I wasn't my problem anymore.

I often wondered if my mother was afraid I'd spew a geyser of family secrets as I lay on the doctor's couch. (*Oh, God. Would I be lying on a couch? That's such a cliché.*) But what secrets? My parents weren't mean or neglectful. If anything, they were the opposite. I certainly hadn't been sexually abused—apart from what had happened with Mr. Goode, and I thought I had handled that with aplomb, especially for a ten-year-old. None of us kids had been physically abused. Sure, my grandfather had a particular fondness for The Strap, but that had been reserved mostly for my cousin Barry. But still, my mother was skittish. *If I am holding on to secrets,* I thought, *I don't want them any longer.* I wanted to talk the energy off of each mystery, to vomit up every last hunched and gnarled fear so that they would never again haunt me.

At Bradley, we sat down in a row opposite the doctor: me, my mother, my father. My mother sat with her legs crossed, hugging her purse, the one with the big yellow smiley-face button pinned to the strap. I don't remember the doctor, just some somber presence behind a big expanse of desk. Nothing like my Coffee Girl. He explained that I had a lot of fears, like that was some great and impressive discovery we should be in awe of. *No shit, Sherlock.* He continued, saying much of the fear and nervousness I was experiencing was actually related to how I dealt with anger. In his opinion, my reactions to *House of Wax* and *The Poseidon Adventure* were actually fear of my own aggression, projected huge and in glorious 3-D Technicolor. I squirmed, like my ass was suddenly itchy. I didn't understand all that he was saying, but his words—*anger, aggression, rage, hostility, tension*—rang true. Hadn't I savagely bitten Barry? Hadn't I thrown that glass at my mother, missing by inches, it shattering on the wall as she hunched away from the shower of winking shards? Hadn't I beaten Duke with his leash because he refused to be tied up in the basement, as he always had for the half hour between my leaving for school and my mother coming home, and he'd borne it as long as he could until he turned on me? And hadn't I sat there weeping, my eyes slits, my nose dripping, bewildered at my behavior, pleading with him to come to me, but he refused? The doctor knew none of this, had no proof of anything, yet I sat there flayed and exposed, shocked, as if he knew every one of my secrets. He leaned in on his elbows, lacing his fingers together, and smiled. It was the first time I liked him. He recommended I start psychotherapy, the sooner the better, and that my parents participate in casework. My mother began flicking her foot like the tail of a pissed-off cat.

He finished, expectant, waiting for a response. That's when my mother stood. "Thank you, Doctor," she said, extending her hand to him, her Courtesy-Booth Girl smile blazing at ten thousand watts. She explained she'd be happy to drive me back and forth as many times as needed, but as far as therapy for them—well, she didn't see the need. But thank you. It was the first time I ever saw anyone in my family say no to a doctor. She then looped the strap of her purse over her shoulder, and she and her smiley-face button stood at the door—twin grins—waiting for my father to open it. He and I thanked the doctor and scuttled after her.

And that's what happened: Every Friday for about two years, she picked me up after school, drove me to the hospital, and waited in that same Jay Gatsby living room as my father had. On the way home, we always stopped at McDonald's, which had just opened in Swansea. I ordered the same thing: two Filet-O-Fish sandwiches, fries, and a chocolate shake. We sat down to dinner with my father at the snack bar in our kitchen, my mother stealing a french fry every so often in between bites of her meticulously measured and carefully weighed Weight Watchers dinners. We talked about everything, except therapy.

I don't remember much about the psychologist assigned to me; most of the details have bleached from memory, like newsprint left in the sun. Thirty, maybe. Blond hair. His name is gone, too, so I'll call him Dr. Copley. Therapy with him felt right. It was logical, the same way geometry class was logical. Practical and logical and familiar. Sometimes, now, I wonder if it was therapy or just the passage of time that made the difference. It was so quiet, uneventful. There was no arc to it. No months of stony-faced silence followed by sobbing breakthroughs, with me a giant fetus curled in a corner, my head in Dr. Copley's lap, drool and snot staining his pants. Yet somehow, my moods lightened, nerves quelled, grades rebounded.

One thing I know for certain: I was heard in a way I had never been before. He encouraged me to talk, endlessly, ceaselessly. And as I did, I found new ways of explaining what I felt. I recounted the "hot molten lead being poured on my chest," the "internal combustion," the sensation of "looking at the world through the wrong end of a telescope." I described a "blackness" that was always ready to consume me; sometimes I called it a "bottomless hole" that I was on the verge of tumbling into. I characterized myself as "frozen," "trapped in amber," "spacey," or "logy."

I came to realize that fear wasn't just a feeling, but a blooming of physical reactions, and I became very good at slicing open my body, an emotional autopsy, to root out where it lived and how it affected me. First, up in my throat, I explained to him. A constriction, sometimes accompanied by a thickening of my tongue and a pop in the back of my mouth when I tried to swallow, signaled a ticky nervousness, the kind I got when I lied or was caught doing something I shouldn't. Kids' stuff. It always passed, easily and on its own.

Lower down, in the bull's-eye center of my chest. That terrifying explosion of heat, which I'd first felt during *House of Wax,* was always a harbinger of a quake of anxiety so massive, it caused me to forget myself and barrel from theaters, friends' homes, classrooms, as if it were somehow possible to outrun the feeling. What was worse was the malaise and muddle that it left behind, with its body aches, disconnection, impenetrable heaviness.

Last, still lower, in my bowels. The most primitive of all the sensations was a sudden thicket of nerves twisting in my guts, which indicated grave dread. It didn't signal a flight response, or even a girding of myself to fight, but rather an immobility, a hunkering down, as if I needed to go unnoticed to survive. It's what I felt when waking to the bluish light of predawn and knowing that to move, to leave the bed, meant I'd be a target for an offensive of feelings I just couldn't handle. Because of this response, I said, I came to understand how people in extreme cases of fear can shit themselves; it's that unnerving.

Due to this white-hot obsession, this *veneta* to verbalize what I was experiencing, I had begun falling in love with language—a slap of a surprise, because I was such a lousy reader. I loved the musty almond smell of old books and how the deckled edges of pages fluttered over my fingers, but what was on those pages often eluded me. I wasn't always able to dive through sentences to their meaning. Words like *to, two,* and *too* confounded me; I couldn't comprehend the difference. Because of that, I can count just three books that seduced me growing up: *The Incredible Journey, Jonathan Livingston Seagull,* and *The Andromeda Strain.*

But in therapy, I saw how *my* words, *my* descriptions, registered with my doctor. They landed like seeds in the space between us and took root, growing into something substantial and vital. The idea that I could take some unfathomable, inchoate sensation deep inside, translate it into language—and have someone understand me—was intoxicating and triumphant in its validation.

Words, it seemed, were a way out of this hell, and I relished everything about them: how they sounded, and especially how they sounded coming out of me. ("Hey, Leite, your nuts finally dropped!"

one of the boys at school had said when my voice lowered to the richness of a string bass. I would never be called "Ma'am" on the phone again.) Their musicality thrilled, hard consonants clanging against one another, soft sibilants whispering, all creating emotion. My favorite letter, if one can have a favorite letter, and I think one should, is *J*, as in "jump" or "judge." The vibration revving up behind my teeth, building power, until it's at last released into the waiting, open vowel.

After one English class that spring, I approached my teacher, Mrs. Barnes. She had mentioned a writing contest for ninth graders and asked if anyone wanted to enter. When she'd first told us about it, I'd ignored her; I still felt stung over the F she'd given me on our assignment to write an original aphorism. For years, my mother had chirped, "Some people eat to live; others live to eat," as a way of reminding herself she didn't necessarily have to devour the contents of the refrigerator in one afternoon. How the hell was I supposed to know she hadn't made it up? It sounded *exactly* like her. When I told Mrs. Barnes my plan, she smiled and handed me the entry form, wishing me luck.

I worked every night for weeks on what I thought was a heart-wrenching story of two boys who went camping together, only to end with one of them killing the other in a car accident. My mother bought me erasable typing paper with red double-margin rules on all four sides. As I typed endless drafts, she acted as editor. Tapping a pencil against her teeth, she read, then every so often attacked the pages, correcting typos, circling confusing words, making suggestions. The story was shot through with clichés, painfully overwrought metaphors, bursts of irrational emotions, and thinly veiled homoeroticism. She mentioned nothing of its themes. I think she was relieved that I was taking an interest in something, and that my grades were buoying back to A's.

I didn't win, but later I did take second place in a civics essay contest. The fact that I lost to Lise LaPointe, the only other person who entered, didn't dampen my enthusiasm. I thought back to when I'd

announced to my parents I wanted to be a writer, but realized I had
nothing to say. I was beginning to see I might have a story to tell
after all.

Words saved me when Vu Costa died from old age, when I was
sixteen. They weren't mine; they were Dr. Copley's. They
pulled me back from the edge where I stood, arms windmilling
against another plummet.

The afternoon of the funeral, I sat off in a corner of the restaurant where we were having the reception. My parents, my mother's
brothers, and their wives were at the door greeting people as they
ducked inside, pumping their umbrellas to chuff off the rain. It was
a gunmetal gray day in October. Some people brought food and
dropped it off on the long table, smiling their Poor-Thing smiles at us
as they shrugged out of their coats. I heard the soft shushing from the
women nearby who were unwrapping plates of desserts and Tupperware containers of hot food. I hunched over, elbows on knees, absentmindedly picking at a *malassada,* one of the fritters that Vo Leite
had made and brought all the way from Boston. I wasn't hungry.

As I sat there, all I wanted was to look inconspicuous, to disappear
into that crowd of grief and avoid anyone's questions. I was scanning
for any internal rumbles of panic again. Like a Geiger counter. *I'm a
human Geiger counter,* I remember saying to Dr. Copley. I was always
measuring, monitoring myself. "That's what being an 'identified patient' means," he said. Something about being the person in the family who registers and acts out the feelings of everyone.

I was still gutted from the wake two days earlier. We had walked
single file into the funeral home, my mother ahead of me. I could
hear the slow rising of sobs and cries from my godparents, aunts
and uncles, cousins, and my father ahead of us. With each cry, I felt
more terror, but it was my mother's scream that ripped through me.
My last hope, my last refuge to get through this was lost with her.
When I entered the room and saw my dead grandfather, I felt myself

become unmoored. That horrid, familiar feeling of hot lead being poured onto my chest and seeping into my arms and legs returned.

I started flapping my hands like dishrags. "It's happening again," I repeated to no one in particular. "It's happening again." I heard my mother somewhere, still screaming.

"Elvira, STOP!" someone yelled. Men from the funeral home, who until then had stood at a respectful distance, like stolid sentinels, bolted to the front of the room, arms outstretched as if to catch something. I looked over, and she was grabbing at the casket. My grandfather was tossing inside, like cold, hard rocks in my father's wheelbarrow.

Dina grabbed me and pulled me through a side door into the parking lot. "Here." She put something up to my nose. I pawed it away. "It's smelling salts," she shouted. She tried again, but I knocked it away and held on to her, breaking down. "I know, I know," she murmured into my ear as I sobbed. "I know." She knew it wasn't my dead grandfather but my very much alive mother who was unraveling me.

"When that feeling happens again," Dr. Copley had said, "try focusing on just one thing."

I looked at the *malassada* in my hand. It was brown and round, the size of a saucer. *Focus closer,* I could hear him say. Its surface was pockmarked with blisters, little bubbles of batter that had formed when the fritter was slipped into the hot oil. *Good, but be more specific.* It was cold and damp, because the sugar had dissolved. I hated that. Why did my grandmother always make a bunch of these, put them in plastic bags, and freeze them? They're never as good defrosted as they are fresh.

I tossed the sticky *malassada* into the trash and wiped my hands on my dress pants. No one likes cold donuts; everyone knows that. My mother walked around the food table and came up behind me. She yanked on a hank of my hair.

"Ow! Why do you always . . . do . . . that?" I asked through gritted teeth.

"Use a napkin," she said. "You don't want people talking." I stared at her, trying to cow her, but I couldn't. I never could. She was imperious, impervious, implacable. *Imperious, impervious, implacable,* I repeated to myself. The rhythm and sounds calmed me.

After Vu's death, I braced for months of pain, but they didn't come. No more hot molten lead, no looking through the wrong end of a telescope, no lying awake waiting for the sun to rise. Although we all were grieving, and, much to my embarrassment, my mother wore a small black corsage for a year, I was able to settle back into my schoolwork without much trouble, despite the fact I wondered how long it would take for two-fourteen in the afternoon, the time my grandfather had died, to lose its charge.

Is this normal?

I'd seen other kids miss school for several days because a grandparent or aunt or uncle died, and they were no different from me: picking up where we left off, catching up on all the drama that is high school. *Normal* felt so oddly anemic compared to the torrents of emotions of the past five years. I didn't miss them—at all—but I did feel suddenly aimless. Gone were the radioactive feelings I had used as touchstones. Vu's was the first family death I'd experienced, something that I'd been dreading ever since he'd had his stroke four years earlier, and now here I was, actually sitting in psychology class listening to Mr. Cote talking about Freudian theory, and feeling perfectly fine. Cocky, even. *He's a sensitive kid,* I remember everyone telling my parents. *Give him time, he'll grow out of it.*

A s we were ending therapy, I asked Dr. Copley what my official diagnosis was. He had told me when we'd started, but it had meant nothing to me.

"Generalized anxiety disorder," he said. We had studied anxiety and panic in Mr. Cote's class, and I had recognized myself in some of the symptoms. Actually, I'd recognized myself in just about all of the disorders we studied—from anorexia and schizophrenia to borderline personality disorder and trichotillomania—an obsessive need to pull out your hair. Ironically, manic depression never rang true.

During my time with Dr. Copley, though, we never once discussed boys, although I was aching to and terrified to, in equal measure. I wanted to talk about my locker-room predicament, about my penchant for blond boys who, of all things, played sports, and about Billy Lyon. Billy had these high, planed cheeks that flushed ruddy when he was embarrassed, and even though he used me to get an A on a project for French class, I didn't care. But I said nothing about it in therapy. I knew what psychiatry and the law thought of homosexuals; I'd read it in *Boys & Sex*. I didn't know if Dr. Copley had an obligation to turn me in to the police, and I wasn't about to find out. More important, I could never disappoint this man, this wonderful doctor who had helped me so much, by letting him know I was a pervert.

13

WATERMELON-FLAVORED DELIGHT

My mother waggled her fingers behind her, motioning for me to take her hand. She led me through the kitchen and dining room, and into the living room, with its expansive tropical-ocean mural above the couch. My father came in and took his place beside her, slipping his hand over hers.

Deep breath. "We have something to tell you," my mother announced.

"Okay . . ." I looked from one to the other, worried.

"We've accepted Jesus Christ as our personal savior. Your father and I have become Charismatic Christians." There was something odd about how she said it. No, not how she said it, but how she looked. Glowing, as if lit from behind, like my old Jesus candles.

"*Asthmatic* Christians? What the hell is that?"

"Watch your mouth, mister," she said. I looked at my father.

"Charismatic," he corrected me, an edge in his voice. His tone told me a boundary had been drawn, a sign erected: "No Smartasses Beyond This Point. All Violators Will Be Spit-Roasted in Hell."

She explained they were leaving St. John of God, in Somerset, where every Sunday since I was six we had sat in the second-to-last row on the left. Where every Saturday, we had taken confession. Where I had attended catechism, received Communion, been confirmed. They were trading up to the more passionate and demonstrative Calvary Temple Assembly of God, a Pentecostal denomination in Fall River. "It's a Bible-teachin', Gospel-preachin' kind of place," she added. This had to be a big deal: My mother dropped her G's for no one.

I knew they'd grown restless with the monotone drone of Father Fraga, so their leaving wasn't a surprise. Something had been changing for a while, but it was so slow and deep—slight, steady tectonic shifts in how they behaved—that I didn't put it together, this drift toward a more athletic kind of worship. First, the nativity scene that was usually packed away after New Year's now resided full-time on top of the bookcase. *Christmas in June!* My mother then banished "Jesus" and "Jesus Christ" as expletives; they could be used only as terms of supplication or ecclesiastical adoration. She applied a bumper sticker—"God's last name isn't dammit!"—to the back of her car, now so patchworked with religious slogans, I nicknamed it the God Squad Car. I said it would've been so much cooler if the bumper sticker read, "God's last name isn't dammit, Goddammit!" Suddenly, she didn't find the humor in that. No chastising slap on the arm coupled with a private smirk of appreciation for the wit.

Later, there were nights I'd return from drama-club rehearsals and my parents, who had always been asleep in their La-Z-Boys by the time *Jeopardy!* started, wouldn't be at home. When they'd return, my mother's face would be flushed, her fingers fluttering as she spoke. Once, she explained they'd been at a service where people were slain in the spirit, falling back with the push of the pastor's finger as if struck dead by lightning. Another night, in the most matter-of-fact way, she said some people had been talking in tongues, as if suddenly losing the flat, broad accent of the South Coast and sounding like weepy Albanian washerwomen were normal. Yet they believed. Me, I had my doubts.

In time, though, Calvary Temple did do something St. John of God and even St. Michael's, in Fall River, never could: It made them better people. It's as if the church polished them, bringing out the luster of their generosity, kindness, and compassion. But back then, standing in our living room, there was still plenty of Ellie Leite, B.C. (Before Conversion), to go around.

"Would *you* like to accept Jesus Christ as your personal savior?"

And here we were once again. Hers wasn't so much a question as a foregone conclusion. When she believed in something—whether Weight Watchers, S&H Green Stamps, or now the Holy Spirit—it was just assumed that I, and the rest of the population, would as well. If not now, eventually. And she could wait—for as long as you needed.

Although I'd been feeling mostly steady for about a year—and had even started going back to the movies (my first, *Blazing Saddles*)—I figured, *Why not?* It couldn't hurt. But I had to negotiate, to make it seem like I had some choice in the matter. I made it clear I wasn't going to Sunday service anymore. Those were my terms, take it or leave it. She took it. All three of us held hands as my mother, with an eloquence so extraordinary I pried open one eye to watch her, asked God to do whatever it is He's supposed to do with fledgling Born Agains.

And that's how, during the summer before my senior year, I eventually found myself at a youth meeting at St. Sebastian's Fellowship, in Fall River, where I met Paul Estrela.

Paul was a popular, outgoing guy, one year younger than me, with a riot of brown curly hair, a formidable nose, and green eyes that crinkled into stars when he laughed, like one of those Hirschfeld drawings of celebrities. He had railroad tracks of braces crossing his easy, broad smile.

He was a blank slate. He lived all the way over in Dartmouth, so

I knew nothing of his past, but I sensed something. Not in his manner or speech, but some familiar shadow, even though he didn't look furtively at other boys like I did. And wasn't remotely interested in even one of the Trinity of Proof we used back then to tell if a guy was gay: art, theater, and fashion. He did have a rapturous love of disco and hair care, though. He was constantly dragging a purple collapsible brush through his mop. Yet that was back in the late seventies, and just about every guy had a brush bulging in a back pocket of his bell-bottom jeans. His interest in disco, on the other hand, gave me pause. And hope. Everyone loved Donna Summer, Gloria Gaynor, and KC and the Sunshine Band, but he was particularly ecstatic about them, and his favorite song was "Best of My Love," by the Emotions. I bought the single and blared it over and over again, lifting the needle every few seconds so that I could transcribe the lyrics.

"Will you knock that bleddy racket off!" my mother shouted, throwing open my bedroom door. "Jeesh! You're going to drive me to Taunton State with that thing."

"I'm trying to figure out the words."

"Why?"

"I . . . I . . . just want to be able to sing along with it." I scrambled to cover the real reason: I wanted Paul to notice me. I wanted to stand out among all the fawners and sycophants.

I was no longer a virgin by definition, human or mechanical. I'd had a bumbling encounter with Greg Martin on his front porch one summer night, which had ended with me pulling splinters out of my ass and us nearly getting caught streaking across a neighbor's yard, as well as a regrettable and painful liaison with our vacuum cleaner. Yet I couldn't exactly consider myself befittingly initiated, and that suited me. I could hide from the inevitable a while longer in those ambiguous last days of adolescence. But it was becoming harder to prop up the fantasy that every boy felt this way. All the guys I had grown up with were now off with girlfriends, coming in late, breaking curfews, bragging about their sexual conquests by using ridiculous and confusing sports metaphors. What "boobs and bushes" had to do with baseball was, like the game itself, a mystery. I'd been damn successful at keeping my life separate and contained in—to use a metaphor that made sense—a jewelry box. School, here. Family, there. Boys locked away in a hidden compartment underneath it all. That is, until Paul.

Our coming together wasn't linear, direct. Instead, we furled into each other, obliquely, first from afar, then nearer, and nearer still, until there was nothing between us but warm cinnamon Tic Tac breath. It began with a wall of people around him, buffering him from me. Occasionally he'd throw a glance my way, over heads, calculated. Fishing, that's what he was doing. Not enough for me to accuse; just enough for me to betray myself. At restaurants, a bunch of us from the fellowship would command a long table. He never sat next to me, but always close enough to lean into our conversation, the others offering safety, proof I was no different from them, before he loped out. I wouldn't hear anything as I strained to listen for the liquid murmur of his voice turned toward the other end of the table, and then the inevitable mushrooming laughter of his audience. Over time, his looks lingered, bore through me, until he, too, betrayed himself, and he chose me. *Me*.

Even alone, we were tentative at first. Just innocent gestures during our Friday-night sleepovers. We'd lie on his floor listening to music, and he'd keep time by tapping my sneaker with his foot, or he'd turn on his side to face me and talk, tucking his hands beneath his head. I might remove a nonexistent eyelash from his cheek. In arguing about who was stronger, we'd strip off our shirts and measure our biceps, me pressing my chest against his back, our arms flexed and straining.

At bedtime, we used the summer heat as an excuse to shed our underwear. Lying there side by side, clearly excited, we still couldn't muster the courage. One night he got an idea.

"I'll be right back," he said, as he tugged on his jeans and tiptoed out of the room. I covered myself with the sheet and rose up on my elbows, waiting for him to return. He slipped back into the room, laughing softly, his eyes two great stars. He stepped out of his pants and slid into bed.

"Okay," he said, holding up a glass dispenser with a gold cap. "Rub this on any part of your body you want me to . . ."—here he paused, trying to find the right word—". . . explore."

"What the hell is that?"

"My sister's lip gloss." Lana, who was home from college, had a purse full of flavored gloss—watermelon, vanilla, cherry, strawberry.

"That's wicked gross."

"Don't worry about it," he said. "I'll wash it off when we're done." I hesitated, then grabbed the gloss and ran the roller-ball applicator all over my nether regions.

Paul was clearly far more experienced than Greg. In a matter of minutes, it was over.

"Now me," he whispered, flopping on his back and grabbing the lip gloss. He was more in tune with his body than I was, because I chased a trail of saccharine-sweet watermelon into creases and crevices I'd never realized were erogenous. It seemed to never end. Just as soon as I was convinced he was clean, he'd gently move my head, and I'd pick up another tributary of sweetness up the middle of his stomach to his nipples, the hollow of his throat, the soft flesh of his ears, the back of his neck, the knuckles of his spine.

He grabbed a pillow, covered his face, and muffled a long, guttural scream as his body tightened and twitched. He pulled off the pillow and dropped it to the floor. There was a goofy look on his face, like he was high. It had never occurred to me to scream, and my mentor, Russell Cantor the Masturbator, had never mentioned anything about it.

"What's the matter?" he asked when he saw me looking at him.

"Nothing. I just . . . does it help . . ."

"What?"

". . . screaming like that?"

"Are you kidding?"

I shook my head.

"*Yes*, dipshit!"

That was how our weekends went for most of the summer. As soon as I finished work at *The Spectator,* a local newspaper where I did a little bit of everything, including writing, I'd pick up Paul in my car, and we'd hang out or catch a movie. Sometimes we headed over to Macray's in Westport for fried clams.

If Paul and I got there early enough, we could find a spot, the car's tires crunching on broken clamshells as we rolled into the parking lot. We'd order, his face splitting open with a sly, metallic smile as he insisted we get fried clams *and* clam cakes *and* french fries. *Fine,* I'd say. Like a kid, he'd hurry back to the car with a cardboard box filled with red-and-white pint containers. Even with the windows open, the greasy aroma of fried foods and the sour slap of malt vinegar filled the car.

Fried clams are a New England specialty that are almost impossible to make sound enticing to outsiders. The clams—big steamers, never littlenecks, cherrystones, or hacked-up quahogs—are tossed in flour and fried until golden and crisp. What made Macray's clams so special, besides the secret flour mix, was their big, profane bellies, which dangled like little beggar's purses and exploded with juicy brininess when you took a bite. They were sweet, salty, with just the slightest pleasant sting of iodine.

Boxes between us on the seat. The slanting light painting the inside of the car orange. On the radio, "Best of My Love"; Alice Cooper's "You and Me"; "I Just Want to Be Your Everything" by Andy Gibb. Us singing along, smiling, suddenly embarrassed by the words, because they now had meaning. I ached to slide over to him, dunk a clam into sharp, creamy tartar sauce and pop it into his mouth, but I couldn't. It was unspoken, but we both knew that there could be no public affection between us.

Sometimes after eating we'd head to Lincoln Park, the amusement park across the highway. And when we returned to his house, stuffed and exhausted, he'd rifle through Lana's purse on the way to his room.

"Do you think your sister's wondering why she's going through lip gloss so fast?" I asked, tugging at my shirt and tripping out of my pants and underwear.

"Who gives a shit?" he said, tackling me onto the bed, laughing.

One morning in mid-July, Lana burst into Paul's room while we were getting dressed.

"Are you two having sex?" she whispered, looking back toward the door to make sure their parents and grandparents were out of earshot.

"Are you crazy?" Paul said, while I toed the shag rug.

"Then how do you explain this?" She held up one of her tubes of lip gloss. I blanched.

Ever cool, Paul replied, "And?"

"Look close." We both leaned in. And there it was: a huge, dark pubic hair suspended in liquid, like some alien specimen.

"Are you doing something kinky with your lip gloss, Lan?" he teased.

"Don't be an idiot. This isn't yours?" He shook his head.

She thrust it at me. "Is this *yours*, then?"

"No. I never saw it in my life."

Doubt clouded her face. "Well, I don't understand how . . ." She looked at the two of us again, then let out a frustrated groan and stomped from the room.

Paul covered my mouth with his hand and shot me a glance that said, *If you make a sound, I'll kill you.*

After we composed ourselves, he opened the door and shouted, "Mom, we're heading out," as we practically tumbled down the stairs. Only when we were in the safety of my car with the radio blaring did we bust out laughing.

"Aren't you worried she'll say something to your parents?"

"Nah. My parents would never believe her over me, and she'd look like an idiot bringing a pubic hair to them." I could just imagine the ultra-religious Mr. and Mrs. Estrela putting on glasses and squinting to see a black crinkle in her lip gloss, their smiles dropping from their faces and eyes widening as they figured out what it was.

As long as Paul didn't care, I didn't, either. I didn't know if it was love, but what I knew to be true was the tug toward him was more powerful than anything I'd ever felt. Everything I loathed about myself seemed so inconsequential when I was with him. He was a tonic. I wanted to drain me out of my body and fill it with him, so I mimicked everything he did. I used the same phrases. I copied the modulations of his voice. I wore the same kind of clothes, but I could never quite pull it off, being heavier than him. I felt unfettered and free about my sexuality for the first time in my life, and I wasn't going to let one of our DNA samples ruin it.

By August, though, Paul had changed. Maybe it had something to do with Lana finding us out, or the start of the school year—senior for me, junior for him—which had a way of deflating us. We were in my car in his driveway when he turned to me and made his announcement.

"I want to start dating."

I laughed. "Why? We already see each other all the time."

"Not *you*." There was a meanness in his voice I'd never heard before. "A girl." When I didn't respond, he blurted, "Don't you get it?"

"No, I don't."

"I'm not that way."

"*What* way?"

He hesitated. "Like . . . you."

Something in my belly slithered over itself and constricted into a knot. I didn't understand. Not like me? *He* had taught me everything I knew. *He* had approached me. *He* had kept pushing the envelope, wanting to have sex everywhere: his house, our house, my car, in the backyard on moonless nights. I had this impulse to claw at him, to gather him up and press him into me so he'd never leave.

"I gotta go." He slammed the car door and went inside.

I moped in my room for I don't know how long, playing "Best

of My Love" endlessly. I felt as desperate and nervous as I had years ago, but there was one crucial difference: I knew what was upsetting me. I could identify the source, and even though I was shredded by anxiety, the knowledge steadied me. And I found I liked it, because I could wade in the pain—proof that I did love Paul.

Proof. That's what was missing now. Without Paul, the only witness to my feelings, it had all vanished. We had disappeared, we had never happened. Around me for years were initials scrawled on lockers, rings exchanged, bodies pressed together in hallway corners, announcements of going steady that were met with hugs and claps on the back. Evidence, confirmation, validation. But not for me. Alone, proofless, I had no choice but to accept that my feelings were sick, lesser than, other, and I had better grow out of this, and soon; otherwise there was no future, except what I began calling the Goode Way, in honor of our pervert neighbor. The irony was that Paul gave in and accepted the limitation imposed upon us by a world that didn't know we as a couple had even existed.

I halfheartedly cast about for a girlfriend, fingering through a mental Rolodex of classmates, but none was right. The only possible contender was Suzanne Fortier, a petite girl with short-cropped hair, intelligent brown eyes, and the ricocheting energy of a hummingbird. She was one of my closest friends, and we spent hours lying on her bed talking; working on *The Chief,* our school yearbook; and, my favorite, baking chocolate chip cookies. She never once lifted her face to me expectantly while creaming butter, or while goofing off over a shared plate of clam strips at Howard Johnson's restaurant. Maybe she suspected, but if she did she never said anything.

No, I needed fresh blood, a girl who knew nothing about me, and I found her in a McDonald's cashier. She was a pretty brunette with everything a guy my age was supposed to find attractive: slim waist, nice-size breasts, revoltingly flirtatious manner.

Our dates, if they can be called that, consisted of my dropping by during her break and chatting over a burger. Once, when we were in one of the back booths, she looked up from her shake with a smile that I recognized as sexy and playful.

"Don't you want to go out tonight after my shift?" Her tone was suggestive, vulgar even. Then more smiles and raised eyebrows. A drill of dread bore through my stomach. It was a weekend, so I had no excuse. But I made one anyway.

"Why don't you like me?" Suddenly, she was a little girl. Her voice plaintive and bewildered. A look of hurt bloomed on her face, and it broke my heart. I said I did like her, very much. More than any girl, ever. "Really?" she asked. I nodded. I told her how I liked her eyes, and smile, and the way she always lit up when I walked in. My words tumbled out of my mouth, unplugged from any meaning, but I could see they revived her, and that was reason enough to say them.

"We'll go out next weekend, I promise." On my way out, I decided never to stop by again.

Then Paul called. My heart caromed in my chest when my mother yelled for me to pick up the phone in my room. I waited until I heard the thunk of the extension in the breezeway before I spoke.

"Hey," I said.

"Hey."

"'Sup?"

"Not much. I was wondering if you wanted to go out Friday night," he said.

Our old routine. "Sure."

"Great. Do you know Lisa Lemaire?"

"Yes," I answered cautiously. Lisa was a classmate of mine with crooked teeth and the corpulent red face of a newborn. "Why?"

"We're dating. Why don't we get together, and then we can swing by her house and pick her up?" I felt *veneta*, that unchecked, monsoon-like anger, rising. I wanted to scream, *You're just a skinny-ass faggot. I know that and you know that. And Lisa's going to know that, too.* But I was trapped. I couldn't say anything about Paul to anyone or I'd implicate myself. Then I found the perfect way to get back at him.

"Well, let's make it a double date. I'll pick up *my* girlfriend."

There was a long pause on the other end of the phone. More was said in those few dead seconds than in all of our conversations. Without any words he expressed his hurt and pain, how he missed and wanted me, his regret over the mistake he'd made, and that, yes, he *was* like me. Exactly like me, and no girl, especially Lisa Lemaire, could change that.

"Um, yeah, bring her along" was what he actually said.

When I picked him up, he slipped into the front seat smelling of Jōvan Musk, his favorite cologne. His expression was so familiar, as if I had seen it just days before. And then I understood: It was my girl's expression: sly, sexy, suggestive. And this time it wasn't my stomach but another part of me that reacted. He put his feet up on the dashboard, as he always did, and being with him felt as it always had. Nothing was different. But when I pulled up to Lisa's house, it was as if a part of him, the part only I knew, had folded up neatly, like an old, worn letter, and been tucked away. He jumped out and opened the back door for her, and suddenly I was a chauffeur.

"Hi, Lisa."

"Hey, Dave!" That was all I got the whole way. I had to watch them, tongues plunging into each other's mouths, every time I looked into the rearview mirror. I didn't exist until I picked up my McDonald's vixen. She was far prettier than Lisa and, even I had to admit, sexier. Lisa didn't seem to notice—she was too focused on Paul—but he did. And I liked it. As I drove, I caught him looking at me in the mirror while his mouth twisted toward Lisa's.

That night there was no dinner, no conversation. Paul instructed me to drive out to a secluded spot by Lee's River, far from any streetlights. And there, he and Lisa sank down in the seat. The smack of wet lips, hissing whispers, muffled giggles. I wondered how he could go at Lisa with such gusto, especially in front of us. It was almost like he was trying to prove something. To himself, perhaps, because I had proof to the contrary.

I, on the other hand, felt no compunction to prove anything. I wanted nothing more than a friendly chat with my date, but, as I expected, she had other ideas. When she slid over to kiss me, I was appalled to find her thick, grape-flavored stump of a tongue pounding its way into my mouth like a jackhammer. I knew what French kissing was but had never experienced it. Paul had refused to kiss, so up to and especially including that moment, I hadn't kissed anyone romantically. Yet I endured, pounding right back, systematically, mechanically, emphatically, waiting for it to end.

When it was over, I dropped off my date first, making a mental note to frequent Burger King from now on. Next was Lisa. She finally unlatched herself from Paul and got out. On her way to her front door, she kept twirling back, bending over to wave goodbye to Paul, who was now in the front seat with me. When she was finally inside, I pulled out and drove him home.

"You want to stay over?" he said, eyes straight ahead, when I turned into his driveway. I hesitated and leaned over, trying to read the expression on his face. "Look," he finally turned to me. "I'm just saying come in—that's all. Or not. It's up to you."

"Sure." Following him up the stairs, I had to hold myself back from grabbing his ass—as I had done countless times before.

In his room, he stripped down to his underwear. I followed his lead and climbed over him to get to my side, nearest the wall. He grabbed me and pulled me on top of him. This time there was no need for lip gloss. There was something animal-like, intense about him. Aggressive, even. This was different from before. A thought spiraled up into consciousness: *He's jealous.* He didn't like that I was with someone else, which is what had fueled his backseat bravado. The pleasure I took in his being hurt was immense. No longer was I on the passive, receptive end of this. No longer was I the person who had to follow his lead. By mimicking Paul and going on that date, I'd succeeded in snatching my own independence, which made him all the more interested in me.

Ironically, when school started a few weeks later, Lisa and I had the same physics class, and when she saw me sitting at one of the back tables, she waved furiously and dragged over a stool while juggling a stack of books in her arms. As Mr. Smith droned, she wrote "Mr. and Mrs. Paul Estrela" and "Mrs. Lisa Estrela" with hearts all around it in the margins of her notebook. I was disgusted, but said nothing.

When Mr. Smith was facing the chalkboard, she whispered, "I think he's wicked sexy," a half–question mark in her voice, and then she paused, making it seem like I was supposed to answer.

"Mr. Smith?"

"No, silly. Paul."

I rolled my eyes. *Does she suspect something? Is she trying to trip me up?* I've often wondered what she would have thought had she known that while Paul got to first base with her in the backseat of my car, he and I were winning the pennant in his bed. (I finally understood what all that baseball talk was about.)

Over the next month or so, Paul drifted away. No explanation, no last talk in the car, his sneakers scuffing my dashboard. He split with Lisa, too, which made me feel better. I could pretend he hadn't left me; he'd just left. As if he'd moved or died. But without him as proof, as confirmation that what I felt was identical to, and as natural as, what those other guys felt for girls, I backpedaled. Shame and self-hatred seeped back in, like blood staining a handkerchief.

I had only one picture of Paul, a Kodachrome slide taken by his sister of us on the hood of my car, saturated with light and color. Him beaming, his head haloed by hair. Me to his right, chunky in a ghastly green shirt, my face blooming with acne. So many times I tried to summon that picture, to say, *Look, it's true. It happened.* But the slide was small, no bigger than my thumb, and I only saw us projected large and sweet-faced once, on the wall of St. Sebastian's Fellowship. It was while driving alone on long stretches of highway that I could conjure him the easiest. It was never that picture of us. Just parts of him: the pulsing divot at the base of his neck, the curve of his thigh, his tan growing lighter, his hair thinner and softer, until at his hips there was nothing but white, smooth warmth. And I'd feel myself grow and press against the crease of my pants. When he was most vivid, I would substitute an image of my McDonald's vixen, wanting to overlay form on feeling. It never worked. I was jarred out of it, aware again of the hum of the road, of who I really was.

"Please, God, take this away from me," I said, suddenly fervently religious. "I swear that if you do, I'll be a wonderful husband and father." I swiped at my face with the crook of my elbow, but no sooner had I done that than tears blurred the road again. I pulled onto the shoulder and laid my head against the headrest, staccato bursts of crying dying out. I closed my eyes and whispered, "Please, I can't be like this."

Jesus is sitting across a table from me. One leg is swung over the other, his big sandaled foot absentmindedly bouncing at the end of his ankle. He's blond and has eyes as blue as lapis. A surfer dude.

"You're not supposed to be blond," I say to him.

"You make me over in your own image," he says. "Haven't you always had a thing for blond guys?"

I'm taken aback. "That's not very Jesus-like."

"What can I say, I'm your creation." He smiles. "So, you have a little issue with your sexuality, huh?"

"You could say that." I'm unnerved by his candor.

Suddenly, game-show music fills the room, and two big red buttons appear on the table between us. One is labeled "HETERO," the other "HOMO." Jesus tells me, with a smile more out of *Teen Beat* than my catechism book, that whatever button I press, I'll be able to live that lifestyle without regret or guilt.

I take a deep breath and contemplate the "HOMO" button. I see myself toddling down a street in New York City, in a pair of red high-heeled shoes and black fishnet stockings. I lean over and see a hole in the stockings, and I curse while I poke at it. I weave over to the front steps of a church, drunk, which is curious because I don't really drink. A handsome man smiles at me, and I call him over, but he just laughs and walks on. I try to change the scenario, imagining different possibilities—entertaining in a penthouse high in the sky; walking down a sweet-smelling autumn road with a lover; being a guest on a *60 Minutes* segment about successful gay men of the seventies—but I always come back to bad drag, alcoholism, and rejection.

"No," I say. "I'm not going to make this decision. *You are.*"

Without checking my mirrors, I jammed the gas pedal and wrenched the steering wheel to the left, bucking the car into traffic. *Kill me now or let me become who I am, but it's not my decision.* My car seamlessly zippered into rush-hour traffic. I took that as an omen that things would sort themselves out on their own.

14

DAVID LEITE SUPERSTAR

Only two things were certain about college: I was going, and I'd pursue something arty. Everything else was an accident.

Sometime that autumn, the door to our senior art class opened, and a guy I barely remembered from the previous year's graduating class walked in. Our teacher, Peggy Grimes, looked up, her giant hippie glasses resting on the tip of her nose, and broke out in a huge grin. They whispered together for a long time at the front of the room, until she dragged over a gray stool splattered with paint and caked with pottery clay.

"Hey, guys," she said, wiping her hands on her filthy hip-hugger bell-bottoms. "Eyes up front, please." She introduced the guy, whose name I forget, saying he was going to talk to us about art school. I looked up from my work—a pen-and-ink drawing of some still-life in the corner with bowls and bottles and cloth that Peggy would change every so often in the name of art.

The guy still sported a head of greasy hair, his bangs little squiggled arms that seemed to hug his forehead like a life preserver. He explained that he was now a freshman at Rochester Institute of Technology, and that his major was communication design, "CD for short." He showed us his portfolio, of which I remember nothing, and described his days in class, of which I likewise remember nothing. But it was this forgettable guy with an unremarkable portfolio who cocked my life in a new and unexpected direction.

That night as I was rushing out to rehearsal for *Romeo and Juliet,* I announced with some fanfare to my parents that I was going to Rochester Institute of Technology and I was going to "study CD."

"What's that?" my father asked. My mother, who was standing at the sink, had the dishrag already clenched in her fist, in case she needed it.

"Oh, sorry," I said, in a patronizing way that made it clear they weren't part of the in art crowd. "Communication design."

"And exactly what's that?" she asked, knuckles glowing yellow.

How I relished that moment. I paused for maximum effect and said, "You would know it as 'commercial art.'" I watched as my mother's fist relaxed, and my father nodded a relieved smile.

We'd been locked in a cage match for almost a year over my future. Since I was a kid I'd loved art, a passion I got from my mother. I had stood by her side night after night as she painted that big plywood Santa Claus that stood in our front yard every December, and leaned over the snack bar to watch as she drew leprechauns, witches, and Easter bunnies. My mother was fond of holidays. It was because of her that I'd asked for private art lessons, which I took for several years. So naturally we all assumed I'd become some sort of artist, although my father had drawn the line at fine arts. "No money in that," he said over the whining of his table saw in the garage one afternoon.

In my early teens, my interest had drifted to photography. I begged them for a thirty-five-millimeter camera, which, after months of torture as my mother sighed melodramatically over their supposedly dwindling bank account, I got for Christmas. I was churning with so much excitement that in the middle of church service, I banged through the doors and barfed up my breakfast over the railing, careful to miss the life-size Nativity. When I was a junior and informed them of my *true* calling—photojournalism—my father just shook his head. "Not practical, Son. I thought you wanted to be an artist?"

"And *that's* practical?" I shouted. I knew he had said it because he was friendly with a few commercial artists at the grocery chain where he now worked as a maintenance man, and they were able to support families. Keeping snotty-faced rug rats clothed and fed equaled "practical" to my father.

He pounded his fist on the snack bar, making the plates jump. "Dammit!" The junkyard dog was back.

"Manny!" my mother bleated.

"Sorry, sweetheart." He lowered his voice and looked at me. "Son—you'll be the first in our family ever to go to college, and your mother and me are not going to pay for something you can't make a living at."

For months I pleaded my case. When that didn't work, and photography was a nonstarter, I tried to figure out what kind of art I wanted to study: fashion (I could still draw one hell of a kick-ass dress and sexy pumps), illustration, or animation. But the answer finally came in the form of a ratty teenager with a dust mote of talent. So what if I wasn't exactly crazy about my intended major? I was certainly hep to the idea of getting out of Swansea and being on my own some eight hours away by car.

I grabbed my script for *Romeo and Juliet* and kissed my parents goodbye. "Ma banse, Dad banse."

"God bless you," they said.

"Son," my father said, "we're happy for you."

"I know, Daddy."

As I drove to rehearsal, I knew there was no way in hell I could ever tell them that I could sense my interest—that unfaithful bastard—wandering yet again, and that this time it was sidling up to the most seductive and forbidden of all the arts: acting.

It wooed me for the first time in the spring of my junior year, when I was cast as a waving party guest in *The Sound of Music,* and continued unstintingly in senior year during *Romeo and Juliet,* in which I played the pugnacious Lord Capulet. (People marveled at my ability to cry on cue. What they didn't know was I had a small Baggie filled with diced onions that I squeezed in my eyes every night before keening over the body of my dead daughter.)

But it was during the spring show, *Carnival!,* in which I played the magician Marco the Magnificent, that I experienced that electric, addictive high of performing. In a number titled "It Was Always You," I helped my assistant and on-again, off-again paramour, Rosemary, into a trick box, with just her head poking out. While I crooned about how she was always my true love, I plunged swords through the box—taking out my aggression by jabbing along to the rhythm of the song. At the end of the number, I gingerly slid a sword straight down in front of her face and pulled out a note that in a previous scene she had tidily tucked into her cleavage. As I held that sword and skewered note triumphantly over my head, the auditorium erupted. Cameras flashed. I could see the jocks pumping the air full of fists, classmates laughing and catcalling, and, somewhere in the middle of the center section, my parents beaming. I was hurtled back to those worn side steps on Brownell Street, where I was always waiting to be discovered, to be found.

As I stand there, arms still raised, someone walks out from the wings and tucks up behind me. "Hello, gorgeous." The voice is unmistakable. "Feels good, doesn't it?"

I nod, speechless.

"It's what I felt every night in *Funny Girl,*" says Barbra Streisand. She walks to the lip of the stage, the lights setting her *A Star Is Born* Afro on fire. She cups her hands over her eyes and nudges her chin to the audience. "They don't know it yet, but you're going to be famous. Huge!" She looks back to see how her pronouncement has landed. I just nod again. "Ya know, for a big mouth, you don't have much to say, do you?" It's her Fanny Brice cadence—staccato-fast and drenched in Brooklyn.

I shake my head, agog.

"Well, take it in, because all this—" She sweeps her arm out across the screaming auditorium. "It's fickle."

I understood in that moment that what I wanted—had wanted for all those years—was to be acknowledged, to be seen. With an ice-water slap of clarity, I knew I was leaving behind any aspirations of a career in art. I was going to be an actor. My only problem? By that time, I'd been accepted to RIT, and my first term's tuition and room and board had been handily paid by bank check—my parents didn't believe in personal checking accounts—with "Jesus Loves You, Bursar" written in the memo field.

From then on I was so desperate to be onstage—any stage—that when Michael Brusella, a former student of our drama teacher, was looking for two actors for a "gig" and approached Trudy Lima and me, I said, "Yes—absolutely!" without even knowing what it was for. When we pulled up to a Catholic nursing home, Trudy and I shot each other looks behind his back.

"Come this way, children." Michael was always calling everyone at school "children," even though he was only a few years older than us. He was affected that way; he liked to flutter his hands in the air and then step back, index finger pressed against his lips like he was shushing someone, as he fitted me for my Marco costumes, which he had designed and sewn himself.

In a large activity room, he instructed me to slip on a shimmery white tunic he'd brought along from the costume room at school.

"But don't I need to learn any lines or something?" I asked, as he fixed the hem of the tunic.

"Nope."

"Does Trudy?" I looked over at her. She was wrestling with a coarse, unflattering tunic of her own.

"Nope."

He magically procured a small stepladder, which he snapped open and instructed me to climb. Grabbing my arms, he spread them out, palms up. "Now," he said, pointing to the ceiling, "look up adoringly." Out of the corner of my eye, I could see him flouncing Trudy's tunic around her as she knelt, her hands clasped together in prayerful supplication.

What's going on? I mouthed to Trudy.

She shook her head, flummoxed.

Finally, the door on the far wall opened, and three women, one of whom was drooling and working her toothless gums, were led to seats in the audience. Once they were settled, Michael hit the "play" button on his boom box, and the song "Jesus Christ Superstar" blared. The women looked on, heads bobbling, lips moving in silent prayer, while Trudy and I looked away to avoid cracking up. When the song was done, the women were escorted out of the room, while we were instructed to remain frozen in ecclesiastical wonderment until the door closed.

"What the hell was that, Michael?" I asked, shirking off the tunic.

"What? They needed to feel closer to God, and you wanted another acting credit. I think that's pretty fair." I had to admit, the thought of adding Jesus to my résumé did have its ironic appeal.

That autumn at RIT, the theater club's show was, of all things, *Jesus Christ Superstar*. By that time, I'd spun the story of my statue-still appearance into a full-fledged, knock-it-out-of-the-park performance so many times that I'd convinced myself I was the *perfect* Jesus. "After all," I was fond of saying, "how many guys can say they have a carpenter father and a saintly mother?" I was so cocky, I didn't even bother to prepare a song for the audition. When I opened my mouth to sing the rock music, the director stopped me after a few bars.

"You know, I think you're better suited for the other theater on campus." A few sniggers floated from offstage. *What other theater?* I wondered.

Across the Quarter Mile, an actual quarter-mile path that separated the academic buildings from the dorms, which was a bitch to cross in windy snowstorms, was the National Technical Institute for the Deaf. The school had significant government funding and a far better theater, and, despite that smart-ass's comment, it was where I would spend most of the next three years of my life—learning sign language and lending my voice to deaf actors in more than half a dozen shows. I even sang the role of El Gallo in *The Fantasticks*. Badly, but I sang.

No matter how much I tried to focus on my classes, month after month, the theater kept stealing my attention. Finally, with just a few weeks left in freshman year, I dropped out of figure drawing, one of the core classes of the program, to audition for Syracuse University's acting program. Not long after, an envelope arrived. It was thin, containing only one sheet of paper with several short, impersonal paragraphs telling me I could always apply again next year. My father demanded I return to RIT for my second year and finish at least my associate's degree. "Son, maybe acting is something you can do on the side," he said on the phone, trying to soften the blow, "for fun."

"Yeah, whatever." I slammed down the receiver in my dorm room and flopped facedown on my bunk.

I limped through sophomore year, putting in just enough work to pass. Sometimes in class, or alone in my room, I experienced an unnerving inversion in my head and felt like I was standing outside of myself, watching, wanting to reach out, to whisper something comforting in my ear. At those times I could sense my anxiety on the periphery, like dark flashes in the corner of my eye, waiting. It'd never gone away completely—more like been pushed back into abeyance. I judged how good my days were by how little I thought of it. Rehearsals and performances at NTID, with their adrenaline and distraction, usually stamped it out for the night.

In time, my social life turned away from RIT, as I spent more time with the deaf community. Entering spring term, I was one class short (technically only a few *weeks* short) of my associate's degree: the freshman figure-drawing class I had dropped. The studio hours conflicted with my schedule, and I asked if I could take independent study so I could finish sophomore year on time.

"*Absolutely* not," the teacher said, plucking pushpins from the critique wall. I wasn't surprised; he had been pissed off when I'd told him I was dropping his class.

"That means I have to wait one full year just to take your spring class—and I've taken three quarters of it already."

"I didn't tell you to drop out, Mr. Leite." He didn't even bother to turn around.

College, I came to learn, had little to do with art history and design theory, and everything to do with who I was and, especially, who I wanted to become. Away from the claustrophobia of my family, I was beginning to rewrite the rules, and some history. I was discovering the shape and edges of me in the absence of my parents, what I liked—and didn't—without the norms of Swansea and my heritage insisting themselves.

Over those three years in Rochester, I gave an ass-whooping to all the confusion and doubt about my sexuality that had dogged me. Well, *ass-whooping* might be a little too bold. I didn't come out, technically. That signifies a single decisive act that can never be taken back, like being unfaithful, or declaring oneself a Barry Manilow fan. Rather, I arrived at RIT faux-straight, and left gay. In between, I *emerged*. First were innocent crushes on upperclassmen. Then I spent nights slumped low in my car, staring at the door of a gay bookstore from across Monroe Avenue. Eventually, I drummed up the nerve to slink in; toss a tight, nervous smile at the guy behind the register, who barely acknowledged me; and buy the first magazine within reach. Something about cowboys—at least I think it was; all the men wore chaps and had their asses hanging out. I used it once and, ripped with shame, shoved it under my mattress. When my roommate, Steve, was asleep, I walked out behind our apartment building and chucked it into a dumpster, making sure to plunge it deep beneath used diapers and spilled garbage. Then came the occasional drunken nights a fellow actor and I steadfastly refused to remember. I even went to gay bars, albeit slipping in, heart thuttering, and then dashing out the minute any man clamped eyes on me.

While I waited to take figure drawing—again—I managed to date this sweet guy named Gordon Rossiter for a bit. On our first date he said, "We're two young bucks going out for a night on the town!" Who says things like that? A WASP, that's who. And just like that, I wanted to shrug him on like a coat. To wear his easy charm, his propriety, his deep sense of entitlement, as if they were my own. In time, though, Gordon's religious upbringing thumped on his conscience, and he suddenly became too busy with classes to call, or return my calls. Heartbroken, I burrowed into my bed earlier each night and slithered out later each morning. I couldn't rally as I'd used to. I had never been affected before by the dark-nickel skies of November, but now they were impenetrable. The air seemed to pull at me, invisible fingers that dragged me back. My sadness began outliving my mourning for Gordon.

A goal—something to accomplish that would forever be proof that I had won, had overcome—was what I needed. In January 1981, I threw myself into preparing monologues for that year's college auditions, held in New York City. I camped at the public library every day, thumbing through piles of scripts. Afterward, I headed to Wegmans, the local grocery chain, and detoured around platters of prepared Kung Pao chicken, lasagna, shepherd's pie, and towering carrot cakes on my way to that sonofabitching produce section. I had to lose about twenty pounds for the planes in my face to find their angles again.

In late spring, I opened the mailbox to find a satisfyingly fat envelope from Carnegie Mellon University, which had one of the most prestigious acting programs in the country. On top of that, I had also been accepted to Washington State University, and wait-listed at NYU. At twenty-one, I was going to be a freshman. Again.

A few weeks later, I was accepted to the University of Rochester Summer Theater program as an intern. In between building sets and making props, I had a supporting role in Molière's *The School for Wives*. The morning after the show opened, I drove to the nearest convenience store for the newspaper and flipped open to the review: "David Leite, who plays Sparkish, the gay delight with a busy little kerchief and cute little bows, is one of the most sensational apprentices to come out of this or any other theatrical season."

A chorus of brakes. "What are you, an asshole?" bellowed the guy who had almost plowed me over in the parking lot while I was running in circles, screaming with excitement.

I held the review over my head. "No. I'm David Leite, superstar!"

15

BLONDE AMBiTiON

Her eyes were what got me. Enormous blue-gray gooseberries, framed by blond hair that kept falling in front of her face like drapes, and that every once in a while she hooked behind her ears. There was a sweet sadness in them, reminiscent of those paintings of kids with saucer eyes everyone had hanging in their houses when I was little. When she watched you, her gaze level and still, you felt seen, sometimes unsettlingly so, as if she alone were watching some private movie of you. She sat diagonally across from me in the circle of beat-up writing chairs, waiting like the rest of us for our first acting class at Carnegie Mellon University to begin.

Our teacher, Angela D'Ambrosia, a tiny hunch of a woman, motioned for us to introduce ourselves. As everyone spoke, I sized up my competition, because that's what they were: Of the sixty or so of us accepted that year, only a fraction would graduate, according to the gossip whispered through the vaulted halls of the College of Fine Arts. I was damn sure I'd be among them, because I had an advantage: At twenty-one, I was older than most of the rest, and certainly

more experienced. They all rattled off their résumés, each subtly trying to intimidate the rest with their achievements. But with the Big-
Eyed Girl, there was no one-upmanship, no trying to knit more from
nothing. She spoke as if what she had done was enough, and enough
had landed her here. When it was my turn, I threw down my creden-
tials, too, but instead of lead roles in high school, I topped that by
mentioning my three years of college. Instead of nonspeaking walk-
ons in summer stock, I told of my role as Sparkish at the summer
repertory theater. The only person who trumped me had been a child
actor in a Disney movie. I predicted he'd be cut by the end of freshman year, and I was right. In all, no one impressed me. Except her.

For the next two weeks, said Angela in between coughs that
sounded like a clogged sump pump, we were going to be crammed
together in that sweltering classroom for text analysis—parsing
theme, structure, mood, characterization, and action—before we
were allowed anywhere near an acting class. Flunk text analysis, and
we'd better have our bags packed.

She passed around handouts on Chekhov's *The Seagull*, the first
play we were to have read before class began, and asked if anyone had
thoughts on the main characters.

A quiet guy raised his hand. Angela nodded at him. "Well," he
cleared his throat. "Ark-a-*deen*-a—"

"Ar-*kar*-din-a," she corrected him.

"What?"

"Honey," she said, exasperation written across that tanned, tight
skin of hers, "the character's name is pronounced Ar-*kar*-din-a. You
do know this is a Russian play, right?"

The class laughed while the poor guy melted into his chair.
Bitchy, funny, sarcastic—as comforting and familiar as the Sisters
of the Spatula. Once we understood who we were dealing with,
the class tried to outdo one another in answering her questions.
They lobbed their comments, which Angela backhanded out of the
discussion—wrong, wrong, wrong. Not the Big-Eyed Girl, though.
She offered her insights and opinions like carefully wrapped cara-

mels. Me, I waited for the precise moment when Angela was most exasperated, her eyes rolling, her sighs dramatic, and said something about the need to look beyond the script, at the artifice of it all. Neither the house nor the people inside ever fulfill their potential. It's all hollow. Angela looked at me a good long time. With that statement, I was permitted to take one giant step closer. To what, none of us knew yet, but in the race to get there, I was in the lead, and that was all that mattered. I looked over at the Big-Eyed Girl, who was watching me. Caught, she flustered and began writing in her notebook.

On the way out of class, I introduced myself. "What's your name again?"

She stepped back a bit. "Bridget Orloff."

"Nice to meet you, Bridget Orloff. Want to grab some lunch?"

She blinked. "Um, no, but thanks." She said it like a question, her voice rising, like she wasn't sure being polite was the proper response to an invitation. She waved as she headed for the stairs.

Stuck up, I muttered.

A few days later, the same. "I think I'll pass," she said, suddenly taking a self-conscious and labored interest in the beat-up bag slung over her shoulder. *I hope she's a better actress than that.* For the rest of text analysis, every time I approached her, she had an excuse: *I'm busy, I'm going with my roommate, I have to go to the library, but thanks, thank you, 'ppreciate it, maybe next time?*

I was emphatically not interested in her. Sure, I'll admit it: I was uncharacteristically charmed by this soft-spoken, bug-eyed creature. Her intelligence, her creativity, and, especially, her social restraint were what I found attractive. She was barely eighteen but had the self-possession of someone twice her age. But that's where it ended. So why did I stand there, stung, every time she walked away?

Maybe she's a homophobe, I told myself. *Or intimidated.* Whatever it was, Bridget proved formidable—and frustratingly consistent—and I eventually took the hint and stopped asking her to lunch. One afternoon a few weeks later, a different bunch of us were sitting in a circle on the Kresge main stage. We had to stand and introduce ourselves, yet again. A handsome black guy stood up and swatted the grime from the butt of his jeans. He looked around, and in a deep James Earl Jones voice said, "My name is Denton-Foster Labette—that's Labette, with two *T*'s." A round robin of amused glances made its way along the circle. I caught Bridget's eye, and she gave me her crooked grin. She couldn't deny it: She thought it was just as funny as I did.

On the way out, I sidled up to her. "Bridget Orloff, may I escort you to dinner—that's *dinner,* with two *N*'s." She let loose a great loopy laugh and rolled her eyes. And, as with Angela, I was allowed to take one giant step closer.

After text analysis, we had to clear one more hurdle—freshman projects—before we were sorted into various acting classes. Unlike other teachers who had their sections perform plays, Angela had us create story theater. We brought "The Wolf and the Fox," "The Fisherman and His Wife," "Chicken Little," and other fables to life through hours of improvisation. She sat there with an unlit cigarette cocked in her hand, electric and engaged. If she liked what you were doing, delight crackled across her face, her laughs punctuated by hacking, phlegmy coughs that she'd wave away with her hand. Mess up, and she could be brutal. She'd halt rehearsal and walk up real close to you. "Honey, that was caca," she'd say, her jaw locked, her head upturned toward yours. It was her most damning criticism. The Disney Kid and this guy who looked like he forgot to bathe got the brunt of it. The rest of us would back off and turn away, but always with one ear straining, trying to pick up on what not to do.

I played the Wolf and turned him into a gluttonous, boozy frat boy. Angela beamed, a five-year-old in front of Saturday-morning cartoons. Apparently, the newspaper review earlier that year, from when I'd been an apprentice at the University of Rochester Summer Theater, was true. And now, with Angela's Canada-goose laughter as proof, I was staggeringly, indomitably, Son-of-Freaking-God gifted.

Her reaction to Bridget, who played Goosey Loosey in "Chicken Little," was the same. Bridget was one of those actors who captivates you. She played Goosey like Edith Bunker, all scattered and clumsy but well-meaning. Nearly every class, she'd bring in something different: a new walk, like she had elastics for muscles, every limb having a mind of its own. She created dialogue that swooped through the scene, adhering to its own brand of logic—dotty and oblique like Edith's. The others chuckled, but I busted out laughing, big and unselfconscious, and Angela glared at me. Bridget smiled, appreciating my compliment—as well as Angela's rebuke. I suddenly wanted to huddle with her on a park bench, Annie Hall and Alvy, cracking her up as we goofed on people walking by.

After projects ended, and we were handed over to a different acting teacher, Bridget and I met with Angela at a bar in the Oakland section of Pittsburgh, away from CMU. The place was ugly. It could have been someone's paneled basement from the seventies, and it stunk of smoke and urinal cakes. We huddled around a pitcher of beer, trying to shout over the music.

"This meeting never happened, got it?" Angela said. We nodded. "So what's the problem?"

"Well . . . ," Bridget started. I could see she was going to be diplomatic, and this wasn't a time for diplomacy.

"Everything," I said, taking over. Angela listened to my increasingly drunken rant about the new class and teacher we were assigned to, while Bridget nodded every so often and pointed as if to say, *Yup, what he said*. It was the first time she'd ever gotten drunk, and the conversation was snaking away from her, much to her surprise.

"All right," Angela said. She looked at both of us, then paused as if considering something. Finally: "I'm going to talk to Mel to see if I can get you two bumped into sophomore class." Mel Shapiro was our department chair. "But if you breathe one word of this—to anyone— it's over. Understand?" We both nodded, Bridget's head jouncing like a bobblehead.

On the way back to campus, we weaved along the sidewalk, playing the Queen and Lady Di, our cheeks sucked in, noses properly cocked in the air. Our cupped hands swiveled on the ends of our wrists as we waved to pedestrians and passing traffic. Over-

come with happiness, I unleashed my most jubilant, regal voice, and
Bridget joined in—just as loud and unthrottled. The looks and bows
and curtsies from strangers only egged on our triumphal march up
Forbes Avenue.

Anointed by Angela, I felt an invincibility rearing up. Bridget, on
the other hand, was thrilled but never let others see it. I began
walking through campus singing "Me," a song from the musical
Rachinoff, which the upperclassmen were rehearsing that semester.
The lyric loop that I belted, arms flung up into the air, working the
sidewalk like a catwalk, went something like:

> *Me!*
> *The only one I think about is me*
> *The only one I dream about is me*
> *Me, myself, and I.*

Eggheads from the engineering and science colleges looked on,
unfazed. They were used to dramats, the nickname for theater students. "You really shouldn't be singing so loudly," Bridget said, looking around.

"Why?"

Complete deadpan. "You're kidding."

"It's in the show," which to me was justification enough.

"People are starting to talk."

"Because I'm singing?"

"Of *course* not. They think . . ."

"What?"

"That you're a show-off."

"They're just jealous, that's all." She winced and cocked her head
in a way that let me know that wasn't exactly the case. "Do *you* think
I'm a show-off?" She paused, too long. "Oh, for crissake," I said, and
walked away.

"David—"

I turned around, vicious. "What?" A *veneta* so disproportionate to the moment, so prepackaged and ready-to-serve, spiraled up my spine.

"Calm down."

"Don't tell me to calm down. What am I supposed to do? Hide? I didn't work my ass off to get here just to be told by a bunch of fuck-heads I'm being a show-off. And if I am, maybe it's because I have something to show off. Ever think of that?"

She grabbed my arm and pulled me toward her. Those eyes, big like headlights, locked on me. Soft and measured: "Why not let them *see* how talented you are instead of *telling* them?"

How someone so young could be so aware, so circumspect, was beyond me. My family pathologically chased down attention, like dogs after the mailman. Paneen drove motorcycles through burning bonfires of packing crates to the screams of fans at Seekonk Speedway. When Uncle Tony and Uncle Joe opened Tex Barry's Coney Island Hot Dogs, they proclaimed themselves to anyone who would listen that they were the Hot Dog Kings of Somerset. We were not a bashful or delicate people. Gifts like ours needed to be shared.

Something shifted that night. I'd loosed a hurricane, a swirling, vehement rage, and Bridget stood unfazed, rooted in place. She wasn't afraid of my outburst; my anger just sluiced off her. And because of her steadfastness, I felt less combustible. In that moment, something inside me leaned imperceptibly into her. Not fully, but just enough to see if she could bear the weight of me.

For the rest of that autumn, we began a slow nautilus spiral into each other. In between classes, we had fierce discussions about the nature of the soul and creativity, went to the movies and argued their merits, huddled in a library carrel murmuring over history-of-theater homework. Because my meal plan didn't include weekends, sometimes we'd meet in her room, and she'd do a little jiggy, *ha-cha-cha* soft shoe while pulling food wrapped in napkins from every coat pocket, like a vaudeville comic. We'd spread it out on the floor, little bundles of pilfered happiness, and have a dorm picnic.

There was a familiarity that spooked and bound us. I knew her, could anticipate her, and she me. We called it karma and fantasized about what past lives had led us inexorably to that precise moment. But what bonded me most to her—drew me closer every time we got together—was her belief in me. She saw what I had always hoped was there—a potential, a specialness I'd felt ever since sitting on those steps on Brownell Street—but, despite my bravado, was too unsure to believe in truly. With her, I felt limitless.

I told her that I was confused. That when I'd arrived at CMU, the last thing I expected to be captivated by was a girl. I explained how growing up I'd never felt like a normal, off-the-rack boy. I laid out, as discreetly as I could, my history with guys. I told her of the anxiety and panic, and how maybe they were related. She grabbed hold of my little finger—a way of connecting, but not too much—and just listened. I'd never been able to talk to anyone about this: certainly not my parents or Dr. Copley, or even the gay guys at RIT. They couldn't tolerate any ambiguity or waffling. Their own sexuality was still too fresh and fragile. I broke down as I admitted the self-hatred and homophobia I couldn't help feeling. If I was to be honest, I said, no matter how much I dressed it up and tossed glitter at it, I'd never quite lost the feeling that I was defective, but being around her made me feel less broken.

Holding her gaze for a long time, I said, "I don't want to be gay anymore."

She was hesitant, unsure of what that meant, unsure of me. But I needed her. Without her, I faded.

Just before the semester ended, we lay on our backs on her bunk, our legs dangling over the side. "I'm going to change for you, you know," I said.

"Change into what? A duck?"

"Bridg—" I tried to get her to take this seriously.

She went on: "A man-duck? A duck-man? Oooh, Duckman. You could be a superhero!" She laughed at her own silliness.

"Bridg, you know what I mean."

She nodded, finally asking the obvious question. "How?" She propped herself on her elbows, and her enormous eyes searched mine. It was impossible to wriggle out from the honesty and vulnerability of her gaze. It was one of the things I loved about her. That and the way she liked to burrow her hands in my coat pockets when it was cold, and how she sent me hand-illustrated cards chronicling our time together.

I thought of conversion therapy, and those Christian weekends where gay men turn straight and stop liking musicals—*all in forty-eight hours!* "I don't know, but I'll figure something out. I promise."

She nuzzled her head into my chest, rubbing the tip of her nose back and forth on my shirt to scratch it, and she looked up at me. Our mouths just inches apart. Expectation hovered in the space between us. I suddenly wanted to be anywhere but there, in that bed, at that moment. Imagining a far-off future for us, one where these wrinkles of impossibility had been smoothed away by time, always made me feel better. So I changed the subject: "Kids or no kids?"

"What?!"

I said it slower this time. "Kids . . . or . . . no . . . kids. What are you, deaf?"

"What are you, crazy? David, I'm only eighteen!"

"Don't you have that biological time bomb ticking inside?"

"Fine. Kids. You?"

"Uh-huh." I propped myself up to a sitting position, farther away from her hope. "Two. Both boys. Joshua David and Benjamin Michael."

"What are you doing, creating your own tribe?"

"I've always liked Jewish names, what can I say," doing my best Barbara Streisand. "And Amelia," I added, "if it's a girl."

"That's sweet. Where would we live?"

"New York," I said, as if there were any other option for our careers. But, I added, I reserved the right to move all five of us to Los Angeles if the right film role came along and wasn't snatched up by Timothy Hutton.

Darlene, Bridget's roommate, who knew my past, clattered in and dumped her dance bag on the floor. She peered into the bottom bunk. "Oh, gross!" she said. "I just don't *get* you two."

Bridget and I looked at each other and laughed. "Us either," she said.

W et snow was falling so heavily, it created soft yellow aureoles around the streetlamps. Giant lemon Tootsie Pops lining Fifth Avenue, one block over from CMU. I was on my way home from class in January when someone called my name. I turned around. Andrew Matas, a classmate, told me to wait up. He lived on my way home, so we walked together, the snow shushing the night, making everything muffled and intimate.

He was this beautiful Catalan with a narrow face; full, brooding lips; deep-set eyes; and a nose that had seen the scraped knuckles of a fist at least once. He was a production student, stage design. Andrew—whose real name was Andreu but who felt "Andrew" blunted his ethnicity (I could relate to that)—had a smooth, practiced way about him, as if he stood in front of the mirror and rehearsed his daily life. A lot of students, including me, made fun of him behind his back, but I could pick up a rumble of insecurity beneath his bluster.

When we reached his place, he asked if I wanted to go in. Pointing to the sky, he said, "You might want to warm up before going home."

I was attracted to him—come on, it was hard not to be—but he was straight; we all knew his girlfriend, a junior acting student named Cheryl. Even though I sensed a slutty undertone to the invitation, I accepted.

His apartment was small—two rooms, really: a kitchen-dining-living room, and off of that a bedroom. The place had that sour-milk

smell of damp gym clothes. He opened cabinets. "I have coffee . . .
tea . . . or . . ." He looked at the bottle in his hand like he'd never seen
it before. "Huh. Bailey's."

"Tea, thanks."

I was standing in a corner of the kitchen, where the counters
made an L behind me. Without asking me to move, he reached up
and over me to grab something, his chest brushing against my face.
He smelled of Drakkar Noir and sawdust. I smiled into his shirt; I
didn't think someone could be this obvious. As he filled the pot and
hunted for mugs, he seemed to be making sure every move accented
the sinuousness of his body. In movement class we had to act like all
kinds of creatures so often that I'd begun categorizing people by their
animality. Andrew was a panther: lithe, supple, with an economy of
motion. He saw the effect he was having on me and seemed to take
pleasure in it. That's when he came up to me, a sly smile on his face,
and put a hand on both sides of me and leaned in. "What would you
do if I kissed you right now?"

I'd be lying if I said I hadn't known something like this might happen when he'd invited me in, but I'm not lying when I say I had no
idea why. He'd never expressed interest in me before. In fact, we'd
hardly spoken. We shared no classes; we ran in different crowds.

I was a lousy flirt around people who were so sexual. There was
no way I could compete, so I didn't. "You're just going to have to find
out" was all I could muster.

He pressed against me and kissed me. I opened my eyes, and he
was looking on expectantly, the same way you wait for that unbidden
sigh after offering someone a sip of a stunning Port, or a bite of a sin-
fully runny Époisses. I must have reacted, because he slipped off his
shirt and T-shirt and walked toward the bedroom. I froze. When he
turned around and saw I wasn't following, he asked, "You coming?"

"I don't know . . . ," I said, screwing up my face. He looked per-
plexed. And then he took both hands and ran them down in front of
his chiseled, furred chest, as if he were the prize on a game show. His
meaning: *How could you possibly say no to this?*

Sex with him was shockingly, unexpectedly mediocre. He lay draped across the bed, like some marble sculpture by Carpeaux whose sole purpose was to be worshipped. When he did join in, it was just a bunch of perfunctory twistings and crankings of my body parts, like I was a slot machine. Or an old-fashioned dial radio. I felt immense pity for Cheryl. When it was over, he hiked on his pants. "Well, *that* was a mistake," he said with a grimace, as if he had just eaten questionable mayonnaise.

Small talk got even smaller as he waited for me to get dressed. Back in the living room, he stood holding open the door. I hurried to scuff on my sneakers.

"See you tomorrow."

"Yup," he said, chunking the door closed.

On my way home, trudging through even deeper snow, I tried to make sense of the night. Clearly, he hadn't invited me into his apartment because he was a loser with women. He was dating Cheryl, for crissake, and women practically melted on him at parties. He had platinum access. Maybe he was one of those guys who, instead of watching football or cleaning sparkplugs, messed around with guys when he was bored. I'd heard of that. But this felt calculated. He'd chosen me, specifically—let's face it, a less-than-cut specimen with the sex appeal of a Labrador retriever—to assuage lingering doubts. "Yup, see? I *knew* I wasn't gay!" I wondered if he would've been so dismissive if he had bedded Darrin, that freshman who looked like a blond Rob Lowe, or that ripped senior who'd left school to star in a Broadway show.

The bigger question, though: Why had I gone through with it? *I wasn't cheating,* I reminded myself. Bridget and I had never officially started dating, and you can't cheat on someone you're not dating. And I'd said I *"wanted* to change," "was *going* to change"; I hadn't said I already had, right? Besides, some people see more than one person—even have sex with more than one person—and they don't feel guilty. (Bad example. She and I hadn't had sex, and I continued to skate figure eights around the topic.)

Dammit. There was no way out of this; I had to tell her. She had rearranged the molecules of my heart.

At first, she crossed her arms and shrugged her shoulders in a way that said, *It's your life.* That was where I should have ended it, right there. But her lack of reaction hurt. *Didn't I mean anything to her?* The previous night's actions notwithstanding, I was willing to change for her. Her coolness made me press on to explain.

"It was a mistake." I suddenly sounded like Andrew.

"Was it?" she said, eyes narrowing. "Or maybe it's what you wanted. Maybe it's who you really are." *Who the hell taught her to throw sucker punches like that?* Then she leaned in, arms still folded: "Are you so self-centered you can't see what you do affects other people?"

This was certainly not going the way I'd staged it in my head. She was way off-script. When I reached out, she batted my hand away and backed against the closet door, her enormous eyes blooming red. Incredible. Couldn't she see I was the injured party here? Andrew had played *me,* taken advantage of *me.* She was making this all about her, when, if you think about it, this was actually good news.

"Good news?"

"Yes!"

"Tell me how this can possibly be good news, David." She spat out the words.

"Because I wasn't that interested in him," I shouted. "I was bored. It's what I've been praying for all my life. Don't you see? It's happening. And that means there's hope for us."

She paused, considering, but confusion won out, and she reached for her coat. "Bridg, wait," I said, turning her around. She stood in the doorframe of the open closet with her head down. I lifted it to mine. Her face had softened, cracked. It was then I saw something I hadn't before: the hurt, rejected little girl she had once been. The one ignored and let down by her father, she had said, over and over again. I put out my arms, and she reluctantly came to me. "Don't even think of wiping that snot on my shirt, Orloff." She swatted me and gathered up a bouquet of Kleenex and honked.

That should have been enough. But I kept on talking, mostly for my sake, trying to convince myself that what had happened with Andrew, as callous and demeaning as it was, meant nothing, that I had felt nothing. And as I bolstered myself against the truth, Bridget became a victim of friendly fire.

16

i'VE BEEN TO THE MOUNTAiNTOP

S it," she said, without turning from the stove.

"Clara, you don't have to—"

She turned around. Two prongs of a large fork were pointed up at my chest: "Sit! You think I don't, but I hear how late you come home," she added. "It's not healthy. It'd kill a *horse*." Ever since starting CMU, I'd been stumbling in as late as two in the morning because of my class schedule, plus stage crew, where we worked for hours building sets, costumes, and props for the upperclassmen. I was used to long hours at RIT and NTID, but this, this was insane. No one at school seemed to mind. I was relieved someone besides me recognized it.

Clara was my elderly neighbor across the hall. She rented out two rooms: a bedroom like mine, and an adjoining bedroom our landlady, Mrs. Mattucci, had converted into a small kitchen. It smelled of grease, onions, and stale cigarette smoke. She wore a housecoat like the kind Vo Costa and Dina wore, except hers was so threadbare I could see through it when she opened the refrigerator. I looked away out of respect.

She put some mismatched tableware in front of me and folded a paper napkin into a triangle. "You don't have to do this; I can eat at school."

She took the fork and fished a few chunks of something out of a skillet and plunked them onto a plate, then forked pasta out of another pan. She slid the dish in front of me: several rolled pieces of stuffed meat held together with toothpicks, a tangle of spaghetti on the side. I looked up at a loss.

"Brah-*jhole*." I must have appeared confused, because she added, "You never had brahjhole?" I shook my head in ignorance; she shook hers in disbelief. "I get me some nice beef," she explained, "and I cover it with some *pro-zhoot* and cheese and bread crumbs and roll it all up like a jelly roll." She shuffled over to the stove and came back with the small pot and spooned sauce over the meat and spaghetti.

"Well?"

"What?"

"Enough gravy?" She tipped her chin to the plate.

"Oh, yes, thank you."

She wheezed down into a chair, in front of an old, dented beer can, and pulled on her cigarette, tapping the ash into the opening as she talked. She asked me where I was from, what I was doing in Pittsburgh, what my nationality was.

"Port-a-geese?" she said, creasing her forehead. She looked like I'd said something wrong. I winced inside at her unknowing slight, but said nothing. My mouth was too busy enjoying what years later I learned was *braciole*.

Her simple act of kindness—feeding a virtual stranger, so much like something Vo would do—added a sense of normalcy to my days, which were beginning to telescope and grow more disjointed.

When I was done mopping up the sauce with a slice of white bread she insisted I eat, I leaned over to kiss her. She offered her cheek, holding her cigarette behind her while waving it back and forth, trying to keep the smoke out of the hall. "Thank you."

"Now, get outta here and go to sleep."

In my room I lay on my bed, satisfied, wondering why she'd finally invited me in after all these months. I knew she sometimes cracked her door and watched me coming home. "Night, Clara," I'd toss over my shoulder while unlocking my room, as if to say *I know you're there.* "Night," I'd hear, then a soft click of her door closing. Did she spy something through the crack this time? I was chronically tired and felt stung, because the gossip about Andrew and me had roared through the department. (Yes, I was the big mouth who'd told the class's other big mouth, Kelly Horowitz, who told everyone else.) In the retelling, I had become the reviled predator pouncing on the unsuspecting, straight-to-the-core foreign student. The cockiness that had buoyed me in first semester was now drowning in self-doubt and second-guessing.

So I wrote. By March, I'd filled hundreds and hundreds of pages in my journal—all a pinball game of ricocheting, clanging feelings. One day everything was dark and lifeless; I wasn't good enough. I had to "try, try, try harder, do better, work smarter." I concocted plots against me, of how my classmates were banding together to undermine me. *Jealous* was the word I underlined so many times I wore right through the pages. They were jealous that Bridget and I had been Angela's favorites. Jealous that she'd gone to Mel Shapiro, our department head, campaigning to move us into the sophomore class—a proposition he'd flatly refused. Jealous we were so close. "Stop being an asshole," I reminded myself in the margins. The next morning I'd awake, journal spatchcocked by my side, and in long, cursive strokes designed to fill up more pages faster, because geniuses wrote fast and big, I'd write how I was the smartest, cleverest, most talented, and vastly superior being in my world. I created my own principles, rules to live by. I theorized that good, true drama—the dramas of Chekhov, O'Neill, Williams—wasn't concerned with the middle, that gray, insipid world where most of us live our lives, but with only the highs and lows. The crashing conflicts and deep, foundering pain. I even drew a diagram that looked like wavelengths, but with the tops and bottoms lopped off by horizontal lines. I extrapolated from there, saying that if drama took place in those highs and lows, that was where I, as an artist, had to live my life—with Bridget, the only other true artist in our class, by my side. By bedtime, though, I would have turned my pen against myself, scrawling that I was cruel and vindictive, grandiose. I made promise after promise—to God and myself, to Bridget and our unborn kids, to my classmates—that tomorrow I'd be different! Better! Improved!

What's weird is that none of this struck me as mental. I thought I was experiencing the near-hyperbaric pressures of the program: the *What doesn't kill you makes you stronger* thinking that was the unspoken motto around the fine-arts building. But this felt different somehow. At RIT, I'd been determined to do well in the communication-design department, but I'd jumped headfirst into the deep end of campus life: I'd gone to mixers and keg parties. I'd gone out for pizza and Genesee beer at three in the morning. I'd joined a bunch of guys who mooned students crossing our quad. I'd smoked some pot and unknowingly shotgunned hashish. (It was only when I was standing in a shower stall in the women's bathroom, belting out the score of *Fiddler on the Roof,* because I was suddenly beguiled by how the acoustics flattered my voice—and most of the residents were convulsing with laughter—that I'd figured out something was amiss.) My school work had been important, but so was having a blast.

At CMU, though, I had to consider socializing a distraction, something trifling; otherwise I could get ousted when the department made its cuts at the end of the year. My determination to be the best in the class was nearly pathological. I had always been competitive, but in acting, movement, and voice and speech classes, not only did I clamor to be the best, I also silently wished for others to fail, gloriously. And when they did—fizzling in an improvisation, tripping during a movement piece, losing control of their breathing—I soared with a wicked, vicious relish.

When the warm weather hit Pittsburgh that semester, I felt an energy vibrating inside me, like an expertly plucked cello string that produces a magnificent sustained tone. Instead of craving sleep, as I had all fall semester and during the rotting black of winter, I got a cattle-prod jolt in the ass from the lack of it. I challenged myself to get up even earlier—six, five-thirty sometimes—and do my voice exercises, read scripts, write in my journal, meditate, scrawl dozens and dozens of affirmations and tuck them in the Bible my parents had given me that I still carried.

I was often out of the house before the morning rush. Pittsburgh's acrid air was bracing, urging me, stroking me to move, to glide. I walked to school, timing myself each day to see if I could make it in less time. Every morning when I walked in front of a resplendent old mansion on Fifth Avenue that had been converted to apartments, I wondered what galas, debuts, and chamber concerts took place in its once-elegant rooms that I could only glimpse if the tenants had their shutters opened.

Standing there one morning, awash in sudden and rapt appreciation for the old façade, I could feel blood coursing through my body. No, not coursing, bounding. Muscles, tendons, ligaments were frizzling, live wires stripped of their plastic covering. I felt like the life-size nude self-portrait we'd had to draw for art class at RIT. Half our bodies skin, the other half flayed to red, striated muscles. And just as I'd been exquisitely aware of each band of muscle while I was drawing it, arcing from joint to joint, I was now wondrously aware of the ripple of them. I was no longer walking, I was gliding, eliding, sliding. When I was a kid, I'd dream that I was floating along, my feet never touching the ground. That was how it felt to walk down Millionaire's Row on the way to school. From my airborne perch of superiority, I grew sad: *If only everyone could feel this way,* I thought.

Riding the bus, I imagined a film camera attached to the side, cap-turing the most nuanced of my expressions at golden hour, the time of day when the sun washes everything in a Crayola-color sunset. With my head turned away from the other riders, I'd cry because my parents had been killed when their hot-air balloon crashed over the Périgord after they'd lost consciousness eating spoiled pâté, leaving their two-hundred-million-dollar fortune to their church. *Cut!* Or, in a stunning about-face, Bridget (who in real life was growing weary of my rever-sals of sexual orientation—"Why don't you install a revolving door on your closet?" she had tossed out one night) ran off with Andrew. *Cut!* I'd scrub the tears from my face and smile dreamily, trailing a finger along the glass as I wrote the name of my newest boyfriend. *Cut!* And when the bus dropped me off, I'd pretend I was arriving in Pittsburgh for the first time, penniless but determined, thrilled by the size of the city and the warmth of the people. If Mary Tyler Moore was happy in her Minneapolis street, tossing up her knitted hat, I was delirious among the gorgeous architecture of Oakland, a section of downtown, with its august library and the awe-inspiring forty-two-story Cathe-dral of Learning, part of the University of Pittsburgh.

My speech went high-octane. I clocked more words per minute than ever before, even in my Chatty Cathy days of high school. No one said anything about the change, because I was funny, charming, arch. (Of course, they may have been terrified I'd rip into them if they did. I never bothered asking.) I was turning into a social beast. A party? *Sure, I'll come.* Dinner downtown? *Of course, let me get my jacket.* My exchanges with others took on a profundity that required me to crack open my heart now, immediately, that instant. Bridget kept a close eye, occasionally tugging back on my sleeves if she thought I was going too far, which pissed me off and sparked spittle-sprayed shouting matches back at her dorm room. Leaps of faulty reasoning were common, which sometimes led to impulsivity and stupid-ass behavior. Like the time I smeared Nair all over my face so I'd only have to shave once a week, leaving my cheeks and jaw looking like mounds of ground lamb.

Then came the eleven-part BBC production of *Brideshead Revisited*. Ditching crew, I slunk off to an AV room in the library with the first few episodes under my arm, not knowing what to expect. Wearing enormous headphones, a giant praying mantis, I watched the beauty of the relationship of Charles and Sebastian unfurl, my face slicked with tears, my chest heaving. The elegance and languor of their lives, the droll elongations and trills of their speech, were so far from the clomping charmlessness of Swansea and my Portuguese family. I ached to be with a man again. To have endless afternoons with his head in my lap, eating ripe figs, profanely juicy plums, and peaches that blushed like a Scot. To wear tuxedos during the day and warm wineglasses over a candle's flame to fully appreciate the 1899 Château Lafite Rothschild. I devoured those riveting, lazy days of eating, drinking, swimming nude—marveling at Sebastian's ruddy cheeks; those blond, blond bangs; his petulant glances at Charles, and wished they were meant for me.

In the shower one morning, that ache turned into an idea. I was seized with the conviction that I would write, produce, and direct a film version of an F. Scott Fitzgerald short story. It didn't matter which, as long as the men had aristocratic noses and porcelain skin and wore white suits and straw boater hats, like Charles and Sebastian. I'd shoot it at that old mansion on Fifth Avenue and cast it using my classmates. All I needed was funding, and certainly there had to be a National Endowment for the Arts grant I could apply for.

"Of course there is, old man!" Anthony Andrews, who played Sebastian, booms as he steps into the tub, his teddy bear, Aloysius, clasped to his chest. He stands there, fist on hip, chin aimed high, eyes glancing over at me to make sure I'm amused. When I laugh, he grabs a sponge that looks like a pink crenelated brain and begins washing my chest. And as he runs the sponge lower, lower still, his pouty mouth curls into a devilish smile, and his already haughty eyebrows raise even higher, suggesting more.

Researching at the Carnegie Library, in Oakland, I took notes in my journal. Pressure. I felt a hard, kneeling pressure. Some force was pushing me to write faster and faster, as if I were hearing dictation I needed to catch before it evaporated into the stale air. The writing caromed from subject to subject. Suddenly, I veered off, and was no longer thinking of Fitzgerald and sculpted chests with blond hair glinting in the light as it swirled down into linen waistbands. Instead I wrote about me, about how special I was, unique, unstoppable. My thoughts tumbled faster and faster and faster, until they began to collide, tripping over themselves, racing one another to the period at the end of the sentence. I couldn't keep up with the words I was hearing in my head and sat there swimming in letters astheybegancrashingintoeachothernotmakingsenseanymore.

And we have liftoff, folks!

Words uncoupled from meaning. Even their sounds clanged foreign, like Norwegian or Czech or Malay. I dropped my pen and closed my eyes. I tried to calm myself, but a night sky's worth of stars suddenly poured through a hole in the top of my head, flooding me with a light so opalescent and blinding, the hairs on my arms snapped to attention, feeling like a million tiny erections. I was so filled with light, I was sure if I opened my eyes, I'd be able to see the shadow of bones and the red glow of blood in my fingers, my nails shining like dimes, just like the young Christ in Georges de La Tour's painting *Joseph the Carpenter*.

I knew with an evangelical conviction the likes of which I had only seen in my mother that I was one of God's chosen. I suddenly understood there were thousands of us across the globe who were part of a Holy Web that protected and healed the inhabitants of Earth. That's why I was so talented, handsome, and passionate, and *that* explained why so many people were jealous of me. That also explained what Bridget saw in me. I was one of the Divinely Divine, and it was only a matter of time before people began to recognize my Special Gifts. (Apparently, when you're touched by God, you Capitalize Everything.) *Maybe I'll leave school and go to India and study to be a guru. But why? Because I can shave my head, wear orange robes, and be a guru right here, right here in the middle of Pittsburgh—I have the power of*

the Infinite Universe on my side, and there's nothing that I can't do or be-
come, because never has there been someone as unique, gifted, and connected
to the Sacred as me.

The stars then coalesced into a burning white geyser and shot out
of the top of my head, leaving me so amped up, I busted out of there
and walked all the way home.

By the end of the semester, I had been rubbed raw—exposed sinew
and bone—by the quickening of my mind. There was no longer a
separation between me and any living creature. I felt a symbiotic connection to everything, which caused me to weep over the tiniest
things—an exhausted housefly banging against the window trying
to find its way out, a smile from the checkout girl at the Giant Eagle.
I saw it as a sign that I was exquisitely sensitive, and that only I could
find the astonishing beauty, sadness, joy, and wonder in everything
around me.

As Bridget and I packed to leave for New York for summer break,
I had nothing but benevolent empathy for everyone at CMU, because
I could only imagine the pain and self-loathing they must have experienced from having me around—a constant reminder of their possibilities and how sadly they fell short. And if I needed proof, when
I burst into the administration office after the semester ended to get
my grades, Mindy, the assistant to the department head, said, "If we
gave out awards, you'd get outstanding freshman of the year. You
had the highest GPA!"

I flashed a smile and thanked her, the first in what I was sure
would be a long line of worshipful fans.

17

MY MAN PLAN

David!" Bridget's mother barked, as if I had told an obscenely off-color joke. And then to the waiter, "He'll have the veal chop." She handed him her menu. "And so will I."

Bridget and I were in New York City, dining with her mother at some marvelously snooty French restaurant with sconces on the wall and silver bread baskets. Whenever I defaulted to the simplest or cheapest dish, Mrs. O, as I took to calling her, would interject and order for me. "Remember," she said, splitting a roll with her knife and spreading a gossamer-thin smear of butter inside, "you can get chicken at Kentucky Fried."

In her lighter moments, Mrs. O had a touch of Auntie Mame to her. Together with Bridget, she introduced me to French wines and prosecco, which I like more than Champagne; duck—confit, seared, and Peking; lasagna Bolognese, the real kind, with plenty of *besciamella;* crisp sweetbreads, with their soft, creamy insides; fondue (nothing hoity-toity; it was at some low-end chain in Pittsburgh); *île flottante;* and the venerable tarte Tatin. Every so often at dinner she'd look at Bridget, who would smile that crooked smile of hers. Clearly, they were enjoying fattening me—like a Toulouse goose—during my Great Gastronomic Education, and I was all too happy to oblige.

Despite our escalating fights—long, dramatic shouting matches straight out of Tennessee Williams or Arthur Miller—Bridget and I had decided to spend the summer together. I wrangled us jobs as camp counselors at Birch Grove YMCA in the Catskills, starting in July. It didn't pay much, but it meant I wasn't going back home, which I would have considered failure. Ever since starting CMU, I'd been determined to prove to my parents I could take care of myself, and spending the summer in Swansea was the last thing on my list.

Mrs. O worked for a group of theater producers and had arranged internships for us at a casting agency for the several weeks before camp started. In exchange for not being paid, we could see as many shows as we wanted for free. And we did. *Torch Song Trilogy* with Harvey Fierstein, *Agnes of God* with Amanda Plummer, *Amadeus* with Frank Langella, *Medea, Dreamgirls, Cloud Nine, Deathtrap, Children of a Lesser God*. I assisted on auditions for countless shows, and loved to walk through waiting rooms of hopeful actors, some in their seventies, a blank clipboard in my arms for effect.

Before the shows, Mrs. O would often take us to dinner on her expense account. That was how I found myself salivating in front of a veal chop the size of my forearm, surrounded by swirls of gilt, chandeliers with millions of winking miniature prisms, tuxedoed waiters, thick starched napkins. Until that summer, the fanciest restaurant I'd been to was a place in Seekonk on a field trip for seventh-grade French class, where I could have sworn I had gotten drunk on the chocolate mousse.

On our own, Bridget and I went on the cheap. We practically moved into the Magic Pan crêperie, near her mother's office. My favorite dishes were the beef Bourguignon crêpe and the orange-and-almond salad. Earlier that year, Bridget had given me a crêpe pan and cookbook as a nothing gift. She knew I loved all things French, thanks in part to Dina and her French stuffing, and that summer I did a face-plant into pounds of butter. I was staying on West Fifty-Sixth Street at the apartment of a friend, Ron Trumble, who was acting in *Children of a Lesser God*. At night when he was performing and Bridget had gone home to Long Island, I pulled out the crêpe ingredients, propped up the cookbook on the back of the stove, and wrapped a towel around my waist. Squinting at the directions, I mixed the loose batter exactly as instructed, letting it rest in the fridge so it could bloom. I had absolutely no idea what that meant, or how to tell when it had flowered. I expected the batter to expand, the way I'd seen soft, cinnamon-speckled domes come to life in Vo Leite's warm kitchen in Somerville, Massachusetts, when she was making *massa souvada*—an eggy sweetbread with a shiny top the color of aged cherrywood.

I carefully heated the pan until a drop of water skittered across its surface. I greased the interior with a paper towel dabbed in butter and poured in the batter, cranking my arm, trying to make a perfect circle. Usually the crêpes looked more like giant eyelashes or great, self-important commas. What I lacked in elegance, I made up for in persistence. Eventually I made what I proclaimed were the finest crêpes known to man: round, thin, with the crispest filigreed edges. Bridget mastered the orange-almond salad. After particularly draining arguments, it was our peace meal.

And that's how I arrived at camp with a sizable paunch, and a plan.

"Lose weight? That'll be mighty impossible here at Birch Grove," the orientation counselor said with far too much cheerfulness in his voice on our first day. "The food is just too darn good." He was so relentlessly cheery, I half expected sunshine to shoot out of his ass when he bent over to fish out our paperwork.

My Man Plan was a regimen of exercise, dieting, education, and self-reflection to get myself in the best physical, mental, and emotional shape to return to school and become the biggest star of the stage and screen the eighties ever saw. "Move over, Tim Hutton and Sean Penn," I'd whisper while running laps on the track, "Joshua David Tealson is here." That was my carefully chosen name, which, according to my study of numerology, would assure me great fame and fortune.

The plan consisted of four parts:

1.) Read plays. I had photocopied a bunch before leaving CMU. Ponderous things like *The Iceman Cometh, Death of a Salesman, Buried Child*. After running through those, I read anything I could find: postcards the kids got, the camp's newsletters, mosquito-repellent instructions. It didn't matter. The goal was to parse meaning from the words, as any brilliant actor does.

2.) Write in my journal every night—without exception. After the kids went to bed, I wrung out every last hope. I was certain that by putting it down on paper, I was making it manifest. I was building my new life one paragraph at a time. That's what all those self-help gurus were telling us in their books.

3.) Lose weight. This was a bitch. I'd dropped about twenty pounds at CMU, mostly through deprivation and walking to and from school every day, but gained back about ten in New York. I wasn't fat, exactly. *Squidgy* might've described me better, but I didn't have the sharp jaw or flat stomach that were clearly the price of entry to stardom and leading-man roles. I vowed to reach an all-time low of 170 pounds. My *secret* goal was to be 169 pounds. Just having that numeral six in the mix gave me a thrill. No one would be able to detect a one-pound difference, and I'd never tell, but I'd always have the delicious knowledge that I had bent my body to my will.

In the three weeks I'd been at Birch Grove, life had been planed down to all square angles: exact and perpendicular. Nothing, including my determination, was off, even by a degree. S'mores, the expected birthday cakes, and ice-cream socials didn't distract—they didn't even register. My attention was locked on the looks of surprise and thinly veiled jealousy I knew I'd see when I returned as a sophomore. I was eating about one thousand calories a day and trying to burn off five hundred. I was physically weak, but I considered that a badge of honor. My skin felt like raw silk, a sure sign that I wasn't carrying any excessive water weight. My jeans from spring were now knocked out at the knees, and so loose they threatened to drop off me if I didn't wear a belt, which I never wore. I would have cut a length

of rope and looped it through my pants if it didn't smack of Elly May
from *The Beverly Hillbillies*. That was a secondary benefit of my Plan:
I'd soon be dressing sharp. Successful men didn't dress like hobos.
They wore corduroy jackets with suede patches on the elbows, argyle
sweaters, Calvin Klein white briefs, fabric belts, and penny loafers
with real pennies in them. (Or if they could pull it off: dimes.)

And finally the last, and most important, part of my Plan:

4.) Be honest. The hardest step, and one that I could only manage
while running. There was something about the metronomic *thwap* of
my sneakers on the track at five-thirty in the morning, before a lodge
full of kids came barreling at me, that allowed me to square with my
most private thoughts.

As long as I was in Bridget's presence, I could connect the dots of
my life. Buoyed by her intelligence and humor, I believed anything
was possible: becoming straight; having sex, which at this point was
still off the table; starting a family. She captured my attention and held
it, like a glinting, sparkly object, and it was dazzling. But then she'd
leave, and it was as if I would shake my head, breaking some sort of
spell. In New York, she wouldn't even be three blocks behind me on
her way home when it started. My feelings for her suddenly seemed
trumped up and suspect, and I was left wondering what the hell I was
doing. Out of her orbit, I basked in the attention of men. Because of
my weight loss, I was suddenly the object of their affection—at the
casting agency, among Ron's friends, in public. I thrilled to furtive
smiles, lingering looks, handshakes that gripped a second or two longer than appropriate. The only difference was that while what I felt
toward her was true, what I experienced with men was right.

On the last lap, I could always smell the deep notes of caramel
from warm maple syrup and the nuttiness of butter browning, wafting down from the cafeteria. My stomach protested, as it always did
those days, but I ignored it. "Deprivation Before Adulation" was my
mantra. I pumped my fists in the air like Rocky and made my way to
the arts lodge. The closer I got, the more that hope would once again
eclipse reality, and I would cast myself into the TV-movie version of

me: tall, thin, heterosexual, soon-to-be father of two boys. In other words, I acted.

W ake up, David!"
    I bolted upright. It took a few long, heart-banging seconds to orient myself. I patted around for my glasses and looked at my watch. It was after midnight.

"Get up! Come on!"

"Shhh!" I was afraid the three girls yanking at me would wake up the dozen or so boys scattered across the floor in their sleeping bags.

After another month of sixteen-to-eighteen-hour days with only two days off, Bridget and I had walked into the camp's administration office and called it quits. The counselor wasn't so sunny this time. I was wiped out after a year at CMU, but tacking on the month in New York City, along with the bone-weary exhaustion I felt from having to keep packs of kids in the arts lodge delighted, interested, and entertained, had proved too much. I was running on fumes. Our last duty before leaving was to look after those campers who had stayed on for more than one two-week session. During the changeover weekend, when kids slumped home and new ones barreled in to take their places, Bridget and I had to oversee a ragtag group of campers from different lodges.

I stumbled over to the girls' side of the lodge. Bridget looked up at me; her expression said, *Be gentle.* She was comforting a girl, eleven or twelve at the most. The girl had her face burrowed into Bridget's neck, and she was rubbing the girl's back. The rest of the girls sat in a circle, sniffling and crying, the hard light casting long, sharp shadows along the floor.

"What happened?" No one spoke. "What happened?" I said louder.

One of the girls who had gotten me spoke up: "We were playing at hypnotizing each other, and then Jennifer screamed." The other girls nodded. Clearly, she was the ringleader. *Just scary parlor tricks,* I thought with relief.

I knelt down. "Are you okay, Jennifer?" She burrowed her face deeper into Bridget's shoulder.

"Just go to sleep," I said to the group. "You'll feel better tomorrow."

"No, no, you don't understand," said the leader. She cupped her hand over my ear and whispered: "She remembered her father burning her with cigarettes. We saw her skin get red bumps."

What? I mouthed to Bridget. She shook her head. She was at a loss, but watching Jennifer cling to her, I recognized the mine shaft the poor girl had tumbled down.

I sat on the floor. A few of the others inched closer, bug-eyed. Bridget and I spent the next hour or so telling stories and trying to make them laugh. I watched Jennifer. Even though she had crawled back into her sleeping bag, I could tell she wasn't hearing or seeing us. She was now looking at us through the wrong end of that telescope.

The next morning at breakfast, I caught a glimpse of her. Her hair was a mess, and she was still in her pajamas. She sat at the table, staring right through her tray of food. I walked over from the boys' table and sat down across from her.

"Jennifer?" Nothing. "Jennifer, sweetie?" Still nothing. "Jenni—" She looked up slowly. The horror I saw buckled me. It was like I was looking into a mirror at my eleven-year-old self. Her face was vacant, sallow, almost catatonic. But it was her eyes that got me. They were pleading, asking for help, but there was also a sense of resignation. Whatever unimaginable cycle of pain she would be returning to, it seemed as though she knew it was inescapable, like a ruined record, playing the same phrase over and over again.

The familiar flashpoint of cauterizing heat ignited in my chest. *Flee, defect, escape, cut and run.*

"I'll be right back," I told Bridget, as calmly as I could.

"What's the matter?"

I looked at Jennifer and the other girls, then back at Bridget. "Nothing. Don't worry." I went over to another counselor and asked him to watch my boys, then I trotted outside and leaned against the wall.

Calm down. Just calm down, I repeated to myself. *You can handle this. You've felt this a hundred times before. This is nothing new.* I tried to picture Dr. Copley and all he had said about anxiety disorders, but as I'd tried to tell him back then, it wasn't the panic I feared—that was like a mortar shell going off: explosive, loud, knocking you off balance. It was the aftermath I dreaded. Months of that lead-dead feeling of inertia, the inability to focus, the insomnia and loss of humor, the hypervigilance—that feeling that I just didn't give a fuck about what happened to me anymore. But nothing could stanch that dread from licking its way through my arms and legs as I stood there. My breathing became so pronounced, my lips started tingling.

After *House of Wax,* I hadn't gone more than a year or two without some kind of episode—but they were always manageable, something deep breaths and frenetic activity could tamp down. This was the worst I'd experienced in the eleven years since. I couldn't get the image of Jennifer's face out of my head. I began beating my head with my fists. *STOP IT! STOP IT! STOP IT!* I shouted. I suddenly saw myself spending the rest of the summer—six long weeks—at my parents' house with nothing to do but obsess. With that, I ran: past the arts lodge, into the field, and onto the track. On the far turn I bent over, lungs burning, put my hands on my knees, and cried. I knew that no matter how hard I tried, no matter what kind of game face I put on, I couldn't outthink this, outtalk this, outpray this. Just like Jennifer. It was back, and I was helpless. I looked up at the faultless blue sky.

"You can't do this to me! Not after all I've accomplished." No answer came.

In the cafeteria, Jennifer's counselors had returned from their days off, and she had sidled up to one of them. Bridget pulled the other three aside and explained what had happened, asking them to watch her carefully. I crouched down beside Jennifer and grabbed her hands. "You're going to be fine, sweetie," I said, trying to sound unshakable. "I promise." I can't imagine she believed me, because I didn't believe it for myself.

18

THE BEST-LAID SCHEMES

When we arrived in New York, Bridget drove me to Penn Station and sat with me as I waited for the train to take me back to Swansea. In the car on the way from camp, I hadn't been able to focus. Half-listening to Bridget, I reminded myself that there were times I had experienced these implosions, and occasionally—well, rarely—they didn't take hold. Life was disrupted for a day or two, as if I had outrun it, and all it could grab hold of was my pant leg before I shook it off.

Knowing I was going off to be alone for week after endless week, I found my need for Bridget mushrooming. I didn't want to let her go. She had become an anchor, a talisman of my new life, not the hobbled, blinkered life I was returning to, with its reminders everywhere: the bedroom with the antique-car wallpaper, the snack bar, the gouge in the kitchen title where the glass I'd thrown at my mother had exploded.

"Come back with me," I pleaded.

"Now?"

I nodded my head.

"I can't, you know that."

"Come visit, then. My parents will love you, I promise." She looked at me, dubious. "It'll be great." As long as I had Bridget with me, I believed I was protected. She was my mathematical proof of growth, my 180-degree validation of where I was a year ago.

"We'll see."

I felt reset, like a top that coggled dangerously out of control but hit a chip in the pavement and righted itself.

Sitting there, I saw an effeminate, overweight young man. As he talked to his friends, he rolled his eyes, made droll, exaggerated expressions, and flapped his hands. (*Put your wings down!* I remember my mother endlessly telling me when I was growing up.)

"I feel like that's how I come across," I said to her, nudging my chin in his direction.

"Oh, noooo," she said with the kind of compassion one might show a child who put his underwear on outside of his pants. She planted her chin on my shoulder and surveyed the crowd. "Let's see . . . ," she said. "There," she added, "against the pillar." I followed her finger. She pointed to a trim, masculine man with a friendly, open face.

I began to well up. "Really? You're not just saying this because I'm—" I twirled my index finger near my temple and whistled.

"Listen to me," she said, grabbing both my wrists. "You're as sane as they come, David." I buried my face in her neck, just like Jennifer had done, and cried. She pulled me tight. "It's okay," she whispered in my ear. "You're going to be fine."

I pulled away and looked into those enormous, loving eyes, as if to say, *I am, right? I truly am going to be okay.*

Sleepy, I made my way to the snack bar on my first morning back. In front of me was a banana with "Welcome home, Son!" and "We love you!" scrawled across it. Little hearts and stars freckled the skin. Nearby was a glass of room-temperature cranberry juice—"for your plumbing," my mother was fond of saying. For as long as I could remember, my mother had been touting the healing power of Ocean Spray.

"How did you sleep?" she asked, coming up from the basement with an armful of folded laundry.

"Great." I hadn't. I'd woken up nearly every hour, until finally I'd given in and lain there, waiting for the sky to lighten so I could get up. *I'm used to getting up early at camp to go run,* I told myself. But it was a lie and I knew it. At camp, I'd had to drag myself out of bed.

The day was sheer, unrelenting hell. By bedtime that night, six massive panic attacks had thundered through me. They were so frequent that instead of counting the years or months between attacks, or "breaks," as I called them, I was now counting hours. The longest I went was two.

For some reason, talking to people about it helped. It was like I was able to infect them with it, pass it along like cooties, and they would take it with them as they left. I cornered Uncle Tony, Dina, Paneen, a cashier in the card store in the mall, even Bob Ledoux, a high school friend I hadn't seen since graduating. But as soon as I was alone again, I would get an iron-pipe swipe to the knees, and I'd crumble onto the bed, wringing my hands.

The next morning, I closed my bedroom door behind me and flipped through the Yellow Pages. My finger trailed down the listings until I found a small display ad. I took a deep breath. When I was a kid, I had memorized the telephone number in case of an emergency, the same way I had memorized my mother's work number and address. It hadn't changed.

"Driscoll Mental Health Center, how can I help you?"

I considered hanging up. This was the place Kevin, my paranoid-schizophrenic cousin, visited. I was burning with shame.

"Yes, I'd like to make an appointment to see someone."

"What's the trouble?"

"I don't feel comfortable speaking about this with you; I'd rather speak to a counselor." There was a pause on the end of the line. I could swear it was filled with judgment.

Finally: "Address and telephone, please?"

"I live in Pittsburgh, but I'm visiting my parents. And I can't have anyone calling me here."

"I'm sorry, sir, but this is a local facility for the residents of the Greater Fall River area."

"I know," I said through exasperation, "but I grew up here, and it's a fucking emergency."

"If it's an emergency, you should go to the emergency room."

"It's not that kind of emergency." I explained I wasn't suicidal, nor was I homicidal, at least not yet, but I needed to see someone right then.

"The best thing I can do is put you on a waiting list."

"How long will it take to see someone?"

"I don't know, sir. Since we can't call you, you'll have to call back each morning."

I slammed down the phone.

"Everything all right in there?" my mother shouted from somewhere in the basement.

"Yeah." I stomped through the house to the garage. I opened the basement door. "I'm taking off on my bike."

"Okay, well, be careful."

"Mom banse."

"God bless you."

Flee, defect, escape, cut and run.

I jumped on my old canary-yellow Schwinn and rode to the far end of Sharps Lot Road to visit Silvia Farm, where I had worked summers. Cora, Mr. Silvia's wife, and Billy, his son, were nowhere to be seen, so I skidded my bike into the wall and walked into the old barn, which was no longer in use. The tomato-packing assembly line was gone, the floor empty. I had ended up at the farm all those years ago because my parents thought hard work and sunshine would be an antidote for their morose teenager. Bobby Ledoux and I had ridden our bikes to the farm in the spring, me on the very same yellow Schwinn, to ask for jobs. We made a dollar and twenty-five cents an hour, working forty- to fifty-hour weeks.

For three ball-busting summers, I'd spent my days bent over picking peppers, green beans, and summer squash; stringing up and popping suckers off tomato plants; and slicing cabbages from their roots with a knife so dull I couldn't have done myself in if I'd tried—all the while getting a redneck sunburn and scratching my ass. (I'd had a run-in with more poison ivy while squatting in the woods.) I'd also had to endure the taunts of the other hired farm boys, who would point to their crotches as they called my name, because they somehow knew I was the rarest of things on a vegetable farm: a fruit. To be fair, no one had escaped the ribbing. It just stung extra-bad, because although I was too young and naïve even to be in denial yet, I somehow knew that what they were so crudely intimating was true.

During lunch I'd sit in the cool shade of the maple tree, fantasizing that one day I'd become as rich as Jay Gatsby, and that I, too, would wear swell Brooks Brothers clothes and drive a yellow Rolls-Royce while the other boys pumped my gas.

Mr. Silvia was an ornery, tough bastard, and if he thought you were slacking, he'd toss the kid next to you off his row and begin hoeing or picking or weeding right across from you—looking at you the whole time. You had sure as hell better keep up, or you might not be picked up the next morning for work when Billy made his rounds with the truck.

When I glanced up at the rafters, which looked as if they'd been washed with tobacco spit, it all came flooding back. I rocketed out of the barn, jumped on my bike, and hooked a hard right onto Marvel Street. My feet were pumping faster than my heart. One afternoon, when I was at RIT, my mother had called to tell me Mr. Silvia had passed. I was deeply sad, I'd told her, because I'd loved the old man, in my way. To get his approval had meant I was one of the guys, and I'd needed that more than anything back then.

"David," she said softly, "he hung himself in the barn." She kept talking, and I could tell from her tone she was saying something soothing, but I felt my brain slip loose, like gears on my bike, trying to catch on. How could this irascible, indomitable man have killed himself? She explained that he had been suffering from depression for a long time. Years and years ago, Cora had taken him to Boston for shock therapy, and it had worked for a long time, but it came back. This time there was nothing anyone could do.

Bludgeoned. That's how I felt, coasting down the hill to the old part of town. It seemed that whenever I stood, I got a baseball bat to my shins. I used to wonder, *How many times can a person be pummeled before he can't get up anymore? Do we have a limited reserve of energy that, once it's spent, we can never recover?* I remembered some of the Vietnam vets I'd see at the Bluffs, Paneen's slot-car racing emporium down in Ocean Grove. They had come back vacant, somehow erased. Had they been beaten too many times? I worried about myself, wondering if I was flirting with that limit, that line in the sand past which insanity, Taunton State Hospital, and hopelessness lived.

I'd manipulated my parents into getting me to a psychiatrist by threatening suicide when I was fourteen. I'd known that I wasn't going to take my life, because I'd had an unassailable certainty—which had nothing to do with naïveté, youth, or faith—that whatever was haunting me would be rooted out, with a rusting garden trowel if need be, but it would be gone. I'd be cured. In time, when I realized a cure might have been over-optimistic, I'd learned to cope with the low-frequency rumble of anxiety and moments of floating disconnectedness. I'd just never bargained with the notion that they could return, full frontal and unapologetic. And I'd never imagined that killing myself could be a relief. But now, I finally understood Mr. Silvia's choice.

The next morning, my mother pulled me into the kitchen. It was her domain, and she commanded it with a no-bullshit, do-it-my-way-or-take-a-hike mentality. But today she was gentle, solicitous even.

"Do you want to help make the marinade for the *carne assada?*" she asked. I didn't. I wanted to burrow into bed, head under my pillow, and awaken when the anxiety was gone, bleached clean like so much black mold.

Vo, sensing something was off, toddled in from the breezeway and sighed herself into a chair to watch, quietly.

"Sure."

I could always gauge how nervous my mother was about meeting someone new by how much she cooked. For Bridget, who was arriving the next afternoon to spend a few days with us, she had packed the upstairs and basement refrigerators with food. "I have no idea what the woman likes" was her reasoning. "She's Russian, for cripes' sake. What do they eat? And don't ask me to make 'paloogies,' or whatever they call those dumplings."

She pulled out the ingredients from the cupboards: paprika, my father's red wine and his onions, tomato paste, bay leaves, crushed red-pepper flakes, and plenty of garlic powder, salt, and pepper. She rooted around under the cabinets for the black enamelware roasting pan with the white flecks, and placed it on the counter. She grabbed the edge of her housecoat and wiped the inside, although it was perfectly clean. Everything in my mother's house is meticulously clean.

"Okay, first pour the wine into the pan." I did. "Next, the tomato paste." I opened both ends of the can and pushed it out with my thumb. It made a little farting noise as the cork of red plopped into the pan.

"Excuse yourself, Ma," I said to her.

"Very funny, Mister Man. Make sure it's dissolved." I used the back of a spoon to smash the paste against the side of the pan and then swirled it, brick red bleeding into the purple. "Now, add the garlic, bay leaves, and red pepper." The familiar smell, *our* smell, started to waft from the pan. It was comforting, and reoriented me whenever I walked into my parents' house after being away for a long time. I could pick out the notes of our heritage: the acidic tingle from the basement, where my father made his wine from the grapes in the back half acre; the heady sharpness of garlic and sting of onions from the kitchen. That was the Holy Trinity in my mother's and grand-mother's cooking.

She placed a hunk of beef that she had cut into quarters in the pan. "Why four pieces?" I asked.

She looked at me incredulously. "Ask *her*," she said, pointing to my grandmother. "That's how she always did it." My grand-mother craned her neck up to inspect the beef. She nodded with approval. *"Bem."*

"Now onions," my mother said, pointing to the six huge globes my father had dug from the garden the previous autumn. "Peel them, then cut them into half-moons." With my fingernail I picked at the onion's papery skin, the color and finish of bamboo flooring, and she hip-checked me out of the way. "We'll be here all day if you keep at it like that." I looked over at Vo, who rolled her eyes and fluttered her fingers over her lips, her way of trying to hide a laugh.

"Open the drawer," my mother said, which she pronounced *droh-wer*, "and hand me the knife." It was the only knife she owned. Its blade had been half worn away by my father, who over the years would trundle to the basement, flick on the rotary grinder, and file off another sixteenth of an inch in the name of sharpness. She held the onion in her left hand and pulled the knife toward her thumb, and in a few deft flicks, it was peeled. She plonked it down in front of me, as if to say, *Get a move on.* *"Pronto."* Ready.

The onions stung, and it felt good. I forced my eyes open, letting them water. My shoulders started hitching, and my mother wrapped her arms around me. I rested my chin on her shellacked beehive.

"Son, I wish I knew what to do for you," she said, which made me only cry more.

"Me, too, Ma. Me, too."

I looked over at my grandmother, and she was wiping her eyes. She didn't understand. She reached out her hand, knobby and tiny, to me. "*Querido*," she whispered, her head tilted to one side. Sweetheart. Her tone was placating, as if to say, *Stop, please stop doing this to yourself.* And I wished I could.

Desperate, my mother hauled out the Funeral Story.

"Do you remember that time Dina, Joanne, and I went to that wake?"

I nodded, already smiling in anticipation, and she began.

"Well, for some reason, the funeral home had all the mourners sitting on risers, one higher than the next, like in a stadium," she said, washing her only knife and putting it away. "I guess so everyone could have unobstructed views of death.

"Anyway, we were sitting on folding chairs about halfway up— me"—she took a step to her left—"Dina"—another step to her left— "and on the end of the row was crazy Jo." To the left of Joanne, she explained, had been one of those accordion walls that locked into place and divided the large parlor into two smaller rooms.

"Always a devil, that Jo, she starts joking with your godmother— you know how she is." She began acting out the sequence I'd known since I was a kid. "So they start *laughing*. Naturally, I poke your *tarouca* godmother to shut her up," she said, giving the air a swift jab with her elbow, "which just makes them laugh harder. So Dina elbows Jo, and, don't you know—Jo's chair slips off the edge of the riser, and she falls against the wall, ripping it out from the ceiling. Now she *and* the wall are on top of all these screaming mourners from the other wake. She's lying there, legs kicking in the air, trying to pull down her dress, screaming, 'Betty! Ellie! Help!'" Here, some of my old mother, Ellie, Before Conversion, came through, and I could see the delicious glint of evil in her eyes. "We just left her there hollering, we were laughing so hard."

The story had its intended effect. Vo was squeaking in her chair, her hand in front of her mouth so we couldn't see she wasn't wearing her dentures. Spurred on by my mother's cackling, I scrubbed the tears from my face. It felt good to bust a gut, to lose myself for a moment.

One morning while Bridget was with my mother, my father and I took off walking up Sharps Lot Road toward the green water tower, which was now painted a battleship gray. I guess to better blend itself into New England's ubiquitous overcast days, although that day it stuck out like a sore thumb. The sky was a startling cerulean blue—the kind people always mention when discussing a disaster. "The morning started out so beautiful," they say. "Who would have ever guessed?"

We turned down the lane to Mr. Silvia's old cabbage fields. The ruts from the trucks carrying all of us boys and piles of produce boxes with flexible wire closures had long ago filled in. It was almost impossible to tell this had ever been a working dirt road; it was so overgrown with grasses.

"I like Bridget, Son."

"Thanks."

I brushed my hands along the top of the grass; a few heavy bumblebees looped away. I grabbed one of the long stalks that looked like they had furry caterpillars crawling on the end. If you pulled up just so, the stalk would release from the lower leaves with a high-pitched squeak and shudder, and when you slipped it in your mouth, it had a vegetal sweetness that, to me, was the essence of summer.

A cargo hold of feelings weighed down on my chest, and I needed to empty it.

"Daddy, I have something to tell you." The grass bobbed in my mouth as I spoke.

"Okay."

We walked farther down the path, with me quiet, him waiting. I don't remember if there was a buildup, or caveats, or tears. The words were just there somehow, out in the sunlight for the first time. "I'm gay." We had reached the end of the lane, where it opened up into the old fields. They seemed smaller than I remembered, less distinct and clear-cut. I looked straight ahead, trying to remain invisible.

"But . . ." He pointed in the direction of our house. "Bridget?"

"Daddy, you know timing has never been my strong suit." After a long pause, I added, "It's confusing."

He rubbed his fingers back and forth across his lips and then under his chin; it was a gesture he so often uses when he's trying to gather himself. Before he spoke, I interjected: "Are you surprised? Honest, tell me. Are you?"

He shook his head.

There were so many questions I wanted to ask: When did he suspect? Did he remember my horror when he had explained sex to me? Was he disappointed? Before I could tell him that I wanted to change, that while I knew I loved Bridget, I was working very hard to become sexually attracted to her, he interrupted.

"Don't say anything to your mother."

I wanted to swallow my words whole. But there they were, glinting in front of us, taking up space and volume, refusing to be ignored. No sooner had I finally unburdened myself, no sooner had I thought I'd put an end to the secret that had festered since even before I was transfixed by the hair swirling out of the top of Paneen's jeans—than he wanted it hidden again. *Don't say anything to your mother.*

Bad timing. That's what this was. *You stupid, impulsive idiot.* If I had told him at a different time, maybe in a different way, he wouldn't have tried to stash it, just like *Boys & Sex*, pushed down into a box deep inside. I have no idea why I waited until Bridget was there, back home with my mother getting lunch ready, to tell him. All I knew was that I was compelled to vomit it all up, relieve myself so I could heal.

But from *what*? In my foolishness, I believed that telling him would magically lance my pain in some great, cathartic Movie of the Week moment, that I would emerge onto Sharps Lot Road changed. As if by simply opening my mouth, all the anxiety and dread and blackness would tumble out onto the lane and shrivel, dead, like slugs in the sun. Instead, I felt no different. Except now I had to live with the weight of this miscalculation.

After lunch, while my mother was washing dishes, my father

called Bridget and me into the living room and pointed to the orange couch. We sat down. He wrung his hands together hard, and I could hear the hissing of his calluses.

"Bridget," he said softly, a kind expression on his face, "this morning, David told me about—" He paused, letting his silence say what he couldn't.

She looked at me, and I nodded. "Oh!" she said, surprised. "Okay." I could see she was as nervous and as confused as I was.

A longer pause.

"Young lady, are you good with this?" he asked, moving his hand back and forth between us. "Is this what you want?"

At any other time, about any other topic, I would have turned on my father, roaring that he had no right to speak to either of us that way. But I didn't feel judged or indicted. It would have been hard to, considering how gently and carefully he had spoken. That's my father, and there was no way he could have lived with himself had he not asked.

Oddly, I don't remember Bridget's response; I wonder if I chose not to.

The night before fall semester started at CMU, Bridget and I scanned the announcement board across from the drama office for classroom assignments. Freshmen, looking spooked, milled around on the periphery, as returning students called to one another, hugged, laughed.

Everyone noticed my weight loss and new clothes, but I took no pleasure in them. I had again lost my appetite and dropped to—what? I had no idea, and I didn't care. I hadn't stepped on a scale since I'd arrived at my parents' six weeks earlier.

As I listened to them speak—some holding me at arm's length, shaking their heads in wonder—I watched their mouths moving, eyes opening wide, fingers pointing. But I heard nothing. It was as if I had gone deaf; their voices were lowered to a muffled murmur. *I won-*

der if I look normal to them. Can they tell something is wrong? Do I seem different from the David of last year? Darlene, Bridget's old roommate, laughed. *Now they're all cracking up. Better laugh so you're not found out.* So I did.

As Marcus King was in the middle of talking to me, I turned and walked away.

"All right, then," I heard him say, "be that way!"

Walking down the center hall of the Beaux-Arts building, with its vaulting beauty, I remembered one of the scripts I'd read during the summer, and the Robert Burns poem that had inspired its title, and of a line in that poem: "The best-laid schemes o' mice an' men gang aft agley."

Outside dusk was falling; the familiar coppery tang hung in the air. I looked down the mall of academic buildings and knew I had lost.

19

MiSE EN PLACE

My heart was pounding so hard I could feel it in the hollow of my throat. I faced the wall. A few pieces of tape curled like eyelashes. Behind me, two dozen or so people were about to judge me. I took a deep breath and turned around.

"It's cold," I said, rubbing my arms to warm them. I wasn't acting when I said my next line: "I'm trembling all over, just as if I'd got an examination before me." A few scattered laughs. *Not enough.* I backed up against the wall and clutched my chest like I was having a heart attack. "I suffer from palpitations, I'm excitable and always getting awfully upset!" *More laughs. Better.* Buoyed, I stole a glance at Angela. She couldn't hide her disdain; she shook her head and rolled her eyes. When I saw her put down her pen and close her notebook, I gave up. I said the rest of my lines mechanically, leaving my scene partner bewildered, her eyes pleading.

It was the start of sophomore spring semester, and I was doing a scene from *The Marriage Proposal* by Chekhov. Ever since I'd arrived back in Pittsburgh, the anxiety that had gutted me during the summer had been slowly replaced by a frightening darkness—"the Gloaming," I called it—that closed in, fading me to black. I cared about nothing. The clothes I bought went unused; the rituals that had given me so much comfort, forgotten. My bed remained unmade and unchanged for weeks. I looked just as rumpled. I had stopped running, and weight piled on; I ate constantly. Days would go by, and I wouldn't touch my journal; then, seized by a sudden, thundering imperative I couldn't ignore, I'd write long, rambling entries about the Quiet Me versus the Loud Me, introverted-self versus extroverted-self, and I didn't understand any of it.

The previous fall semester, my grades had plummeted so low that I'd been put on academic probation. Even my grade in voice and speech, which in freshman year had been an A, had fallen to a C. At first, Angela had tried to rally me in acting class, joking affectionately, finding every way into my work to pinpoint my problem. Once, she had even pulled me into the hall to verbally bitch-slap me into the moment. Nothing had worked. By December, she had given up. In the coup de grâce, she transferred me out of her class and into another section. A demotion. If I'd been myself, I would have been gutted by her abandonment. Instead, I was relieved. I was out from under the heft of her disappointment. But just before the semester started, my new teacher had gone on sabbatical, and Angela had taken over his class. Which was how I ended up standing in front of her, defeated, bracing for her critique.

"That was caca," she said through her clenched jaw. "You were indicating all over the place. I didn't believe a minute of what you did. What's *wrong* with you?" Everyone fought hard to find a place to look at that wasn't me. My scene partner was near tears. I couldn't disagree with Angela: I was vacant.

At the end of class, everyone filed out, and I pulled Angela aside. She was hugging a notebook to her chest, as if trying to protect herself. Wrapped around her shoulders, a black shawl with lots of fringe. She looked like one of her beloved Chekhov characters.

"I think I need to leave school."

She scanned my face, as if looking for a sign—the reason for my spectacular headfirst plunge into mediocrity.

"I think you should, too," she said finally, and walked away. At the door, she paused, as if considering an apology, then turned around. "David, do yourself a favor and come out of the closet. And for God's sake, leave that poor girl alone."

I stood gawking for a long time. Nothing was registering. I was swaddled in a dissociative blankness that was like thick cotton batting. The next class trickled in, staring at me staring at the door. Caught, I grabbed my bag and walked out of the fine arts building, and across campus to the administration offices to take a leave of absence.

Flee, defect, escape, cut and run.

With my scholarships and work-study on hold because I'd dropped out, I was broke. My parents floated me for several months, but attached to each money order—covered with little hearts and with "Jesus Loves You" written in the memo field—was my mother's implied plea to come home, forget about Pittsburgh. To burrow in where I belonged.

"This will always be your home, Son," my father said on the phone. I could hear the TV, which meant my mother was on the extension.

"I know, Daddy. I just need to make it work here." A soft click. She'd hung up.

"God bless you, then."

I'm not sure how I found the job, whether it was listed on a bulletin board in the administration offices, or Bridget had heard about it and passed it on, but there I was across town in Squirrel Hill on the doorstep of a CMU professor, about to interview to be the family cook.

"Come in, come in!" Professor Hollis said, waving me into the large foyer.

I was stupendously underqualified. My entire repertoire consisted of hamburgers, tuna-salad sandwiches, Toll House cookies, crêpes, and the Magic Pan salad. I had one cookbook that, along with my dictionary, thesaurus, and Bible, I took wherever I moved: my beat-up copy of *Betty Crocker's New Boys and Girls Cookbook*. And that was for sentimental reasons.

As he patted his rumpled shirt and sagging trousers for the glasses lost on the top of his head, I followed him into the dining room. Skyscrapers of papers, magazines, and bills rose from one end of the huge table. Shelves lining the wall were crammed with books, wadded-up newspapers, board games shoved in askew. There was a dog somewhere; I could smell unwashed fur and Fritos—that unmistakable scent of canine paws. Every surface was dented and burnished by life, and I instantly felt at home. I began to wonder if pigs in a blanket and s'mores, or maybe even my lasagna (but this time made with mozzarella, Parmesan, and ricotta), wouldn't be so out of the question.

In the kitchen, Professor Hollis scraped a worn wooden chair away from the table for me. He leaned against the counter.

"So, are you a student at CMU?"

My stomach rolled over on itself. It was the first time it had dawned on me that I had no role, no appositive after my name that defined me: David Leite, scholarship recipient; David Leite, acting student; David Leite, top of his class. I considered lying; it seemed less complicated. "I was. I left."

"Probably for the best. I find it almost always is." Not a hint of judgment in his voice. I fought the impulse to hug him.

"You have cooked before?"

"Of course." Technically true.

"For others."

"Yes." Again, technically true.

"Good. There are four of us," he continued. I nodded, trying to ignore the waft of garbage coming from under the sink. "We eat everything, so no worries there." I nodded again. "Whatever you make, just leave it on the stove or in the fridge with a note of how to reheat it. That's it, really."

"Sounds . . . great."

"And feel free to use those." He pointed to a line of ragged cookbooks above the refrigerator. Pieces of paper sprouted from their tops, like so many weeds.

"Let me guess: favorites?" I asked. He looked baffled. "The bookmarks."

"Oh!" he laughed. "Hardly." He pulled down a book and handed it to me. As I flipped through, forgotten shopping lists, dry-cleaning receipts, and articles cut from newspapers fluttered out. "I think things get swept up when we clear the table." Another flip, and a wedding band clinked onto the table. "Ha! My wife's been looking for this for months," he said, sliding it on his little finger. I was enchanted.

He explained that all I had to do was arrive by three o'clock and be out by five-thirty. I was responsible for cleaning up after myself and setting the table. On Fridays, I was to leave a grocery list for the next week, and someone would shop and stock the fridge and cupboards.

"Well?"

"I'll take it." He handed me a key to the house, and we agreed I'd start the following Monday.

Even though leaving school had been my choice, grief still hollowed me. For months after, I was living on theater-department time. In the morning, while I stared through a cup of cooling coffee at a breakfast joint on Walnut Street, I knew everyone was in voice and speech, warming up, asses pitched high while moving through sun salutations. While watching TV, I'd suddenly lift my head, as if on cue, and realize they were now at lunch in the Kiltie Café. Sitting in the office of Kim Mueller, the shrink I'd started seeing during fall semester, I was aware that at that precise moment, someone was in the basement of Margaret Morrison, unpacking a bag full of props and getting ready for scene-study class. Talking to Kim, who was stony-faced in her expensive Eames chair, I could feel part of myself in that basement, a phantom gliding among once-friends.

But at the Hollises', it was different. In the kitchen, time shape-shifted. It was no longer linear or linked to anything. It was free-floating and independent. Being alone for those few hours, rummaging through their gouged and sagging cabinets, was like watching Julia Child all those years ago. It was a chance to forget for a while. I'd lean over the counter and tumble into the cookbooks, zig-zagging my finger down the instructions—*Read the recipe all the way through,* Julia had instructed—and then I'd lay out the ingredients in the order I'd use them. *Mise en place,* she called it. Translation: Put in place. There was a kind of pleasure in being able to impose control and order on something, even if I couldn't impose it on myself. At times, rare and unexpected, I'd feel small, almost imperceptible shivers of happiness.

I was learning, too. I had never cooked with fresh herbs other than frizzled, curly parsley, with its wild green Afro. I'd crush them between my fingers and inhale, trying to understand them. The licorice of tarragon, the pine of rosemary, the wet woodiness of thyme. The family were chicken lovers, I discovered. So I made chicken in sour-cream sauce; chicken à la Kiev; curried chicken, which, with its frontal assault of garlic, ginger, and cayenne pepper, was a revelation. I exhausted the chicken chapter in a battered original edition of *The New York Times Cookbook* by Craig Claiborne. Flipping to other chapters and thumbing through more books, I learned that the "Lorraine" in quiche Lorraine meant bacon and Gruyère cheese. I had never heard of *blanquette de veau,* essentially a veal stew in cream sauce, but when it was requested for a dinner party, it wasn't just a hit for the family, but for me, too. I accomplished something I had never done before. And there were no critiques, no two dozen pairs of eyes watching me. If anything, I got notes of thanks stuck to the fridge with magnets.

When I wasn't happily lost in the Hollises' kitchen, I slumped. The Quiet Self, a marionette with cut strings. Bridget was never

around because of class and crew, and I refused to see my other former classmates—I could just imagine their pitying looks and karma-
is-a-bitch smirks. So in the mornings I burrowed in my bedroom,
listening as Clara started her day across the hall. Anxiety frizzled as
I heard the murmur of the TV, the clinking of fork on plate, the soft
thwump of the refrigerator door closing, an occasional bray of laughter. At one time, it had been the exceptional in life that had made me
feel less-than, incompetent. Now, it was the mundane. The idea of
merely getting up, sun splashing into the hall between our rooms,
wracked me with panic. Small, everyday pleasures caused such
angst and guilt. They reminded me I was constitutionally unable to
be buoyed by something outside of myself. I craved gray, obliterating skies, or better yet, night; the cold shoulder of winter; lashing
storms—anything a normal person would consider depressing, because I found refuge in them. Unlike an animal that changes its appearance to blend into the background, I felt camouflaged by bleak,
gloomy surroundings, and I didn't have to explain myself to others.
Didn't everyone get down on rainy days and Mondays? They even
wrote a song about that.

Despondent one night, I called Kim Mueller from a pay phone. I
was too scared to call from home and risk anyone overhearing.

"I think I need to be hospitalized," I whispered, looking up and
down Fifth Avenue.

A pause. "Do you *want* to be hospitalized?"

"Everyone, say hello to our new patient, David," says Nurse Ratched.
She's stern-looking, her hair wrapped into two giant rolls that look like
beer cans hanging off the sides of her face.

A bunch of men are shuffling around the day room, some with their
asses exposed, some smelling of dirty armpits, others of piss and shit.
One guy looks like his face is melting, his left eye dripping toward his lips.
They form a circle around me.

"Wha-wha-whadja say your name was a-a-gain?" says a thin, wiry guy
with eyes like billiard balls.

"David."

A wild-looking dude in a leather jacket offers me some Juicy Fruit gum. I shake my head no.

They start pawing at me, pulling at my clothes, molding my face like clay. One short stub of a guy grabs me hard in the balls. "Now *this* is a man! He doesn't have a thimble for a dick like me," he shouts, eyes rolling, as he lifts his hospital gown for us to see.

Shit. I didn't think this through. I'd heard stories of people being voluntarily committed to a psych ward, and they never got out. What if that was me? I hadn't breathed a word of hospitals to Bridget; we weren't seeing each other much these days. Our lives were spinning in different orbits. Hers: a tight circle of school, friends, performances. Mine: a weightless drift of slowly losing my mind.

"Maybe we should talk more about this during our next session." Then I hung up.

Late that spring, I dragged myself to the Hollises' after a particularly fruitless therapy session. Kim had leaned forward in her expensive chair, her impassive face a mask, battering me with questions I was at a loss to answer: Did I see my mother as a Madonna figure and all other women, who couldn't live up to her, whores? (Thanks to that one question, I was besieged with nightmares of being chased by a phalanx of women wearing nothing but rosary beads and fuck-me pumps.) Was I, perhaps, gay as a way of punishing my mother?

"Punishing her for *what*?"

"You tell me."

I had only Dr. Copley back at Bradley Hospital as a comparison, but I was beginning to think Kim Mueller of the Eames Chair sucked as a therapist.

Deflated, I flipped through the Hollises' massive music collection and slipped in a cassette tape. Prince told me to party like it was 1999, a date so, so far away. *I'll be thirty-nine,* I said to myself, as I slid the cast-iron skillet onto a burner. I imagined living in that house, married to Bridget, a pair of arguing teenagers upstairs—just like I'd told her that day on her bed. Joshua would take after me, but Benjamin would be all Bridget. I dropped a knob of butter into the pan and watched as it melted and slumped to the edge. I took a wooden spoon and swirled it. I had no idea what I would make, but I knew if I started with butter, it would turn out okay. I remembered the note Professor Hollis had scrawled to me several weeks earlier: "You can make your mustard chicken for us anytime. My wife loved it." Chicken, then. Yes, mustard chicken. And for that I didn't need a cookbook anymore.

As much as I found refuge and healing in their kitchen, I had to leave the Hollises. The pay wasn't cutting it, and I was broke. Sensing things were getting worse, my mother campaigned hard to get me to move back home. During calls, I could feel her gripping the phone, knuckles yellow, as she tried to contain herself: "Sweetheart, you can go back to art school at Rhode Island School of Design. Remember how much you liked taking photography classes there when you were in high school? Then you can act in Providence, or," trying to make it sound enticing, like she was holding out a candy dish of Hershey Kisses, "Boston."

"Ma . . ." It was less a protest than a plea.

When I gave my two-week notice, Professor Hollis looked as if I'd gut-punched him. "Isn't there anything we can do to get you to stay?" *Yes, pay me more money, so I can live and not have to keep borrowing from my parents,* I wanted to say. He couldn't afford to pay me a full-time salary, which is what I needed, and I had to begin living for more than two and a half hours a day. This time, I did lie: "I have another job."

"Well, then . . ." He offered his hand, and as I shook it, he clasped his left hand over mine like a big paw, engulfing it. "We'll miss you."

I nodded vigorously, a fist in my throat preventing me from speaking.

Flat out of options. I had played my last hand, called in every favor. My resistance was so low, anyone with a half-cocked solution had my full attention.

20

THE WALKiNG DEAD

I t's a kind of philosophy," said Judith to Bridget and me, cutting a quiche and nudging slices onto plates. "It teaches you about the world." Judith was a friend of ours, and the only person left rooting for us as a couple. I was half-listening as I folded paper towels for napkins. All this talk about "opposites" and "liking the world" sounded like a steaming pile of therapy horseshit worthy of Kim.

"Part of what they do is help gay men turn straight." *Now* she had my attention.

"What's it called again?" Bridget asked.

"Aesthetic Realism." *Weird name*, I thought.

During lunch, she told us her brother-in-law Tom had been gay, but now was married and lived with his wife and two kids in Greenwich Village. "You'd love him, too. He has a great sense of humor about it." Tom was the first person I'd ever heard of changing; I had to meet this guy.

"How do these aesthetes turn straight?"

"Oh, the gay thing is just one part of what they do. You could study, too," she said to Bridget. "And you don't have to live in New York, where they are; you can do it by phone."

Taking the number from Judith, we ordered literature from the Aesthetic Realism Foundation and began brushing up before our first phone session, called a "consultation." Aesthetic Realism, we read, had been founded in 1941 by the poet Eli Siegel. Its core belief is that beauty, in art and in the world, is the "making one of opposites"—his poetic way of saying we're all trying to grapple with opposing forces in ourselves and in the world. That was a fascinating concept when I first read it, and I still believe it. It seemed to address my periods of extroversion and introversion, the extreme highs and lows I'd been experiencing.

But as I curled up on the couch reading, I grew itchy from what came across as sycophantic adoration. Siegel's followers believed he was the greatest man who ever lived, and his *Self and World* the greatest book—trumping Shakespeare and the Bible. No small feat for a practically unknown writer. And they were fervent in their belief that his was an entirely new concept, that no one in the history of man had ever come up with the notion of opposites. "Oh, come on!" I yelled, flinging the book across the room. I remembered sitting in art-history class at RIT as our teacher had mumbled on about the light and dark of chiaroscuro in the work of Caravaggio, or the shimmer and structure in a Monet painting. If my *Janson's History of Art* was to be believed, both of them were trending long before Siegel wrote his first poem.

I read on. Another tenet is that we're constantly in a battle between the crucial opposites of respect and contempt for the world, and that "contempt causes insanity." Aesthetic Realism, they said, was the only way out of the morass of mental illness and into the world of mental health. This was the cause of my same-sex predilection, too: "All homosexuality arises from contempt of the world, not liking it sufficiently," and "this changes into contempt for women." Little of this tracked for me, but I assumed it was because it was all so new. My consultants assured me otherwise: My lack of understanding was actually rooted in a colossal and unmitigated contempt for Eli Siegel, the world's greatest thinker. I couldn't comprehend how I could have contempt for a man I'd never met, but I decided to keep that to myself.

Still, I spent what free time Bridget had discussing this, trying to squeeze meaning from Siegel's convoluted words.

"Does this stuff make sense to you?" I asked, lying on her couch, almost whispering for fear of offending the spirit of Siegel.

"Not totally," she said, screwing up her face, "but I do like this respect thing. We could use a little respect around here."

I didn't have to tell her. She knew exactly where to go. "R-E-S-P-E-C-T! Find out what it means to me—" we belted out together.

It felt good to be united again behind a common cause. We couldn't share acting, but we could share this. I could feel hope once more warming our relationship. Lying on her bed during freshman year, I had promised her that, Goddammit, I would change, and here was the only thing I found that promised I could—and would still let me love musicals.

It didn't take Bridget long before she ditched Aesthetic Realism. When she announced to her consultants she was leaving for a summer tour of Europe, they roundly criticized her. "Miss Orloff, don't you think your place is with Mr. Leite as he works on his change from homosexuality?" Even Judith pressed her to stay, to see me through my change. Bridget's answer to all of them was a flat and unequivocal no. They tried to get her to see she was being contemptuous of me and the world by turning her back at such a critical time.

I urged the opposite: "Bridg, go, get the hell out of here! Have a great time. Chances are I'll still be gay when you get back. We can work on it then."

And that's what she did.

While she was gone, I had a few halfhearted phone consultations and decided to move to New York within a year to pursue acting. Oh, and to start liking the world, so I could turn straight.

That summer, the anxiety and sadness ebbed, but nothing rushed

in to take their place. I felt like I was stuck in that moment right before being photographed: face slack, impatient, waiting like I had
when I was a kid, sitting on the stairs on Brownell Street. For someone to prompt me to smile. For a brilliant flash. For anything.

That "anything" certainly wasn't the undead. I'd heard about an
open call for extras for a zombie movie that was shooting outside
of Pittsburgh. All I had to do was show up at an appointed date and
time. When I arrived, I was shocked to find a park filled with wan-
nabe actors and zombie fanatics milling around. A casting person
about my age took one look at me and pointed to the left, to a waiting
bus. I think it was my Neanderthal brow that got me the job.

"I've seen every zombie film the director's ever made," said the
woman who was sharing my seat. She said it with the kind of whis-
pery adoration reserved for minor saints. Or Meryl Streep.

"Oh, you mean he's made more than one?" My comment had the
intended effect: Her mouth tightened into a hard little dash, and she
didn't talk the rest of the way. Me, I pulled out a pretentious collection of Greek tragedies, meant to intimidate the others, and read un-
disturbed for the next hour or so.

On set, which was some kind of underground facility, we changed
into hideous torn and shredded costumes. Some zombies were ushered into a makeup room, while the rest of us were smudged a few
times on the face and hands with gray makeup, then told to follow a
production assistant. He referred to his clipboard as he positioned us
throughout a cavernous section of the facility, with me dead last—
the farthest goon from the camera.

A geyser of *veneta* shot up. I hadn't busted my ass since I was sev-
enteen, and nearly dropped dead at CMU, to be a frigging zombie
stuck in the back row. As the crew was setting lights and adjusting
camera angles, I slowly threaded my way through the crowd, some of
whom were actually rehearsing their dead moans. *Morons.* The closer
I got to the front, the more detailed everyone's makeup got, I noticed.
Some people even had prosthetic brows. *Jesus!* I had the real thing,
and they'd stuck me in the back? I kept my head low so no one on

the crew could see a zombie going rogue, and slipped into the second row, behind a woman with huge hair. As I studied my torn shoes, I could see out of the corner of my eye a circle of people fussing with the back of Big Hair's wig and costume.

"Everyone, listen up," the director said through a megaphone. "When I say, 'Action,' I want all of you to shuffle toward the camera. Got it?" The zombies nodded. "Then these guys," he pointed to several actors dressed like soldiers behind him, "will run through and shoot at you. Remember: Don't react. You're dead!" Conspiratorial laughter rose from the filthy crowd around me.

The director waited as the crew made a few last adjustments to Big Hair. When they were done, they nodded and left the set.

"And . . . action!"

I lifted my head and shuffled and moaned along with my dead brethren. The director waved on the actors, who pointed their guns at us and shot off several rounds. Instantly, the back of Big Hair's head exploded, spraying the zombies behind her. Unaware of this impending gorefest, I screamed loudly. (Because I wasn't an official member of the second row, I hadn't been privy to the conversation about how a giant squib of fake blood and brains would detonate all over us.)

"Cut!" shouted the director.

"Reset," said someone else. The rest of the zombies watched as a production assistant led me away. He instructed me to clean up, paid me my one dollar, and told me to wait. In the extras' room, I sat with my book of Greek tragedies propped up in front of my face, trying to block out their derision. To them, with their filthy clothes and peeling skin, I was something repugnant: the only undead in the history of cinema to recoil at the sight of blood and guts.

Desperate for money, I auditioned for commercials. Nothing. Local theater and voiceovers. Nothing. I considered returning to CMU for the fall semester, but knew I couldn't hack it, so I officially withdrew. Nothing. Finally, I did what I'd sworn I would never do: become a cliché and wait tables. I was hired at Gullifty's, on Murray Avenue, around the corner from my new apartment. If I couldn't get a job performing, I decided, I'd turn my job into performance art. The dining-room floor was my stage; families, early birds, and couples my audience. I borrowed from voice and speech, improv, and acting classes. Describing a spinach salad with hot bacon dressing, I said, "Ladies, a delight even your thighs wouldn't hold against you." A red-stuffed pizza became a meal of Falstaffian proportions. "Imagine if you will, a gigundous pizza topped with another gigundous pizza, stuffed with mozzarella, Parmesan, and provolone, and ladled over with spicy tomato sauce." Of my favorite dish, the almighty Meshugna—corned beef, coleslaw, and Russian dressing between two potato pancakes—I said, "Don't worry, order it! We have a fully charged defibrillator with your name on it." If kids were at a table, I'd do my best Buster Keaton, suddenly losing control of my tray of food, tipping it left and right over their heads, all to squeals of laughter. That always got me a huge tip. Through talking about, eating, and serving food, I was surprised to find myself making my way back to the contentment of the Hollises' kitchen, to the peace of watching Julia on TV.

After two and a half years, and despite my work in Aesthetic Realism, my relationship with Bridget had become a long string of arguments and apologies, with an occasional afternoon of laughter to remind us of what we loved in each other. Even though her withdrawal from me happened gradually, the way sunlight fades the fabric of a favorite chair, I still felt blindsided. In time, she told me she was with Douglas Isay, a pompous older directing student to whom I had taken an immediate dislike when he had become her housemate two years earlier, and whom she would later marry.

When she turned those huge, warm eyes, which had been trained on me for so long, toward him, I felt the potential drain; my limits returned. That family, that life, that house with its swinging kitchen door, would never be.

"Why did you stay with me for so long if it never worked out?" I asked her. Despite my proclamations, my halfhearted fumbling attempts, our relationship had remained chaste.

Tears spilled down her cheeks. She lowered her head and butted my chest gently. "You were the first person who was willing to fight for me. To try the impossible, for *me*. You made me feel seen. How can you not love a guy who does that?"

The idea of continuing to fight for her, trying to charm her, holding her back for my benefit, would have been unfair, even cruel. I finally understood that.

On an innocuous morning in December 1984, I watched Pittsburgh drop away, clouds wrapping me in white silence. I recalled the day I had arrived, more than three years earlier, in the backseat of my parents' car, the trunk filled with boxes and hope. I remembered the ambition I'd felt staring up, agog, at the statues as my parents and I walked through the empty marble halls of the College of Fine Arts, which were being cleaned before classes began. The air was heavy with cold stone powder. It smelled like wet pavement at the start of a downpour.

"Beautiful," my mother had said, head swiveling left, up, and right. "Just beautiful."

My father had nodded his approval as he'd looked around. "We're proud of you, Son." That's all he'd said, but I could sense the dream he had for me—an immigrant's dream for his child to do better than him, to surpass him—burning in his chest. I had beaten hundreds of others to earn my place in one of the most prestigious acting programs in the country. The building, so grand and imposing, was my father's proof. He'd put his arm around my shoulder, and my mother had wrapped hers around my waist. "You're where you belong."

This wasn't how I was supposed to leave Pittsburgh, ignominious, done in not by a lack of talent or drive, but by an enemy I had no name for. "I'm a failure," I whispered to my reflection in the window. And then I felt what little shreds of *veneta* I had left, rumbling. The Loud Me answered myself with a smirk: "No fucking way, Banana."

21

i HEART NY

It hit me at the oddest times. Riding Duke Ellington's famous A train. Flipping through music at Tower Records. Eating a falafel (which until that time I had thought was a kind of loofah). "I live in New York City. I live in *New York City!*" I had to stop myself from breaking out into a dopey grin walking down Tenth Street, or humming Eva Gabor's part from the opening sequence of the sitcom *Green Acres*.

I had a hunch that if I moved to the city to be an actor, and studied Aesthetic Realism in earnest, the poles of my world would shift, just slightly, and things would warm; the frost would recede. A new place, a new start, a change in luck.

A friend had given me the name of a woman she'd heard of who was looking for live-in help to look after her four-year-old son. "It's a great building, and you'll have room and board, and you'll get paid." What could be bad about that?

After announcing me, the doorman of the Brevoort East sent me up, and I stood in front of the door in my only jacket and tie. I knocked, and a woman who introduced herself as Regina answered. "But ya can call me Reggie," she said, her accent musical. Jamaican or Dominican. I reminded myself to ask later.

"Reggie, who is it?" came a voice from another part of the apartment.

"The young man who's applying for the job."

"*What* job?" I could hear the slur in her voice.

She rolled her eyes at me and shouted down the hallway. "To take care of Timothy." Then to me, "Don't mind her, she's . . . slow to get goin' in the mornin'." It was two in the afternoon.

"Send him in." I pointed to what I assumed was a bedroom, and Reggie nodded and sighed.

Laurie Dannenberg was the very unemployed and overindulged daughter of a Broadway composer. Her father had created some of the best shows in the previous thirty years. When I entered the room, she was lying in bed, halfheartedly clutching her brown satin bathrobe with one hand while pouring a tumbler of Georgi vodka with the other. When she saw me, a slutty squiggle of a grin crossed her face. She tried to lift herself up on an elbow to run her fingers through her ratty hair, but she slipped, dousing herself and the bed in liquor.

"Ah, shit." Giving up, she just lay there and conducted the interview horizontally. "What's your name?"

"David. David Leite."

"Do you have experience with kids?" I explained that I had worked in a day-care center back in Rochester and had been a camp counselor. After a few minutes, the interview loped away from her. She began talking about how the building was filled with gossips, all of them trying to stick their sanctimonious schnozzes into her business, and how I needed to be circumspect.

"Can you be discreet, Daniel?"

"David."

"Wha'?" She looked at me as if I had spoken Zulu.

"Nothing. Yes, I can be discreet."

"Good." Here she called me over and patted the bed for me to sit. I lowered myself slowly, avoiding the wet spot. She explained she was dating Joe Montana *and* Dan Marino. She paused so I could take in the momentousness of that. I had no idea who they were—maybe actors in her father's shows? Part of my job, she said, was to make sure one didn't get wind of the other. "They'd kill each other if they knew I'm seeing both of them," she said, nodding.

"What about Timothy?"

"Oh, right." She said it as if she'd just remembered her overdue taxes. "Just keep him out of here in the morning and when he gets back from school. We usually spend dinner together, if he doesn't jump all over the bed. I have migraines."

She pulled down her sleep mask against the early-afternoon sun and dismissed me with an unsteady wave of her hand.

Reggie motioned me into the kitchen. "You hungry?" Before I could say yes, she pulled Tupperware containers from the fridge and made me a sandwich and poured a glass of Diet Coke. She sat down with me and placed her hand on my arm. She explained that it was a good job, and Laurie was a good person, really, even if she drank too much. I'd have a room, all the food I could eat, a car and driver, and a paycheck. I could smell the desperation coming off of her.

Swayed by the apartment, the fancy address, and a cook and driver to call my own, I took the job. I'd never known any alcoholics, but how bad could it be?

Timothy was in preschool, so every morning I had to wake, feed, and dress him, then get him out the door, all while keeping him from crashing into his mother's bedroom, where she was usually splayed diagonally across her bed, that robe once again in much need of clutching, passed out from drinking and, I began to suspect, snorting too much coke.

A few weeks later, after I'd dropped off Timothy at a playdate, Laurie summoned me to her boudoir/bar and asked if I could pick up a package for her. "Performance contracts," she said. She didn't trust bike messengers, because if they got into an accident, confidential information about major Broadway stars and their salaries would be fluttering in the wind for anyone to grab. "No, I need someone I trust to pick them up."

"Here." She slipped a fifty in my pocket, a little too deeply for my taste, and told me to bring home some dinner for Timothy and me.

I stepped out of the car and looked up at the building, and then again at the address scrawled in Laurie's loopy cursive on the front of a take-out menu. I looked at Javier, her driver, who nodded. He seemed to know the place. I'd been expecting to be dropped off in front of that tall building with the Robert Indiana *LOVE* sculpture in front. Instead, I walked up to the third floor of a ratty building that smelled of piss and Chinese food from the restaurant below, and knocked on the door. A guy whose eyes were rimmed in red and looked as if they were coated in corn syrup answered.

"Um, I'm here for the contracts for Laurie Dannenberg." It was more of a question than anything.

He grunted a laugh. "Hey, d'ja hear that?" he shouted to someone in the room. "Contracts."

"Here are your 'contracts,' kid." I could hear the quotation marks in his voice. He handed me a package the size of a baseball, covered in brown paper and wrapped with packing tape. "Now get the fuck out of here before you cause me trouble."

Back at Laurie's apartment, she met me at the door, all twitchy. It was the first time I'd seen her vertical. I thrust the package at her and started screaming, "How dare you! I am *not* your drug mule!"

"Shhhh!" she hissed, falling against me, as her fingers tried to pinch my lips closed while she looked up at me through crossed eyes. I heard rustling in her bedroom and looked down the hall to see an enormous man dressing. He tried to slip one foot into his cowboy boot, but he weaved back and forth, finally falling face-first out of view. He lay there, immobile, just his stockinged feet visible, like the Wicked Witch of the East in *The Wizard of Oz*.

"Open the package," I demanded. More shushing and lip-pressing. "Open it!"

"Awright, just be quiet. Please." She put her hand out to steady herself as she bit at the tape.

"Oh, for *crissake*, give it to me." I yanked it from her and tore it open. The tape stuck to my hands, and as I tried to shake it off, an enormous roll of hundred-dollar bills and little packets of white powder dislodged through the hall. She fell to her knees and started stuffing them into her pockets. "Those are not contracts, Laurie!" I screamed. "Those are *not* contracts."

Running to my room to pack my bag, I wondered: *Could I be arrested for aiding and abetting a drug deal and not reporting a possible overdose in the other room?*

On my way out, Laurie and the enormous guy (was this Joe Montana or Dan Marino?) blocked the door.

"Open your bag!" She was suddenly stern, and her words weren't skidding into each other.

"What?"

"You heard her. Open the bag," said her Sasquatch drug fiend.

"There are plenty of worthless things in this apartment a certain someone could be tempted to take," Laurie said. She was oblivious to her mistake.

"Fine." I opened the bag, and Sasquatch riffled through it.

"Satisfied? Can I please leave now?"

She swung open the door, and I stormed out. She waited until I was at the elevator to holler, "And you're fired! I don't want you around my son! Ever!" A pathetic attempt to steer suspicion away from her and onto me, for the benefit of the neighbors.

On the street, still trembling and with nowhere to go, I dug into my wallet and pulled out the only telephone number I had.

22

OPPOSITES DON'T ATTRACT

Nice to meet you," said Tom Junger, shaking my hand as he ushered me into the Greenwich Village apartment. Tom was Judith's brother-in-law, the one who'd turned straight through Aesthetic Realism.

"We were just getting delivery when you called," his wife, Maggie, said, digging through a drawer in the kitchen. "Hope you don't mind."

"*I* definitely don't," Tom said. As he walked behind me, he whispered—not particularly softly: "Maggie's a much better sculptor than cook." The grins on their faces told me this was part of their daily jousting.

"Delivery's fine," I said to Maggie.

"Indian? Chinese? Italian?" She held up a fan of menus. Over her shoulder, Tom mouthed *Chinese.*

"Chinese sounds great." He gave me a thumbs-up and started setting the table.

I'd been in the city for only a few weeks and was blown away by the idea of Any Food, Anytime. Of course, I'd had delivery before, but it had been mostly pizza in college, and those pillowy chow-mein sandwiches Dina used to order for us back on Brownell Street. In New York, though, *authentic* international cuisine was delivered right to your apartment. Thai, Sichuan, Israeli, Jamaican, Mexican, Spanish. I'd answered the door at all hours of the day for food deliveries for Laurie, and it was always something new.

"So, what exactly happened?" Maggie asked. She saw I was still shaken and poured me a glass of wine.

I explained about Laurie, her drinking, my short-lived career as a drug trafficker, and Sasquatch. "And so, when I saw all that cocaine flying through the air, I called. Thank God you were home."

"Well, I'm glad you did," Tom said. He took my bag from me and tossed it on a bed in a small room off the kitchen. "You can stay here as long as you need while you look for a place of your own."

About an hour later, significantly mellower thanks to several glasses of Chardonnay, I was sitting at the table, an army of take-out containers in the center. I tried to take in this family, a family that wouldn't have existed, if what Judith had said was true, without Aesthetic Realism. Heather, who couldn't have been more than four, kept fluttering her feet in the air, determined to show me her ruby slippers, which she pronounced *sli*-piz, with an accent straight out of the Bronx. Nicholas, who was older and surprisingly adept with chopsticks, was lost in his food. Over their heads, Tom and Maggie exchanged beleaguered, tired smiles. This is what I had envisioned for Bridget and me—kids, mess, happy exhaustion—except we had burned through each other before we had the chance.

Maybe it was the MSG or the wine, or Laurie's one-hundred-percent, grade-A freak show, but I was wiped. "Does anyone mind if I go to bed?" I finally said. "I got to start looking for a place and a job tomorrow."

"Of course not," said Maggie. She gave me a set of sheets and towels and pointed out the bathroom.

"Night," said Tom.

"Good night. And thank you. Both."

A week or so later, I found a job waiting tables at Fiorella, on the Upper East Side, and an apartment share in the then-low-rent, high-crime police state of Fort Greene, Brooklyn, where gunshots and cries for help were an almost nightly occurrence.

On one of my first nights on South Oxford Street, I pinged awake to the screams of a woman, who was pleading to anyone in earshot to call the police. Someone was trying to rob her. I thought of the story of Kitty Genovese, and how dozens of neighbors had heard her cries for help as she was being murdered in Kew Gardens, yet no one had called the cops. I crawled on my hands and knees to my desk and yanked the phone to the floor. There was no way I was going to let anyone identify me, and I wasn't about to be bullet fodder at only twenty-four years old. I dialed 911. Someone had beaten me to the punch, which made me feel relieved. At least when it was my turn to get mugged, I could rely upon an unseen neighbor to help me out. I considered making a casserole of thanks, to grease the wheels of community goodwill, but I had no idea who the Good Samaritan was.

Tom and Maggie picked up on my reluctance after work to go home, where I'd lie on my futon in the dark, shutters closed, reading a book by flashlight. "What with all your crime-fighting these days," Tom said over the phone, "you must've built up quite an appetite." That was all it took for me to sprint the eight blocks to the subway and head to their place for more takeout.

After dinner, Tom and I sat in the living room, his long legs telescoping out in front of him. Maggie was in the kitchen, soft clinking coming from the sink as she washed the dishes. Shrieks and laughter uncurled their way from the other end of the apartment. Tom looked at me, waiting.

I didn't know how to broach the subject. Had he and Maggie discussed this? Could he speak freely about this with her so near? I wanted to ask: *How did you get unbent, become not gay?* But what came out was a tepid "How did you get involved in Aesthetic Realism?"

He shifted in his chair, lifting himself a bit straighter—the raconteur claiming his ground. He began by telling me of his time working and living in Bangkok. He filled his story with embellishments, non sequiturs, and sotto voce asides designed to tease Maggie, who could plainly hear from the next room. He explained he had been a tax consultant for a U.S. company, a position that came with local perks. One of them being a houseboy, who, besides his official duties of cleaning, ironing, and running errands, also offered a nonsanctioned assortment of services of which Tom availed himself. "Often," he added, with a big, unselfconscious laugh. However, it was the punch line—the verbal rim shot to his story—that got me: "David, I wasn't a practicing homosexual," he said, a wry grin on his face. "I was professional."

The room itself held its breath. *Should I laugh? Is it right? Would that be contemptuous?* Just then Maggie turned from the sink with an *Oh, you!* smile and shook her head, as if he'd just told me how he'd convinced some tourists that the watchman of the Statue of Liberty lived in an apartment in her breasts—a harmless frat-boy prank.

Taking that as permission, a laugh hiccuped out of me.

Tom went on to recount his experience with Consultation with Three—one of the trios of Aesthetic Realism teachers that dealt with homosexuality—and how being criticized thoughtfully had helped him change. What got me was that the whole time I stayed with them, he never lost his bewildered tone, as if he was the luckiest guy in the world. And his candor floored me. He could have been talking about a suit he'd decided he didn't like and exchanged for another.

If it weren't for my *Scarface* afternoon, I probably wouldn't have bothered looking up Tom. And I doubt I would have ever taken Aesthetic Realism seriously. Until then, it was all theoretical: tenets on papers, examples in books, voices over the phone. But Tom, with his magnanimity and easy sense of humor, was the closer. He was big and colorful and full of swagger, and clearly beloved by his family. I ached for what he had and would have done anything to get it.

om's bonhomie and wicked wit bore little resemblance to the
moony-faced stolidity and emotional lockstep of everyone else I'd
later meet at the foundation—especially my consultants. For an hour
a month, I sat on one side of a table while Neal Hartley, Dylan Redmond, and Arturo Wolfe—three men who, like Tom, had changed
from homosexuality through Aesthetic Realism—sat on the other
side, hurling questions at me. They each had their style. Hartley, on
the left, was a beautiful man—he could have been a Paco Rabanne
model—who had the slightly haughty air of a European aristocrat. "A
piss-elegant queen," they used to call his type. He spoke the least.
Redmond, in the middle, had a face that was all angles and points. He
was the kindest, speaking with warmth and wonder in his pronounced New York accent. And then there was Wolfe. He felt like a
black, heavy presence to my right. I always half-expected him to
slouch over, his bored, slack face cutting me a look that said,
"Mr. Leite, you know what? You're full of shit." I had to stop myself
from turning my body away from him.

On the table, between us, was a cassette tape recorder—witness
to it all. My homework each month was to study my tape, listening to
it as many times as needed to glean an understanding. And that was
the problem: I never could. Not the listening; I did that ad nauseam.
I could never wring meaningful truth from their words. Part of the
problem was the pace of their criticism; it was assault-weapon fast.
Before I could come up with a thoughtful answer to one question,
someone fired off another. And then another. They piled up, few ever
getting answered by me. Almost all were leading questions that left
no doubt as to how I should answer. Just a few:

"Mr. Leite, do you think you're being tricky, getting one over on
the world?"

"Mr. Leite, are you *truly* grateful?"

"Mr. Leite, did you cozy up to your mother as a child and find a
way for both of you to be superior to your father?"

"Mr. Leite, do you think it was intelligent or stupid of your mother to be so devoted to you?" I thought of my mother, and imagined what her reaction would have been had she been in that room at that moment: She would have coldcocked these assholes into the middle of next week with the butt of that knife of hers. I bit back a smile.

"Mr. Leite, are you having a problem with the idea that you have more gratitude and more respect for Eli Siegel than you ever thought possible?"

"Mr. Leite, do you want to have conquest over a man?"

"Mr. Leite, do you use your accomplishments and interests to make yourself important and offset your great respect for Eli Siegel and Aesthetic Realism?"

"Mr. Leite . . ."

"Mr. Leite . . ."

"MR. LEITE . . . !"

I sat there, hands fidgeting, feeling verbally gang-raped. It's hard to comprehend, but I never considered standing up for myself, because I'd been programmed to think that it was me and not the philosophy that was problematic; that I was flawed, like a piece of handblown glass that they could see right through. And that flaw, no matter what we were discussing, was always my "terror of respect for Eli Siegel," the greatest man who ever lived. Yet the only thing I was *truly* terrified of was my consultants. Every time I tried in earnest to comprehend, and take what I was learning and shape it to fit my life, I was jumped on, like in a bloody three-on-one fight in a schoolyard, and told that I was reprehensibly disrespectful. Aesthetic Realism wasn't there to serve me, they said, fingers jabbed into the table for emphasis. My job wasn't to pick and choose what I wanted, "like on a Chinese menu," but instead I was to study it deeply, respect it, heed it, because it was "the most beautiful explanation of the world that history has ever seen." They said it could put an end to war, racism, poverty, and crime. I wanted so much to see that.

During one consultation, I questioned Wolfe, whom I'd seen smoking in front of the building.

"Mr. Wolfe, don't you think smoking is contemptuous of yourself and others?" He reminded me of a king cobra, expanding his chest and shoulders like a hood, rearing up in what the foundation called "beautiful anger," staring right into my eyes. The other two flew into paroxysms of self-righteousness, denouncing my disrespect for the three people, they said, who cared most about me in the world.

"But I'm simply asking, because I'm trying to understand—"

"You're *not* trying to understand, Mr. Leite," Wolfe finally roared. "You're trying to manage us, to get one over on us. You, Mr. Leite, want to be superior to us and Aesthetic Realism, so that you don't have to be affected by it."

"I feel sorry for you, Mr. Leite," Hartley said.

"Why?"

"Because you're in the business of making everything around you dull and not coming to much, aren't you?"

All I could muster at that point was what I felt they wanted: a guilty and ashamed "Yes."

I slumped out of my sessions, wondering why they weren't working for me, why I wasn't being affected the way my consultants told me I should be. So many of the other students, especially the men who were changing, seemed to bound down the stairs from the second floor of the Terrain Gallery after a consultation. Across their faces was a gleeful, almost euphoric expression that reminded me of the rapturous look my mother had when she came home from her prayer meetings, where people were slain in the spirit and talked in tongues, and devils were cast out.

Consultations had the opposite effect on me. Instead of having "stirrings" for a woman, as Aesthetic Realism called them, I felt driven toward men more than ever. At my kitchen table, with my books spread around me, I fracked my heart, trying to flush out any feelings of superiority or conquest I had when a man looked my way on the street, or flirted with me at Fiorella. But all I could come up with was that I felt seen, acknowledged, grateful even.

After work, I'd sometimes walk around Times Square, which in

the eighties was still seedy enough to terrify tourists and comfort lo-
cals. I tried to sniff out the reek of contempt my consultants assured
me was there. I tried to make myself disgusted by the squalor of it
all—the male hustlers, the lurid posters in front of gay movie theaters,
and what I called Stop-and-Pops: booths in porn shops where busi-
nessmen in suits on their way home would duck in for a quick hand
job and still make the 6:15 train to Rahway or Croton-on-Hudson. No
matter how I smutted it up, the ache for men never lessened.

On Eighth Avenue, I'd pass a gay movie theater—each time determined to go in, and each time I'd walk right by. One afternoon,
I approached the door and at the last second veered away, acting as
if I'd forgotten something. I walked down the block, turned around,
walked straight to the door, and peeled off again to lean against a
pole. *What would your consultants think?* I asked, as a way of trying to
shame myself into not going in, but the pull was too strong.

"Yes," I said to the guy behind the window, "I'd like—"

"Six bucks." I slid the money into the booth, and he jerked his
head toward the door.

To say the theater was charmless would be a compliment. Enough
light from the screen spilled onto the audience to allow me to see
just about every head swivel my way. I dropped the average age of
the room considerably. Embarrassed, I ducked into a seat. A few men
stood and walked slowly up the aisle, trying to lock eyes with me.
When I looked at the first one, and saw him nudge his chin toward
a door where men were walking in and out, fussing with their belts,
I froze. It reminded me of Mr. Goode, whom I had forgotten about
for years. I shook my head and looked down. I had made a mistake.
Revulsion started to swill in my gut. There was nothing remotely
erotic about the droning moans from men with shag haircuts and
mustaches that looked like sleeping otters on their upper lips, doing
things I'd had no idea were physically possible. But despite what my
consultants kept hammering into me, I didn't feel superior to these
men; I didn't feel contempt. What I did feel—which surprised me—
was the opposite: compassion.

A man slipped in behind me and wedged his knees into the back of my seat, bouncing it to get my attention. I got up and moved one seat to the right, which was construed as an invitation to another man to take my empty seat and loosen his pants. His buckle jingled like Christmas bells. *What if they don't let me out of here unless I have sex? Is this whole place a Stop-and-Pop?* Shaken, I had to step over Mr. Ho Ho Ho to get out, and he took the opportunity to brush my ass with his hand.

I step out into the furnace blast of the afternoon heat, stumbling headlong into a crowd gathered around the entrance. I try to duck into foot traffic and be carried away unnoticed down Eighth Avenue, but someone catches my arm. It's Barbara Walters, with a huge microphone in her face.

"Excuse me, excuse me, sir," she says, pulling me to her. A TV camera closes in on my face. "What's your name?"

"Um . . ." I look at the camera, then back at her. "David."

"David what?"

"David Leite."

"Mr. Leite, were you just inside of this homosexual movie house?"

"Me? Inside? No. Well, I was inside, but not inside of the movie," I stumble. "I went into the bathroom." She throws a skeptical look toward the camera.

"Oh, God—oh, no—not for that."

"Mr. Leite, we're here because there are allegations that men, such as yourself, have been locked in this homosexual establishment and are forced to have sex with strangers before they can be released. Can you comment?"

"Haven't other men left?"

"You're the first in more than a week."

"Really?"

"We've counted. Three hundred and forty-seven men have gone in . . . you're the only one to come out."

I lean in close to whisper. "Barbara, is this live?"

She whispers back, "Yes, it is. But you're doing great."

"These people"—she waits for the camera to pan the crowd—"are the relatives of the men believed to be locked in there. Do you have anything to say to them?"

"Um." I lean closer to the microphone she shoves in my face. "No."

"Do you know these men?" She motions to my consultants. Hartley is dripping with haughty superiority, an *I knew this would happen* look on his face; Redmond just shakes his head, disappointed; and Wolfe takes the cigarette he'd been sucking on and flicks it into the gutter with his middle finger. A long, disgusted stream of smoke snakes from his mouth.

I nod, tearing up.

"And who are they?"

"My consultants—" I try to say more, but my throat clenches.

"I'm sorry, who?"

"My consultants from Aesthetic Realism."

"And how do you think Eli Siegel would feel if he knew you were here?" I break down, sobbing. Barbara has a travel packet of Kleenex at the ready. I blow my nose.

"Why do you always make people cry like this?"

I walked up the aisle toward the door, praying it would open. I pushed, but it wouldn't budge. Freaked, I rattled the crash bar and threw my weight against it. Startled by the noise, people on the sidewalk turned around just as I hurtled out. A woman screamed and grabbed at her throat. With my face burning, I shoved my hands in my pockets and walked toward the Brooklyn-bound subway.

As I sat on the R train to DeKalb Avenue, a thought gnatted around inside my head. No matter how much I tried to swat it away, it buzzed loudly: I didn't want to end up *like* these men—desperate and hollow-eyed, with belts jangling in the dark—but I knew, deep inside, I was *of* them. There had to be a different way to be gay that had nothing to do with pedophiles in their basements, or men groping in the dark. I also understood that I had to exorcise Bridget, get her out from under that bell jar in my head, a preserved specimen of what my life could have been. The truth was that the primal hip thrust I felt toward men was stronger than any "stirrings" I had for her. And, despite what my consultants said, it was more logical than anything I'd heard in Aesthetic Realism. Yet by the time I turned the corner on to South Oxford Street and climbed the stairs to my apartment, I had tucked common sense and gut instinct in on themselves, to become the crisply folded, neutered version of David others expected—the Origami Me—just like those men from Rahway and Croton-on-Hudson.

From almost the beginning of my consultations, the greatest acrimony had been reserved for my refusal to wear the "Victim of the Press" button. Believing that the teachings of Siegel had been perniciously and purposefully ignored by the press, which, in the foundation's impenetrable logic, was just another example of snubs pointing to the enormity of the world's contempt for the greatest man who ever lived, consultants and students took to wearing the pin. Small and white, with black serif letters, it was a brand, marking their intolerance of the intolerance of the media.

The pressure to wear the button was enormous. My consultants, fellow students, anyone involved in the organization, felt it was their duty to challenge me as to why I wasn't wearing one. And so, eventually, like a cheating husband who slips on his wedding band just as he's skulking home and pulls it off the minute he leaves, I did the same. Right before turning onto Greene Street, I pinned it to my shirt and hurried along, zippering myself into the line for the gallery, hoping no one saw me.

Home should have been a refuge from all this. Instead, my roommate, Darrin, the beautiful blond Rob Lowe from Carnegie Mellon whom I'd introduced into the organization, was by now a zealous adherent and my greatest critic.

"Why don't you want to wear the pin in the apartment?"

"Because I have no one to make my point to," I said wearily. "And *I* know I'm a victim of the press, so it's redundant."

"Wearing it all the time is a reminder. Just think how different our lives would have been if we knew about Eli Siegel and Aesthetic Realism when we were small." He had adopted their monotone delivery, as if reading a liturgy.

"But, Darrin, *I* know it. That's all that matters." *Where did that happy, carefree kid go?* I wondered. The one who'd thrilled to be running around naked on CMU's stage as the dead man in Strindberg's *The Ghost Sonata,* or who'd cracked us up at dinner in the cafeteria with the sexual possibilities of a slice of pizza.

During a break in a presentation at the Terrain Gallery one warm spring night, a student approached me. She was exotic, with dark hair, perhaps Brazilian or Argentinean. Definitely one of the very few people of color in a vast sea of prim white folks in khakis, oxford shirts, Ann Taylor dresses, and sensible shoes. We were at the back of the room, near the door, and I could feel the press of her criticism.

Criticizing one another was something students were encouraged to do by consultants. It served two purposes: It kept us on the defensive, as well as allowing the organization to ferret out any threats to itself, as nothing was secret. Because most students lived, studied, and socialized together, ratting out one another was a favorite pastime. Emboldened, they often took this as an opportunity to let their hatred, animosity, jealousy—whatever negative feelings they'd been bottling up in the name of conformity—gush like water from a hydrant, blasting anyone in their path. All in the name of caring deeply for that person's life.

She questioned why I wasn't wearing my "Victim of the Press" button (I had stupidly forgotten it at home), and she challenged what she considered my obvious contempt for Eli Siegel and Aesthetic Realism. "Otherwise you'd be straight by now."

Oh, no you didn't.

My vision began telescoping—a sure sign that an anxiety attack was galloping my way. Fight-or-flight flooded my body, and this time I chose to fight. I decided to ride this one out, to root myself to that spot and take whatever shit she had to sling.

Come on, bitch, I thought. *Give me all you got.*

I was practically vibrating off the floor with a *veneta* so virulent, it felt like my skull was shrinking, crushing my brain. As she lit into me, I shocked myself by imagining vomiting all over her. The image came uninvited, and I allowed the fantasy to carry me. I pictured her disgust as orange Kool Aid–colored puke dripped down the front of her tailored champagne dress, with its shoulder pads and bulky gold buttons. *Don't fuck with me, lady! I'm Regan in* The Exorcist. I envisioned her arms out from her sides, like the broken wings of a bird trying to take flight, and the slow, hateful gaze as she lifted her head to look at me, as if to say, *See? See how deep your contempt is?!*

She hammered on, even corralling another woman into the conversation, so I was getting criticized in stereo. I nodded at the accusations, agreeing with a false solemnity that startled me. When they were satisfied that they had done Siegel's work, they threaded themselves back into the crowd. I stood there, my body rocking slightly in time to the pumping of my heart.

It wasn't as if a fever had broken and the pain and writhing and sweating were gone. But something was extinguished that night. I left the building and walked up Greene Street, taking a right onto Houston Street, into the real world—one I loved, hated, admired, resented, embraced, feared, and, yes, at times had delicious contempt for—and went home.

On a Saturday afternoon around my twenty-fifth birthday, I rummaged through my apartment, gathering Siegel's books, all the musty newsletters I could find, and the box of my old cassette tapes from consultations that I had stashed away out of shame. This was to be a solemn and ritualized ceremony; I wanted it to have the whiff of those endless Sunday masses, where Father Fraga would mumble in his heavily accented English about the body and blood of Christ. And just as the bread and wine used in the Eucharist are supposedly turned into the body and blood of Christ via transubstantiation, there was to be a transformation here. I was going to transform all the rhetoric, double talk, and what I'd experienced as disgust thinly veiled as helpful criticism during the past two years into something truly glorious: freedom.

I crumpled up pages of the *New York Times* and made a crinkly bed under the grate in the fireplace in my bedroom. Next came a Duraflame log, the only kind I was allowed to burn in the apartment. I knelt down in a prayerful way in front of the hearth, my pile of Aesthetic Realism propaganda to my left, and lit a match. As the flames ate through the paper crumples and started licking at the log, I thought back to all the people who had asked me, "But you're so smart. How could you get involved with a cult like *that*?"

I'd never had a sufficient answer. I tried, "It just makes sense." Then: "There are so many successful people who are students—the actor William Atherton, who was in *The Day of the Locust* and *Ghostbusters*, for crissake! How could it be a cult?" Tired of defending myself, I defaulted to, "They can help me change."

But after all these years, the answer was obvious, like a crossword clue that eludes you for days. I'd gotten involved at a time when I'd been bereft. I had believed my life was a cheap polyester knockoff of the real thing, and Aesthetic Realism came along promising me a real life, with real, true feelings for a woman, in a real relationship: what I'd coveted in Tom Junger. But in time, I came to see that what I'd admired so much had nothing to do with his sexuality. I'd been taken by who he was—that larger-than-life, confident, irreverent man. It was his *personality* that I'd fallen for, not where he put his junk.

When the fire plumed with heat and size, I took hold of *Self and World*. I flipped through it, reading my margin notes, which were just regurgitated AR-speak. Then I ripped off the cover and tossed it in the fire. I felt such guilt, as if I were defacing the Bible, or a first-edition Nancy Drew mystery. That didn't last long; on its heels came fury. Fury at having bought wholesale this business of turning straight. Fury at the accusations that I wasn't trying hard enough. Fury at their insistence that I had contempt for Eli Siegel and Aesthetic Realism. (And if any of them is reading this, I'm sure they'll use it in a lecture, as proof of my contempt. That's their way.) I tore at the pages, feeding them into the fire faster and faster, until a tower of pages balanced on the log.

Ariadne, my cat, was lying on the hearth. She scooted as the pages tumbled. I had to beat at them with a kitchen spatula; not much need for a poker set with a Duraflame-only fireplace. With the fire now burning more steadily, I ripped the tapes out of their cassette cartridges, yanking and yanking until each had puked up its insides. I was sitting among skeins of shiny brown threads. They went up in an instant, curling and hissing, the cassettes melting like thick slices of cheese.

The "Victim of the Press" button was last. I contemplated keeping it, and writing "NOT" in Magic Marker above, but I wanted a clean purge, so I tossed it in. I watched as the white button turned the color of caramel, then tea, and finally black.

After the fire had died out, all that was left was irony. It was ironic that Aesthetic Realism, whose greatest goal was to help people to like the world, made me justly leery of it, especially of any organized thought. It made me distrust myself, my gut, my thoughts. Also ironic: The world they claim to have such love and respect for is the very same world they came to fear and grow paranoid about, because it had failed to see the greatness of what they, the keepers of the One True Knowledge, were trying to share. But perhaps most ironic: Within five years, Aesthetic Realism would no longer offer Consultation with Three for men and women who wanted to become heterosexual, saying they preferred not to engage in the anger surrounding the issue. Which is hypocritical, because they triggered that rage by creating, promoting, and defending the absurd and completely erroneous idea of the possibility of change.

The next morning, I knelt on all fours at the fireplace, Ariadne making figure eights between my legs. I swept up cinders, chipped off gnarled hunks of plastic from the andirons and floor, and scooped it all into a bag. Outside, I tossed the bag on top of the mound of garbage waiting curbside and headed toward the subway, smiling.

23

QUARTER-MiLE-HiGH CLUB

Looking up at the Twin Towers made me dizzy. It was an enormous study in perspective, like the kind we would practice in art class at RIT. The steel columns reminded me of train tracks that, above the lobby level, split into three tracks each, all of them soaring to a vanishing point beyond sight.

I took the elevator to the 107th floor, where Windows on the World was located. When it pinged open, I was dazzled; it was like standing inside a giant kaleidoscope. The long, imposing hallway to the front desk was lined with huge geodes and crystals from around the world. Behind them, the walls were all chrome and mirrors. I was instantly ashamed of myself. Reflected back were a million me's—a million lopsided and scuffed black sneakers, a million black polyester pants that I could now see were sagging in the ass. I couldn't wear a suit because right after my interview I was headed to work at Fiorella, and I didn't need that smug French waiter, Joël, who'd had it in for me from the day I started, pointing out my clothes to our manager.

After I introduced myself at the front desk, I was escorted to the right, to a corner booth in the Hors D'Oeuvrerie, the bar and smaller restaurant of Windows on the World, where a woman in a tan naval uniform was perched in front of a splay of papers. The booth was on the highest tier of tables. All around, nearly unobstructed views east, south, and west.

"Impressive, isn't it?" she said. I was gawking out the windows at the Statue of Liberty, Governor's Island, Staten Island, and New York Harbor beyond. The restaurant, she told me, was so high that guests looked down on helicopters, and sometimes sat above rain clouds while the sky above remained infinite and blue. Suddenly, I wanted this job more than anything, if only for those views I knew I would never grow tired of seeing.

Around us, waiters in white naval jackets and waitresses in officious tan dresses were setting up their stations, polishing flatware, hip-checking chairs into place, folding napkins. Moira—that was the manager—looked at my application. I had little New York experience, so I talked up my almost yearlong stay at the Grand Concourse in Pittsburgh, where I'd moved after Gullifty's. I think it was my prattling on about table-side service—the flourish of deboning Dover sole, shelling lobsters, assembling and igniting desserts—that got me the job. She told me I'd start with lunches, plus one breakfast and Sunday brunch. Lunch, she explained, was a private club for members only, or for the occasional civilian willing to pony up a hefty surcharge.

"When can you start?"

I looked out at the light stippling the water of the harbor. "I'll give my notice today," I said.

After a week, I wondered if I'd made a mistake, if perhaps I was more suited to a job with the common folk a quarter of a mile beneath me. I felt choked by my starched military uniform, and the atmosphere. I'd been instructed to stand erect, never to interact with a table unless invited, and never to laugh or speak loudly. I was invisible unless serving. "You never know," Moira told me, "when some multimillion-dollar deal is being made under your nose." Day after day, we all stood prim and silent. So I was shocked when I worked my first night shift a few months later. Gone was all the military precision. Instead, the lights were dimmed to an opalescent gold, the better to see the winking lights so far below. A trio played while couples swept around one another on the dance floor. The rigidity of the staff during the day melted into a dreamy sultriness. Our outfits had a lot to do with it. The women dressed in jewel-toned satin cheongsams with sinuous slits up the sides, while the men wore pants and short kimono robes, a dragon snaking up the one side. The robes flopped open whenever we bent over. Some of the better-built waiters would strategically reach in front of a group of young women or enthralled drunken matrons, giving them the briefest view of their chiseled, manicured chests. Me, I safety-pinned my robe closed in several places. I needed my tips.

Every night, even when we hovered anchorless in a haze of clouds lit pink and orange from the lights below, the place was packed: moony newlyweds; gawking tourists, who never listened when we explained that taking a flash photo out a dark window would only result in a nuclear blast of white; and, new to me, courting Orthodox couples on Saturdays. They'd quietly occupy tables by the windows all night, the highest-priced real estate in the joint, nursing two Cokes and leaving a five-dollar tip. Other times, those same stations could easily pull down 135 bucks—a small fortune in 1986.

And then there was the menu—a paean to Asian hedonism.

Wildly exotic to me, it featured nearly three dozen dishes. Thai spring rolls, crispy coconut fried shrimp, chicken yakitori, sushi and sashimi, Kyoto beef rolls, Indonesian lamb saté. One of the most popular dishes, Bangkok avocado dip, was a mix of mashed avocados, cubes of ruby-red tomatoes, thinly sliced Thai chiles, and lime juice. "Think of it as an Oriental guacamole" was how I described it to guests. Whenever anyone unfamiliar with the dish leaned in and stared, I added, "Don't worry, those Styrofoam-looking things on the side are shrimp chips. They're weird, but they're *wicked* good. Trust me." That usually unfurrowed a couple of foreheads and added a buck or two to my tip. My favorite? Szechuan hacked chicken served on rice noodles with a spicy sesame sauce. It was made by a volatile Ecuadorian prep cook, who every day before service whipped out a menacing cleaver and made short work of a heap of cold chicken breasts. Watching him, I thought of my mother's only knife, the one so worn from my father's grinder, and considered buying her a cleaver. But then again: no.

I schooled myself in these dishes, adding to that inventory of flavors, aromas, and textures I'd begun creating in my dark bedroom on Brownell Street. It wasn't the restaurant, but my guests that taught me. Let me explain: All us waiters had hiding places in the kitchen where we'd stash plates of half-eaten food from the dining room. A guest wouldn't have descended fifty stories by the time I'd grabbed her plate, hidden in my spot down by the dishwasher, and torn into the leftovers. With shoulders turned to the kitchen, I cataloged the nasal burn of wasabi, the tingle of ginger, the oceanic purity of Cotuit oysters in their crenellated shells. This overlooked food gave me my first understanding of fine cuisine and ingredients.

Breakfast was no less of an object lesson. Working dinner the night before a morning shift usually meant my head would barely hit the pillow before I had to be up and at the restaurant by five-thirty in the morning. Never a caffeine addict, I nonetheless needed a way to wake up, so I'd stumble to the dessert case and cut a generous slice of dacquoise, a delicate cake of hazelnut meringue layers with coffee buttercream filling. The dacquoise, made the day before, was best then; the crunchy meringue had turned slightly chewy because of the filling. I'd install myself at one of the east-facing tables and, with my feet up and my starched uniform falling open, I'd watch and wait. My reflection would fade while the sky turned from black to battleship gray to a luminous mauve, as if the world had just discovered Technicolor. On the clearest of mornings, as the sun rose, I could see almost ninety miles, or so the bartender would always tell me.

One morning after breakfast, the doors to one of the private dining rooms opened. We were all folding napkins and polishing silver.

Moira led a small man with a shock of bleached hair into the room. His shoulders were somewhere up around his ears, like he was in a perpetual state of uncertainty.

"Everyone, this is Ronnie. He's starting today." A chorus of "Hey" and "Hi" burbled up. She looked around the room. "David, let him trail you."

"Sure." From the looks of him, I gave him two days, three at the most.

Without my asking, he grabbed a bunch of knives and began dipping the blades in water and buffing them with a napkin. "I don't need to trail; I've been a waiter for years."

"And I don't need a wiseass with an attitude bothering me all day." He made a face, as if to say, *Nicely done.*

"Who's that?" he said, cocking his head over to the table of Bangladeshi waiters. I knew exactly who he meant.

"Mayur. And he's not gay."

"What makes you think *I'm* gay?"

I stumbled. "I just thought—" I said, pointing from him to Mayur and back.

"Relax. I'm just busting your balls." Ronnie was never one to let you have the last word.

Over time we grew close, but only at work. Ronnie took immense delight in shocking me, which wasn't hard back then. Sometimes at morning announcements, when we all were lined up in our spotless naval whites, he'd slide in beside me, late and bleary-eyed. He'd lean in close, smelling of stale cigarettes and vodka, and recount his sexual exploits of the previous night—just to watch me blush. What struck me most about Ronnie was he never judged. His greatest gift to me was a shrug from his already-hitched shoulder, no matter what I said. He didn't give a rat's ass that I had tried to be straight, or never walked in the gay-pride parade, or didn't know a single person with AIDS. He knew I had no idea how to be gay yet. But anytime I mentioned Aesthetic Realism, he dragged me to the far side of the cappuccino machine, cooing at the Ecuadorian cook to put away the cleaver he had pointing just inches from our crotches, and tilted his face up close to mine. "They're fucked, you know that, right?" he'd say, stone-cold serious. I nodded. "Good. Say it."

"They're fucked."

"Again."

"They're fucked."

"Now get out there and find a rich guy to marry, so that I can mooch off you the rest of my life."

I couldn't see it then, as steeped in self-loathing as I was, but Ronnie was like a lot of the staff: nonjudgmental and supportive. I've often wondered if I stumbled into that circle of people at the moment in my life when I needed them most, as if we were shuffled together for a reason. To heal, perhaps? For me, certainly. I ask because after more than thirty years, so many of them have remained bright and saturated with life in my mind, whereas hundreds of other coworkers since have faded into nameless nothingness.

There was the giantess, Brett, with her short hair and smug British superiority. At first she wanted nothing to do with me. (I think she thought I'd last only a few days—the same thing I'd thought of Ronnie.) Eventually, I could tell from the way she'd purse her lips and look down that she'd grown fond of me—not that she'd ever deign to tell me. Mayur was the sexy Bangladeshi object of Ronnie's affection who, like Daniel, the premed student, knew how to work his robe for bigger tips. The pixie-faced actress Kellie had a mean son-of-a-bitch boyfriend who we suspected beat her, and we tried our damnedest to help her leave him—even enlisting her mother—but she never could. Aurora, the former model from Senegal, asked me every day in her musical, sweeping accent, "How was your acting day, David?"—which by that time consisted of calling my answering service several times a day only to be told, "No messages." She had a rip in her earlobe where an earring should be, which Kellie said hinted at something sinister and violent. The loudest of our group was Angie, a single mother straight out of Jersey who sported a mullet, proudly. And then there was Deshi, the gentle older waiter from

China, who said little. Once, he stood motionless in his section, looking shattered because he was slammed with guests, so I took out his
food and served it for him. Afterward, he laid his hand on my arm
and looked up at me. No words, just a nod and a soft smile.

"You'll never guess who's in my section!" Angie said, barging into
the kitchen one evening. Celebrities were everywhere in the Hors
D'Oeuvrerie at night. Even the handsome piano player was rumored
to be a protégé, some said lover, of Leonard Bernstein. He would
only smile and sip his coffee if you asked him. We all bunched around
one of the service doors to peer out. Sitting quietly one row from
the windows was Cher and her son Elijah Blue Allman, who couldn't
have been more than ten years old.

Even Brett, the most cynical of us all, was impressed.

"The least they could have done was seat them by the window,"
I said.

Suddenly, we all found reasons to visit Angie's section. We
watched as Ronnie, clutching a fork behind him, dropped it just as he
was passing the table. He stopped, picked it up, and said something to
Cher, who looked confused at the appearance of a third fork. I refilled
the nearly full water glasses, and Aurora, who usually acted like she
was above it all, suddenly swooped in to replace something on the
table. And then there was Angie. Every time I walked by, she was
hugging her drinks tray to her chest, chatting with Cher as if they
were sitting side by side getting a pedicure. When they moved to the
main restaurant for dinner, we all watched from the kitchen as Angie
slid a cocktail napkin in front of Cher and handed her a pen.

"You gotta give it to her," Brett said. "She's got balls, that one.
Good thing Lewis isn't here to see that."

Alan Lewis. He was the general manager of Windows, and the
right-hand man to the temperamental Joseph Baum, one of the famed
restaurateurs responsible for the Four Seasons, the Rainbow Room,
and Windows. Every day Mr. Lewis would come in for lunch, most
of which he never touched, and read his paper, every so often lifting
his head, watching, and waiting to spot something out of place. Al-

though only in his midsixties, he reminded me of Truman Capote's bulldog in its later years. Everyone hated to wait on him.

The first time I waited on him, I climbed the stairs to his table, terrified. He mumbled his order into his newspaper, never looking up, which suited me just fine. A few minutes later, I slid a plate in front of him, and he hesitated.

Shit.

"You're new." *How could he have possibly gleaned that from my hand putting down a plate?* He glanced up.

"Yes, sir."

"What's your name?"

"David."

Then he returned his formidable gaze to his newspaper.

After that, he asked for me by name.

"So what do you do besides this?" he asked me one day, sweeping his hand across the room. Knowing he was famous for tripping up unsuspecting staff by revealing their less-than-fanatical devotion to the industry, I smartly sidelined acting—which in the two years I'd been in New York had amounted to one MTV commercial as an extra: Guy Holding Pizza Box.

"Baking."

"What do you bake?" he asked, as he looked up with an arched eyebrow that clearly telegraphed, *Don't disappoint me.*

"Um, well," I stalled, mentally flipping through the sticky pages of my cookbook—a bargain tome with recipes from around the world that weighed as much as a Sunday brisket. "Éclairs and gougères."

"Bring me something."

Because Lewis's descent on the Hors D'Oeuvrerie was capricious, I carted a homemade chocolate éclair in a brown paper sack on the subway from South Oxford Street to the 107th floor of the North Tower almost every day for a month, as cautiously as if I were transporting the Shroud of Turin. That meant every morning boiling water and butter, then dumping in flour and mixing with a wooden spoon until my arm ached. Watching the mess go from pallid gray to slick yellow with each addition of an egg fascinated me. When the batter shone, I piped stubby fingers onto a baking sheet and crouched in front of the oven, watching them breathe and heave to life.

When our orbits finally aligned, I presented Lewis with my éclair with just a whiff of self-importance.

"Here's one of the pastries I was telling you about," I said, sliding the plate into his field of vision. He looked up confused. "You know, the one, the pastry I told you I make."

He took a bite and grunted.

That was it. A grunt. A single frigging grunt. I stood there until he looked up over his glasses at me, and I withered back to the kitchen. When I returned to clear his table, though, I was stunned to see the éclair was gone. Lewis's imitation of high praise.

Up there a quarter of a mile in the sky, popping open Champagne for movie stars and convincing Midwesterners they wouldn't die from eating raw fish, was the most normal I'd felt in more than four years, since my break at Birch Grove. *Break* was the only word I dared use back then. *Break*down threw up images of jittery sixties housewives who had come undone—my mother grasping at her housecoat, screaming that I would send her to Taunton State. A "break," on the other hand, was nothing more than a snap in the routine of life, like the crack of a bone that can heal, seamless. I was whole again.

24

A BEAUTiFUL CORPSE

Ronnie snuck behind the bar in the private dining room we'd just cleared and poured himself a sizable shot of vodka. He did a cartoon double take, as if he hadn't seen me standing there watching him the whole time. "What?" he said with faux innocence, his already-high shoulders hiking higher. "You can't expect me to face a PG movie—a movie for *kids*—sober, can you?"

Having worked Sunday brunch and a Christmas party for a group of suits bent on drinking their bosses dry, we both were off the rest of the day. I was too wound up to pack it in at five in the afternoon, and there was no way I could bear sitting at home listening to instrumental music one more night. I'd had it up to my cojones with George Winston's plinking piano solos and trying to meditate. I asked Ronnie if he wanted to go out, maybe see a movie. To my surprise, he said yes. He liked to steer me clear of his social life, for reasons I think had to do with leather, rubber, and stainless-steel accoutrements in graduated sizes.

His choice: an indie flick downtown that was way too violent for me. I lobbied for *Young Sherlock Holmes,* which had opened up a few days before in Times Square. The mention of Steven Spielberg as producer was what sent him barreling for the vodka.

I'd been picking up extra shifts at the restaurant since Thanksgiving, tumbling into bed at two in the morning, and getting up some days at five-thirty for breakfast. Yet I was humming with energy. That turbine inside was back. Gone was the Quiet Me, the clomping, oafish me. In his place, a guy who liked to wink a lot and crack jokes and toss zingers straight out of those 1940s Tracy-and-Hepburn comedies. The lady at the Laundromat got a kick out of it. So did the homeless guy in front of McDonald's, whom I bought breakfast for on weekends. Where did it come from? Damned if I knew; I just didn't want it to stop.

Seized with energy. That's a good way to describe it. And that old-fashioned word, *feverish*. My apartment became the Cradle of Possibility. Slips of paper were scattered everywhere. Lists: of presents to buy, awards to win (Tony, Emmy, Oscar, and—I have no idea why—a Clio for advertising), the number of sit-ups and push-ups I set out to accomplish. I wrote down all the things I needed to do for my first-ever Christmas party, with a real tree, handmade ornaments, warm cheese puffs, and a badass punch. *Hell, maybe I'll even invite Mr. Lewis!* During meditation, a habit I'd taken up as a way of harnessing this 220-volt surge, I began hearing words, so I took dictation. Someone named Amarok decided to borrow my body for a while each morning, so I let him. (Don't judge me: This was the era of Shirley MacLaine and her spirit guides. Everyone was speaking to the disembodied.) In a tone that was vaguely pretentious and British, he told me things like "The gifts you perceived were always inside of you"; that consciousness was like "fluffy pastry dough, with all its layers and flakes"; and that I should play the lottery on a particular day. That afternoon, I slapped down a dollar and a dream at the local bodega, cocksure I was going to wind up on the news as New York's newest multimillionaire. I had not one number. When I questioned

Amarok, he seemed to have suddenly—and without warning—vacated the premises of my body.

At work? Well—that was all showtime, boys.

Everything is dark, and suddenly a spotlight hits me. I'm wearing a black skintight bodysuit. My belly is flat and tight, which means I can see that I do my dance belt proud. I hear the strains of a song. My body responds automatically. My wrists turn in tight circles, fingers extended. My pelvis thrusts, small and controlled. Knees knock. When I beckon with both index fingers, boys—a whole bunch of boys—in bowler hats and spats step out of the darkness to frame me. I'm in *Chicago*, the musical!

> The person everybody loves is gonna be: David
> The big guy making all the tips is gonna be: David
> I'm gonna be a superstar,
> Y'know, somebody dripping with class,
> They're gonna idolize my style, my hair, my laugh, my voice,
>   my ass.

One Saturday night I was working the section of the restaurant that faced Brooklyn and Queens. "David, what bridges are those?" said a handsome woman in a flowing top the color of a French manicure. She was pointing to three sets of lights arcing across the East River. The whole table turned to me. Ha-cha-cha.

"The easiest way to remember this is to think of my favorite car." They shouted out different models, all wrong. I shook my head in dramatic exasperation. That got a few laughs.

"Well, what then?" the handsome woman asked.

"B-M-W." And moving from right to left I counted off, "Brooklyn, Manhattan, and Williamsburg Bridges." A round of chuckles and delighted *oh*'s rose from the table.

When I returned with their drinks, I slipped on a patch of wet marble floor and skated into the table. Instinctively, I tilted the tray against my chest to prevent the cocktails from spilling on my guests.

But the heavy silver pitcher tanked forward, splashing water down the front of the woman's blowsy top and causing her to yelp and jump up, which knocked me back into another guest, who was drunk enough to stay upright by holding on to me with one hand while nursing his drink in the other.

Now, a woman has the right not to wear a bra any damn time she pleases. But in my section, she does so at her own peril. The fabric of her blouse, so soft and opaque while dry, was nearly invisible and cupped her, giving all of Brooklyn and the east-facing part of the restaurant proof she'd never gone to a plastic surgeon. She clapped a hand on to each breast and was immediately descended upon by Angie and Brett, who draped several napkins over her as they ushered her into the bathroom.

After she sat back down, windblown and flushed from the hand dryer, all it took was a few well-timed comments and a neon-bright smile and—*bingo!*—they were thanking me for making their holiday. And their tip confirmed it.

> *I'm a star*
> *And my customers adore me*
> *I adore them*
> *And they adore me for adoring them.*

At the movie theater, Ronnie and I grabbed some Diet Cokes and popcorn and made our way to one of the rows in front. Slouching way down in the seats, we got a huge, perspective-distorting view of the screen. Ronnie was snorting at my running commentary on the people around us, stuffing his face into my arm to stifle his laughs.

The lights dimmed.

A man with enormous muttonchops makes his way through snowy streets in fin de siècle London. Outside of a restaurant, he stops to read a menu as a hooded figure lurking in the shadows raises a dart gun—*thwip!* Muttonchops swats at his neck, inspects his empty hand, and looks around. Inside, a waiter brings the man his favorite dish: roast pheasant. ("Look! Its ass feathers are still attached!" whispered Ronnie. I elbowed him to shut up.) Muttonchops slices into the bird, which begins gushing blood. Its head worms its way out of its body and pecks at the man's eyes, gouges his raised hands. He grabs it, trying to hold off the attack. Cut to the view of the other diners: The man is grasping at air and howling. He's hallucinating. He's going insane. I was watching this man become unhinged right in front of me.

I felt it gathering. *This is a PG movie. A* Spielberg *movie, for crissake.* Diverting my attention from the screen, I said something to Ronnie, but he was too engrossed. I knew what was about to happen, and I was powerless to stop it. I could check off its plan of attack—chest, heart, face, skin, joints, excuse, escape—like a pilot to a copilot.

A landmine detonated in my chest, shooting up my esophagus, throwing sparks against the back of my throat. *Check.*

My heart heaved against my ribs like a broken washing machine. *Check.*

A million needles prickled my face. It felt like they were embroidering my lips, nose, eyes, ears, cheeks. *Check.*

A wave of heat almost annihilated my skin. Tiny beads of sweat popped up on the back of my hands. *Check.*

My knees and ankles were pumped full of fire ants. I needed to move them. I couldn't sit still any longer. I needed to run. *I need to run now! Check.*

I lied to Ronnie, something about having to be somewhere else. He looked at me, jaw slack, confused. *Check.*

I ran up the aisle, through the doors, across the lobby, and burst into Times Square. Humiliated. *Check.*

I hoped the explosion of noise, chaser lights, and billboards—massive sensory overload—would bulldoze this back where it had come from, so I could return to Ronnie saying, "False alarm!" Instead, I could feel the bastard elbow aside my insides, digging through its filthy, reeking bags as it unpacked.

The nameless, homeless fear was back.

Unlike with my other breaks, there was no grace period this time, no wobbly days that could be chalked up as semi-successes. A headfirst plunge into an airless, dry well, that's what this was. Everything went from light to dark in the span of a minute, a few thousand frames of film. All that had come before—the elation, the camaraderie, the rocket-fueled late nights, and the hopped-up mornings—vanished.

I analyzed it obsessively. "Fear of my own anger." Isn't that what the doctor at Bradley Hospital, the one who met with my parents and me, had said about movies? All my rage played out big on the screen? Desperate, I tried that on, like a new sweater, but it didn't fit. It could have been watching Muttonchops go mad, but that, too, didn't make sense. This had nothing to do with movies. I'd become a film buff, and I'd seen countless flicks since I was sixteen, and nothing like this had ever happened. This was about something else, something more. Being gay, maybe? No, that felt wrong. I was beginning to suspect films were just a trigger, a portal to the other side, the crazy side, the upside-down. It wasn't movies, but The After, that made me want to evacuate my soul.

The days that followed at work, when I wasn't avoiding Ronnie out of shame, were bleaker than any I'd experienced. I'd heard alcoholics talk about hitting bottom, a hard, mean place. Maybe this was mine. I slipped into the back of AA meetings, hoping to hear someone describe what I felt, so that afterward I could sit with them over coffee in some fluorescent-lit diner that stank of old french fries and ask questions. I couldn't be the only one who experienced this. There *had* to be others—but I found no one. In time, I gave up on AA. Liquor wasn't my demon, and I had no idea what was. I just knew I no longer had the energy to fight. Worse, for the first time, I didn't care.

At home, when I wasn't sleeping, which could at least liquidate the pain for a few hours, I ate. I'd shuffle into the kitchen, which was no more than a pass-through from the living room to my roommate's bedroom in back, and pull out a pot from under the sink. I had read somewhere that when you're at a loss for what to eat, start with boiling water. I'd open and close the same four cabinets and the refrigerator. Carbs. I wanted carbs. Listless, I'd flip through my international cookbook and check out the dog-eared pages. Gougères speckled with Gruyère cheese? No. Mr. Lewis's éclairs? Didn't want sweets. Coq au vin, which the Hollises had liked so much, or chicken paprikash? No and no. Too long. Eventually, I'd end up on the same page: spaetzle. The kind of food that demands nothing of you in terms of skill and offers everything in return, namely comfort.

Mix flour, salt, pepper, and a pinch of nutmeg in a bowl. The steam from the boiling water collected on the edge of the hood, a tiny string of transparent garland. *Beat the eggs and milk in another bowl with a whisk.* Vovo Costa never used a whisk. Always a fork. I did as she'd taught me. *Stir the egg mixture into the flour until smooth.* Again a fork would do. I fitted a colander on top of the pot. Steam rose up in a million tiny smokestacks. *Scoop the batter into the colander and, using the back of the spoon, pass the batter through the holes.* Little worms of batter dripped into the pot, roiling over themselves. *Cook for five to eight minutes.* Dammit, I'd forgotten to look at the clock. I tasted one. Too soft. I waited. Again. Almost ready. Finally: chewy, dense, perfect. *Drain and toss with butter.* Sometimes, if I was mindful enough, I'd take half a stick of butter and swirl it in my mother's Revere Ware skillet that she'd given me. I'd watch it spread into a puddle, spitting as it turned dark yellow, tan, brown. Brown butter has a nuttiness to it that I liked. Hazelnuts, some say. *Sprinkle with Parmesan cheese.* (That was my addition, which I'd written in the margin of the cookbook.)

I leaned against the counter, by the light of the hood, the only light on in the apartment, chasing doughy worms across my plate with my fork.

One morning, after I'd deep-sixed my Christmas party and thrown out the unopened box of holiday cards, I considered calling in sick. But the idea of lying in bed and watching game shows and soap operas was even less appealing than catering to the whims of privileged, overweening megalomaniacs who thought having a membership to the world's tallest lunch club was something.

In the locker room, I slipped off my shirt and grabbed a clean jacket. Lyle, another waiter, snuck a glance at my belly and looked away. I wasn't wearing a T-shirt, and all the eating I'd done over the past several weeks showed. A few days before, Mayur had looked at me as I was bending over in the kitchen, my Japanese robe falling open, and remarked, "Look at you, man, you're disgusting. You have tits. Do something with yourself."

"You better hurry up," Lyle said, slamming his locker shut. "You know Moira." I nodded in thanks.

After he left, I sat there, elbows on knees, head hanging. I wanted to cry, but I just couldn't summon the strength.

"David, come on!" Ronnie said, running into the locker room. "Moira's screaming for you."

I trotted after him up the stairs and out into the sleek dining room. My jacket was still open. If Moira wanted me in lineup so bad, she'd get me in lineup. I stood there, defiant, staring her down. My belly protruded between the open folds of my jacket, hairy and round. I saw others lean over and gawk. *Let them. I don't give a rusty fuck what they think.*

"Get in the kitchen," Moira shouted. I didn't move. "Now."

Instantly, all of that inertia rolled over on itself, uncovering a welter of rage. I ached for a confrontation, a bruising head-on collision. The last time I'd felt like this was back in Pittsburgh, when Bridget and I had been on the fritz and she'd invited a guy to her house for dinner. The next day she and I had a screaming match. After she stormed out to class, I opened the window of her bedroom, which faced a steep drop into briars that tumbled down to the highway, and chucked out all of her stuff. I screamed as I heaved clothes, stuffed animals, books, photos, anything that would squeeze through the square of the window frame. Later, in a fit of regret, I climbed down the hill, ripping long bloody gouges up my arms, to collect everything before she got home.

"What do you think you're doing?" Moira said, busting into the kitchen after me.

Veneta pinballed in my head. Scream, punch, kick, bite, stomp, rip. Somehow, I eked out a lie that could half-explain my behavior. *My grandmother died, her head blew up because of an aneurism, been in a car accident, something.* I don't recall, but it must have been big enough to melt her, because the next thing I remember, I was buttoning my jacket, head down and contrite, and walking out to my station.

Waiting for service to begin, I felt compelled to go over everything, one more time. A thought came. Not really a thought; more like a small bubble breaking the surface that, if followed deep, deep to its source, would lead to something ugly and big and frightening. I can see it so clearly: I was gripping the brass rail that surrounded my section, tapping my turquoise ring against the metal—*plink, plink, plink.* Lost in that murky depth, I heard it like it was someone else's voice, like in the underwater game we would play in the O'Shannons' pool, holding one another's faces close and speaking, bubbles gushing out, trying to figure out what the other had said. Inexplicably I heard: *Maybe I'm manic-depressive.* And just as quickly, the thought floated away, to be forgotten for a decade. I turned to the guests being seated, a smile taped to my face.

That night, I rolled over and squinted at the alarm clock. The red numbers fishtailed into view from across the room. I was wiped; still, it wasn't enough to knock me out. When I was alone in the dark, with the light from the streetlamp splashing across the ceiling, was when the press of hopelessness was heaviest. I didn't want to do it, but it was all I had. *Just one more time,* I told myself. Since Christmastime, the seduction of planning my own death, the relief of suicide, had become the only thing that could calm me so I could vault over insomnia into sleep.

I went through my usual list in the usual order. Guns were too violent, and messy. What was it James Dean had said about leaving a beautiful corpse? Carbon-monoxide poisoning was a possibility, but I needed a car for that, and I didn't have a clue how to hook it up.

Hanging myself was out of the question: I was too fat, and I'd just end up ripping out the chandelier, which meant I'd have to pay for the repairs on top of explaining the hole in the ceiling to my landlord. Pills. Pills always did the trick.

I pictured myself carefully pouring out a bottle of pink pills onto the floor beside my futon. I would arrange them into a smiley face, like on my mother's big button, so they wouldn't seem so lethal. I watched myself taking them one by one, slowly, as if they were tiny handmade Jordan almonds, hoping I'd slip away before I finished off the smile. I wanted the person who found my stinking corpse to see that smile. To know that despite it all, I'd had the hope of a happy life. Eventually, a blackness would strum through my body, but I wouldn't fear it, because I was calling this blackness, this sleep, to me, and it would mercifully obliterate thinking, obsessing, worrying, feeling.

Over time, imagining my death lost its somnolence. I needed more. I needed a plan. Walking home from the R train at night, I found myself thinking specifics: *Where can I get my hands on enough pills to whack me? What is enough? What kind? Should I leave a note? Or a tape recording? Or is that too* Valley of the Dolls? I looked over my shoulder and down side streets. Surely in *this* neighborhood I could score something that would make short work of me.

The only thing that stopped me from knocking back a handful of lethal pink pills by the glare of the streetlamp was the fact that my mother was now the executive director of the Samaritans, a suicide hotline back home. And I couldn't bear the headlines that would be splashed across the front page of the *Herald News,* the local paper: SUICIDE DIRECTOR'S SON KILLS SELF. Or the jokes: "What's worse than getting a busy signal when calling the suicide hotline? Picking up the phone and hearing your mother on the other end."

I woke up early one April morning and looked around the room. The gray walls, which had for so long depressed me, and every morning unlatched a spiral of dread, looked almost cheerful. I didn't move my head but shifted my eyes, across my desk, to the club chair, and over to the dog-shit brown couch, and tried to understand the lightness inside. I waited for this bubble to pop. That sometimes happened in the morning: I'd awake and for a moment I'd feel happy, until I remembered I wasn't. Something was propelling me out of bed, but I was scared that if I got up, the illusion would fade, and I would be back to slumping through my day, dragging my blanket to the couch, ticking off the minutes until I had to go to work at four-thirty.

Slowly I propped up on my elbows. All good so far. I pushed myself off the futon and stood up. Still good. I squinted my eyes almost closed, which threw everything into focus so I could find my glasses. Sitting on the blue club chair, I looked out at the sky, the color of slate. It couldn't have been later than seven-thirty. I wanted to laugh myself silly, like Alastair Sim as Scrooge in *A Christmas Carol*, who couldn't contain his joy after his long night of ghost-busting. Sitting there, I couldn't remember why I'd been so despondent. That's not true. I *could* remember, but it felt more like shards of a dream from the night before, rather than something that had dragged on for four months. The longer I was awake, the more it receded.

Every other time these breaks had happened, it had been a slow slog back to normal. It would take years, sometimes, for me to feel my head was tethered to my body, my heart cupped in my rib cage the way it was meant to be. So to wake up suddenly, magnificently fine was indescribable. I thought of alien abduction—I kid you not; it was popular at the time, and I thought maybe a lizard-headed doctor with cold, scaly skin had performed some kind of surgery on me. The change was that dramatic.

I kept waiting to be sucker-punched back to reality, but it didn't happen. I found that I could go a few hours without thinking of my break, the sadness, the fear. And even when I *did* remember and my stomach clenched—always a tense moment, like being stuck in an elevator as it jolts to a stop, not knowing whether it'll plummet or judder upward—nothing happened.

Walking to the subway a few days later, I began weeping with exultation while listening to Dvořák's *New World* Symphony on my banana-yellow Walkman. As the music played, it flushed every part of my body with euphoria: It felt like hoses were attached to the soles of my feet, pumping liquid joy into my toes, legs, knees, groin, torso, then spilling over into my fingers, hands, arms, neck. And when it reached my head, another type of explosion happened, far different and far more pleasurable than those of the past. I saw an entire production unfold in front of me, a production so fully formed, so ripe with meaning and symbolism and pure genius, that the Brooklyn Academy of Music, just down the street from my apartment, was sure to mount it.

I saw flashes of enormous tableaux filled with huge, gorgeous puppets of Jesus, Hitler, and the Buddha that would require five people each to operate, if they made them to my specifications. (To make sure, I made mental schematics in my head.) In there somewhere—I had yet to figure out all the stage directions—were multi-ethnic versions of the figures from Millet's painting *The Gleaners* and the characters from Steinbeck's *The Grapes of Wrath*. A chorus of traditional Greek players sang contrapuntally (I didn't know what that word meant; I heard it in my head and had to look it up later) with bands of Holocaust victims. Angels made a thunderous racket, stamping their feet on catwalks above. Demons sniggered from boxes on the side of the auditorium. Unaccountably, the Rockettes were there. And I knew if there were Rockettes, I wasn't just back to normal. I was back to fucking fabulous normal.

25

A COTERIE OF PENISES

ecca and I were draped over each other, watching *When Harry Met Sally,* one of the movies we'd rented from the deli-video store on West Eighty-Sixth Street. It was Love Day, one of those Saturdays when we lounged all afternoon watching romantic comedies, the air conditioner beating back the swelter that is New York City in August. Becca was my closest friend. Mercurial and passionate, she was as fiercely devoted to me as I was to her. Although we were looking for love in opposite directions—her straight, me gay—we hung out almost constantly, even spending the night at each other's places several times a week. After work, we'd walk arm in arm all over the city. People smiled at us like we were newlyweds, something neither of us discouraged. I got a kick out of playing Happy TV Couple; we considered it practice for when we found our future husbands. On weekends she'd drag me into Tiffany and Gucci so she could try on engagement rings. Salespeople would watch as she slipped on a ring and held out her arm, wrist cocked, so she could see it sparkle. Then she'd waggle it toward customers, asking their opinion. When they nodded and offered congratulations, she would thread her hands—ring showing—around my arm and squeeze. I would just shrug at the clerks and smile.

My parents adored Becca, and my mother practically exploded like a dirty bomb of delight whenever we visited, especially when someone called her asking to be put on the church's prayer list. "Oh, poor you. Rheumatoid arthritis *and* irritable bowel," she'd say into the phone, scribbling down the maladies in need of divine intervention, all the while giving us a wink and that megawatt smile. "Well, can't talk long!" she'd say with an air of innuendo. "David and Becca are here. They're spending the *weekend*."

I allowed her this indulgence. When I was twenty-eight, I had told her in bald, no-uncertain terms I was gay. In the silence over the phone, I could hear the thunder of her *veneta*—this was one thing she wouldn't be able to control. We didn't speak for several months, and it wasn't until years later that she told me she would call my answering machine when I was at work just to hear my voice. Still, all this time later, the woman believed that if she willed it otherwise, so it would be.

Becca had a *veneta* second only to my mother's. When we were at a gay bar and some guy would call her a fag hag, I'd turn away and wince. It took everything for her not to smash him over the head with her lemon drop, our preferred cocktail. "Let me tell you something, sweetheart," she'd say, leaning in close. "Every girl needs a gay, and he's mine. Where's your girl? Oh, wait," she would add, leaning back, as if suddenly recognizing something about him. "You're too much of a dickhead to have one." By the end of the night, she'd have a bevy of boys surrounding her, laughing, buying her drinks.

She delighted and scared me in equal measure.

Pointing to Billy Crystal on the TV, I asked, "Do you think everyone has a Coterie of Penises?"

"A *what*?"

"You know, all the bad boyfriends you had in your life."

"You mean a bunch of guys who were dicks?" she asked.

"That's a vulgar way of putting it, but yes."

"Absolutely." She took a big swig of her two-liter bottle of Diet Coke and burped. "What about you?" I shot her a look that said, *Are you serious?* My coterie was as populous as it was unsettling.

It was 1993. I was thirty-three years old. By the time I met Becca, I had lost seventy pounds, and had a thirty-inch waist and hair so thick and full, it was practically muscular. Plus, I had a gorgeous parlor-floor apartment in Cobble Hill, Brooklyn, all to myself, where I spent my nights gold-leafing the ten-foot mirror in my living room and crying to the soundtrack of *The Bodyguard*.

Five years earlier, I had grown weary of the shape of my life. I'd been waiting tables for four years, with nothing to show for it but a dangerously wide ass and a bank account that required regular CPR, in the form of money orders from my parents. Under Scotch tape so rain wouldn't splotch it, my mother had written on the envelope in red marker: ♥ ♥ ♥ *Jesus Believes in You, And So Do We, Son!* ♥ ♥ ♥. After they'd witnessed all my failures, I marveled at how they were capable of generating such unending hope.

I have no idea if it was my manager's codependent relationship with Stoli on the rocks, or customers who sent back food because, among other things, there was eggplant in the *parmigiana di melanzane*, but I'd had it. One night I ripped off my apron and stormed out of a little Italian joint on Seventh Avenue in the middle of dinner. I have a vague memory of flipping double birds at everyone in the dining room, but that could be the story I told people to make me look a little more like Norma Rae.

With the help of an art-director friend, I eventually got a job as an advertising copywriter. For the next two years I worked for a kind, gentle Israeli who had no head for business, then for two years for a financial genius who had no clue for fashion. He sported a mullet, acid-washed soccer-mom jeans, and cowboy boots. In time, seduced by a hefty six-figure salary, I defected to another agency, which was how I could afford all that gold leaf.

During that time, life had slowly stitched itself back together. I'd become stronger and more resilient. Therapy, which I'd stayed away from since the train wreck that had been Kim Mueller of the Eames Chair back in Pittsburgh, helped. A lot.

David Lindsey Griffin, my new therapist, reminded me of Truman Capote—short and perennially boyish, with a shock of strawberry-blond hair. He was tough, fierce, irreverent, and gleefully iconoclastic, but he communicated with me in a way no shrink had before—the way of the Sisters of the Spatula. Like them, he joked, cajoled, and never passed up an opportunity to tease me, but it was always done with affection. And it worked. Unlike with Dr. Copley, I held nothing back from him, and he made deep and lasting sense, unlike Kim.

I hadn't had any of those A-bomb explosions, which he'd diagnosed as panic attacks, in years. And without panic attacks, there were no periods of lumbering, weighty blackness that inevitably followed. Sure, I still had my moments when *veneta* got the better of me—mostly with cashiers at Fairway, bank tellers, and those frigging perfume pushers at Bloomingdale's. But in time, that tension in my gut, like I was bracing for the next punch, relaxed. Life, I was beginning to believe, was good.

With one exception: I was chronically single.

I longed to be in a relationship—a real, loving mutual relationship—but so far it had eluded me. I couldn't even cop to having *had* one. The longest time I had ever been able to cobble together with a guy was three months. I'd sit in David Lindsey's office, mourning my single status.

"David Leite!" He always called me by my full name when he wanted to drive home an important point. "The only thing you're going to pick up at a gay bar is a drink," he'd say in his Southern accent. Then he'd pause theatrically and add: "And maybe the clap." I figured that as a recovered falling-down drunk, he just might know a thing or two about the machinations of the bar scene, which were still new to me. "You're going to meet your future husband in front of the dairy case at Zabar's, or at tap-dancing class, when you're having fun. Imagine that—you actually enjoying yourself." He pulled on the word *enjoying* as if it were a fat piece of saltwater taffy. "Like when you were with Cameron."

About a year before starting with David Lindsey, I'd met Cameron Lamott, himself a therapist, at Pottery Barn while shopping for a gift for a friend. Cameron always reminded me of one of those Ivy League wrestlers in vintage photos. He had Chiclet teeth, straight blond bangs, and a muscular build, with a low center of gravity that anchored him wherever he went. And there was something about his thick, hairy wrists that just did it for me.

Despite the fact he walked like a fullback, Cameron had a penchant for women's high heels. He claimed it was a healthy fetish because he expressed it in a supportive environment, at his tea parties. I wasn't so sure about that. A few times a year, a bunch of guys would sit cross-legged around the coffee table, their size-thirteen Guccis, Diors, Chanels, and Manolo Blahniks bobbling in the air as they reached for cucumber sandwiches and mini pavlovas. I had absented myself from their most recent festivities, which Cameron psychoanalyzed as internalized homophobia. (And, for what it's worth, David Lindsey later agreed with him.)

I much preferred our times alone after work. He enjoyed cooking, too, and we spent evenings in his spare, starkly lit kitchen in the West Village. Guy food was his thing, so we made hearty dishes: minestrone soup, meaty pastas, steak, pulled pork, meatloaf topped with a woven cap of bacon. Every once in a while, he'd come up behind me at the stove, pull me close, and nibble on the back of my neck, making me almost buckle. It was as if every nerve ending in my body had decided to move crosstown and gentrify the real estate back there below my hairline. I'd stand wrapped in the hardness of his arms and feel safe, grounded, like him. Nights in that bright kitchen gave me my first glimpse of domestic life with a man. Until then it had only been an idea, a concept whose possibility was far from certain. But suddenly, there I was in my sweatpants and a cruddy T-shirt, reaching across him for garlic or Parmigiano-Reggiano or a spatula, as he

poured wine and argued with me about my chintzy hand with butter. He didn't have a swinging kitchen door with a round window,
but other than that I had a real TV-worthy relationship.

My participation in Cameron's high-heel tea parties could have
been negotiated. Hell, I would have been willing to teeter around in
Judy's ruby slippers, for crissake, if he hadn't pushed away his dinner
one night and said, "I just wish I'd get AIDS and be done with it."

"What are you talking about?" Until then we'd never really discussed AIDS, even though he had lost so many friends.

"If I got it, I could finally stop worrying." I must have looked horrified, because he began jabbing the air with his finger. "Don't judge
me," he snapped. "You weren't living in New York when it all started.
You have *no* idea what it's like waking up every morning for years
and thinking today's the day."

"Cam . . ." My voice was soft. I walked around the table and
wrapped my arms around his wrestler's shoulders, but he broke my
hug, throwing me off like a cape. "What the hell is wrong with you?"
I shouted.

He swiveled toward me. "Don't pity me. Don't *ever* pity me."

"I'm not. I just—"

His fear and anger must have emboldened him, because on his
way to the kitchen he turned around, a plate in each hand, and admitted he hadn't been exactly faithful, or safe. The look on his face
screamed, *And don't say a fucking word about it.*

"So you put me at risk, too?"

"Well, we've been safe, haven't we?" His voice rumbled with derision. "You've always demanded it. So *you* have nothing to worry
about, do you?" I couldn't tell if he was angry or jealous.

The truth was that he pushed the envelope when it came to
safety. Once, he'd found these mini condoms that covered just the
head. When he strutted naked out of the bathroom, thinking I'd be
as delighted as he was with his discovery, I horse-laughed. "You gotta
be kidding me. That looks like a shower cap for your dick." He and
his junk visibly deflated. Trying again, he crawled across the bed to

me with that silly shower cap swinging. I made it clear: "You are *not* putting that thing anywhere near me." For the rest of that week he was too busy with patients to see me.

When I tried to take the plates from him, he yanked back and threw them in the sink. "Please, go." I stood there until I realized he wasn't going to turn around. I grabbed my coat and left.

The next morning, I fidgeted in a chair at a health clinic, getting tested for HIV. Again. I was tested about every six to eight weeks, whether I had had sex or not. It got so the staff of the clinic would grill me as to why I felt the need to be tested if I'd been safe or abstained. I tried to explain that ever since I was a kid, I'd believed that if I worried about something—earnestly, punishingly worried—I'd always be okay. Nothing bad could happen, because I'd been vigilant. But the minute I stopped worrying, when I dropped my guard, *that's* when a door would open and let in a landslide of shit.

"You're what we call the Worried Well," they would tell me.

"Nice to meet you," I'd say, rolling up my sleeve and sticking out my arm. Some were better than others at hiding their anger and frustration. In time, instead of trying to be talked out of the test, I just rotated clinics throughout the city. And when the tests came back negative, as they always did, I'd relax for a few days, until I began jabbing my lymph nodes in my neck or groin so hard they began throbbing, and I invoked my Mantra of Worry for protection.

Cameron was right, though. I hadn't been around when it all started, and, as I'm sure he suspected, I'd purposely kept myself off the front lines. I'd been so brutalized by Aesthetic Realism that getting caught up in the rage and power of ACT UP, or even the compassion over at Gay Men's Health Crisis, would have broken me. Back at Windows on the World, when I came out for the last time, all I wanted was to buy matching flannel pajamas and gold-rimmed china from Macy's.

I tried to rationalize staying with Cameron: He was handsome and a good cook, after all. But I couldn't ignore the fact he was sleeping around, willfully trying to get sick. One afternoon a few weeks

later, a mundane disagreement ended with me standing in the middle
of his living room, screaming, "This is over!" I considered picking up
the blue satin high-heel shoe perched on his coffee table and winging
it at him as punctuation to my point, but thought better of it. To this
day, I Google his name, hoping to find him, hoping he's still alive.
Nothing.

Meeting Eddie Sheer convinced me David Lindsey was all wrong
about bars. A friend and I were at The Works on Columbus Avenue
holding up the wall and trying not to look desperate, when this
beautiful blond man with a body that belonged on magazine covers
caught my eye from across the room and smiled. I had that cliché
movie reaction: I gave him a quizzical look and turned around, sure
he was smiling at someone much prettier behind me. Considering
all that was back there was the wall, I had no other option than to
assume he meant me.

"Here we go again," my friend said. "See ya." He gave me a kiss
and headed home. He'd been trying unsuccessfully for two years to
make us a couple, and he was tired of watching my affections lock
and load on everyone but him.

All that's really important to remember about Eddie is his perfect
build. His perfect, flawless build. Not that he wasn't smart; he was.
Probably the sharpest guy I've ever dated. And cultured. He had sub-
scriptions to just about every ballet, opera, and symphony in the city.
His body, which I was convinced had a lower BMI index than a tree
frog's, was the problem.

When I went to his apartment for the first time, he showed me
around, and we ended up in his bedroom. He said nothing, letting
me take it in. On the floor were free weights, neat stacks of fitness
magazines, enormous containers of protein powder in the corner. On
the wall was some sort of vintage poster of a boy feeling the ripped
bicep of a body builder. It was creepy—not in a lecherous way, but
close. Maybe he meant it to be ironic or nostalgic? Or maybe it was
a comment on gay culture? Or he could be the kid in the poster, like
Jodie Foster, who was the little girl in the Coppertone ad where a dog

was pulling down her bathing suit. I looked back at him to see if I could get a read. He smiled sheepishly.

My gut went into overdrive when he asked me if I wouldn't mind taking off my shirt and facing away from him. Still, I did as he asked.

"You know," he said, surprise coloring his voice, "with a little lifting, you could be in great shape."

"Um, but I *do* lift weights," I said, facing his altar of manly adoration. "Three times a week."

"I mean a real program with a trainer."

I nodded and buttoned my shirt, unsure what had just happened. *Was that a vote of confidence or a criticism?*

"That's so degrading!" Becca said when I told her the next day. She was so mad, she bugged me for his number so she could call and ream him out.

"You're not going to do that," I said calmly.

"And why not?"

"Because I'm seeing him this Saturday." I told her maybe I agreed with him; maybe I could do with a little bulk.

She held out her arms and wriggled her fingers at me, her way of summoning me into a hug. "Oh, sweetheart, the only six-pack you need with *me* is Diet Coke." I could feel her voice vibrating in my shoulder.

I planted my chin on her head. "Well, until you grow a penis, I'm out of luck."

That Saturday night, after a long, frustrating time in bed, Eddie shared what he thought was a secret. My jaw, which had spasmed several times, and I were way ahead of him. He could only get it up for muscle boys. His room said it; his poster confirmed it. But, he said, they repulsed him intellectually. "Their nuts have higher IQs than they do." Then he went on: "Men like *you*, on the other hand, are smart and funny and passionate . . ." I didn't need my nuts to fill in the blanks.

Still, I continued seeing him. On weekends, we rented a car and took long drives through Connecticut in autumn, a state I'd always wanted to live in. To me, it was the epicenter of locked-jaw WASP-dom, where people wore tartan, swapped wives, and imbibed clear drinks with impunity. "I want to be a Connecticuter," I said, walking down some Main Street speckled with yellow leaves. "Or is it a Connecticut-ite?"

"I don't know."

"Nah, sounds too much like Walter Cronkite."

When I veered in the direction of a sweet ye olde ice cream shoppe, he glanced at my stomach—a look that said, *Do you* really *need that?*—and I demurred, slinking away from the window, empty-handed and full of resentment.

At night, we'd lie next to each other, his inevitable "I'm sorry" the last thing I'd hear as I fell asleep.

Before I could find a way to wiggle out of seeing him again, he pulled the plug when he found a guy he thought was the perfect mix of brains, abs, and ass.

"I never really liked him, anyway," I said to Becca, holed up in her apartment, spooning into pints of Ben & Jerry's as we watched TV on yet another Love Day.

"Yes, you did."

"Yeah, you're right. I did."

"C'mere, baby," she said, letting me put my head in her lap. "Someday the right guy will come along."

"You think?"

"I do."

Neither Peter Adler nor Gabe Newman was that guy. Peter was a dull dentist with hair plugs, eighteen years my senior, who, I found out several weeks into dating, like Eddie couldn't perform. In his case, it wasn't muscle boys that turned over his motor, but rather straight porn blaring from the TV.

Gabe was a short, compact podiatrist I met through a personal ad I'd placed in the *Village Voice*. It was early January, and we were on our second or third date—drinks and, if all went well, dinner. On our way to Temple Bar, we passed desiccated Christmas trees piled on slumps of filthy snow, waiting for the morning's garbage trucks. In front of the bar, Gabe shooed me inside, telling me he needed a minute. Just as I settled onto a stool, a blast of cold air and commotion came from the door. Gabe was yanking a huge de-needled tree into the bar, probably the same tree the bar had just ditched. The room fell silent and stared as he dragged the tree across the floor and over to me, propping it up between us.

"I'd like a Scotch," he said to the bartender, and then, pointing to the tree, added, "And one for my friend"—here he paused, to make sure the guy got the joke—"Mr. Tannenbaum." He explained to the man that the tree was meeting its end the next day, and why not give it a glorious send-off before it faced the chipper?

I was burning with humiliation. "Are you serious?" I said under my breath.

"What?"

"A tree? In a martini bar? What are you, fucking twelve?"

The room slowly came back to life with low murmurs of disbelief. All eyes were on us; some, thankfully, were warm with sympathy. And that was when I needed to say, *Enough*. Enough of guys who have a grossly misguided notion that they're hysterical. Enough of guys who can't get it up or can't keep it in their pants. Enough of guys who, pissed off that you broke up with them, call every phone-sex line impersonating you, and give out your name and number—on your frigging birthday. Enough of guys who leave you alone in the emergency room with a painfully swollen thumb they dislocated in the name of gymnastic sex. Enough of guys who try to make you over in the style of their dead boyfriend, and then drop you when you try to be yourself. Enough of guys who insist you wear a condom just to cuddle. Enough of guys who fake an orgasm. Yes, apparently, it's possible.

Enough.

26

GAY WHiTE MALE SEEKS BALANCE

The first batch arrived from the magazine after a week. A fat manila envelope, full of letters from self-described eligible men. I dropped onto the couch and stared at the packet in my hands. *I should be more excited*, I thought. The last time I'd placed a personal ad, the one in the *Village Voice*, it had been a sideshow of gay oddities. It reminded me of Mystery Date, a board game I used to play with some of the girls on Brownell Street. In the middle of the board was a plastic door. When it was your turn to open it, fate would match you with a swimmer in sexy tight trunks, a dreamy Ivy Leaguer wearing a Baracuta jacket and carrying a bowling bag, a tow-headed skier in his lodge-appropriate sweater, or what I dreaded most: a bum. Filthy clothes and all. If recent history was any indication, my chances for a happy date had been better when I was eight.

Which is why I worked for days on this new ad. I approached it like I was one of the products I sold at the agency: IKEA, WordPerfect, IBM, President Bill Clinton. After many drafts, and reams of cor-

rections from Becca, I sent this to *New York* magazine. It appeared in
the September 27, 1993, issue.

> **Gay White Male Seeks Balance**—This honestly
> handsome (33, 6', 185 lbs.) creative professional whose
> days are filled with deadlines, clients, and chaos is
> looking for another very successful, self-aware, car-
> ing man (35–48) for quiet autumn nights of courtship.
> Must like the beach in November, long walks, lon-
> ger talks, antiquing, a good laugh over a good meal,
> car trips to nowhere, and anything subtitled. Caution:
> the confused, anxious, and intimacy-phobic need not
> apply. Send heartfelt letter with photo/phone.

I heaved a sigh and tore into the envelope. The first letter I pulled
out was written on light blue stationery lipped in royal blue. Inside,
a picture of a man. A short intake of breath. He was beautiful. He
was wearing a sapphire-blue sweater (obviously, blue was a favorite
color) and white shorts, and was standing in front of a split-rail fence.
Beyond were craggy cliffs and, farther, the ocean, bleeding into fog.
He had his left arm slung over the top rail, his hands clasped, his legs
crossed at the ankles. Casual, but not in that studied way I'd seen before. Decorous, even. No private parts practically pressed up against
the lens. No possessions stuffed into the frame to clue me into his
financial status. In fact, he took up so little of the picture, it was more
a photograph of the ocean than anything. I flipped it over. On the
back he had written, "Terrible picture, great beach!" I stood and held
it under a lamp to get a better view. I was right; his eyes were closed.
And his hair, dirty blond and receding, was ruffled by the wind, like
a rooster's comb. I was beguiled and relieved. Although this man was
very handsome, there was no vanity in the picture.

He wrote that his name was Alan Dunkelberger, "a 35-year-old
man who sells Manhattan real estate to make a living." *What an odd
way to put that.* Most men would have said, "I'm a real estate broker,"

or "I sell real estate." I wondered if perhaps he was foreign. As I read on, the photograph made sense. He wrote that it was taken on Martha's Vineyard, one of his favorite places. He explained that the beach was his getaway, where he was most himself. He closed with, "You said to write a heartfelt letter. I feel as though I've written a book . . . so, why don't you pick up the phone right now and call me. Don't wait!"

Minutes later we were talking. His voice was deep, and I could hear the smile in it, curling up the ends of his sentences. The conversation veered from work to theater to the beach to books. It was peppered with all sorts of questions, always followed by "And what about you?" Unlike the guys who had answered my previous ad, he wasn't halfhearted or preoccupied, dividing his time between me and *Entertainment Tonight*. Plus, the phone gave me distance to focus on what he was saying and not get caught up in his looks, or how I looked, or what we would look like on our Christmas cards.

We agreed to meet at Top of the Sixes at nine forty-five on October 4. I chose the times—after my group therapy with David Lindsey and seven other gay men finished. Alan picked the place—for the atmosphere. I'd never been to the restaurant, which was on the top of 666 Fifth Avenue, hence the name. He said he liked the view, and the understated elegance and quiet of the bar.

Walking down Fifth Avenue, I felt the frisson I always experienced on blind dates. The potential, the hope. Then I saw him, and my heart sank. Once again a man had misrepresented himself. He stood at the entrance to the building in a camel jacket, white dress shirt opened one too many buttons for my conservative tastes, spray-painted-on jeans, and cowboy boots. *Fire Island queen,* I thought, and I was drained of hope.

It was a polite date, the kind you smile through wanly, the whole time wondering if you can make it back in time to catch the end of *Murphy Brown*. The conversation didn't exactly ping-pong like it had on the phone. On the other end of the line, safe within the fantasy of his being an unaffected guy—one who unselfconsciously admitted

to loving McDonald's, and who actually said things like "Holy go
to war!"—I had been curious and interested. But seeing that he was
one of the Beautiful People who, I was certain, did Beautiful Things
in Beautiful Places, the kind who moved effortlessly from parties in
Fire Island to East Hampton and who was, in all likelihood, fond of
under-eye night-repair cream, nude sunbathing, and drinks with umbrellas in them, I just couldn't muster the energy.

I was about to call it a night when he asked about my other experiences with personal ads. I told him about the seventy or so letters I'd
gotten in response to my *Village Voice* ad, which I'd winnowed down
to about a dozen dates with exhibitionists, fetishists, utterly nice but
utterly boring suits. I mentioned that peculiar little man Gabe Newman, the Christmas-tree hugger.

"Wait," he said. "Did you say 'Gabe Newman'?"

"Is he a friend of yours?" I answered, glad that I hadn't said anything insulting.

"Not really. I dated him, too. Through his ad."

"Get . . . out . . . of . . . town. When?"

I waved over the waiter and ordered two more gimlets and another bowl of nuts. Flipping through our Filofaxes, we figured out
that I'd dated Gabe first. I recounted Gabe's need to rescue Christmas trees. Alan's eyes grew big. I could see he was trying to reconcile
someone he'd found to be a pretentious, onerous man with the self-
proclaimed "Jewish rapscallion" I'd had drinks with.

"That little shit!" I said when Alan told me some of the things
Gabe had said to him about dating, men, and relationships. "Don't
believe him for a minute," I added. "Those are my lines. *I* said those
things to *Gabe*."

"And he made believe he came up with them."

"I hope you were impressed."

"I was."

"Well, you're looking at the real thing. I'm the original Broadway
cast. He's merely a bad bus-and-truck company."

The rest of the room fell away as we laughed about Gabe and the many men we had met, the few we had dated. Although Alan looked like the guys who intimidated me, who stared right through me on the streets and ignored me at parties, he wasn't one of them. He hated the pretension and the posturing of the gay scene as much as I did. When I relaxed, I found my way to that man in the picture. His easy charm, his honesty, even innocence. I knew at that moment he would never sunbathe in the nude.

Eventually, the waiter slipped the bill on the table between us. "Let me give this to you," he said, pointing to the room. "We're closing." I swiveled in my seat. The restaurant, which had been packed when we'd arrived, was empty. Waiters were flipping chairs and sliding them on top of tables. I looked at my watch. We'd been there for hours.

Outside, Alan stood under a streetlamp that painted everything a ghastly orange. Through the liquid haze of several gimlets, he seemed on fire, the light burning through his hair and the edges of his jacket.

"What's the matter?" he asked.

"Nothing." I took in Alan, that horrid light, the street behind. I wanted to imprint it, a caramel-colored Kodachrome slide, so that, regardless of what would happen between us, I would always remember what a wonderful first date felt like.

We stood facing each other, suddenly silent and awkward. I tapped the point of his very *Urban Cowboy* boots with the toe of my penny loafer.

"Dimes, huh?" he said, pointing to my shoes. I suddenly felt silly, self-conscious. Then, "I had a great time."

"Me, too."

"I'd really like to get together again."

Relieved, I answered, "Me, *too*."

He didn't try to kiss me, which I found endearing, and refreshing. Instead, we shook hands. As he headed up Fifth Avenue, I waited for a cab back to Brooklyn. I watched to see if he would turn around, and he did. Once, twice, three times. You could fall in love with a guy who turned around three times.

27

LOVE FOOD

lan, I soon discovered, was a diner. He loved everything about the ceremony of the table. Whenever we were at his apartment on West Eighty-Fifth Street, he'd lay out placemats, those gold-rimmed plates from Macy's, silverware, glasses. He slipped rolled napkins into shiny rings, like wedding bands, and lit candles and played music—Kenny G, of whom, for some reason, he was inordinately and unfortunately fond.

He especially enjoyed lingering after a meal. He'd push away from his plate, cross his legs, and fold his hands in his lap, like he was ready to be told a story. We were to talk, I came to understand. About our day, about a book one of us had read, about the news. Anything, really. Company and conversation were what was important. I figured it was something he'd picked up from his family. Not so, he told me. When he was a kid in Baltimore, dinner had been a hit-and-run. At suppertime, his stepfather rarely spoke to him. Instead he would glower across his plate at Virginia, Alan's mother. Alan would sit in his chair, head down and silent, waiting for the first chance to slip away unnoticed.

I didn't get this concept of lingering. My people are not lingerers. We'd sit down, platters passing in both directions, a raucousness rising from the table, even when it was just my parents and me. Ten minutes after finishing, regardless of how many of us there were, there was no evidence we'd ever shared a meal. Tables were stripped, dishes washed, food covered and put away. The women then gathered in the kitchen, getting ready for the next meal; the men sat outside on lawn chairs, waiting for the next meal; the kids played in the street, building up an appetite for the next meal. We were eaters, not diners.

Weirdly, food factored in little in Alan's dining ritual. It wasn't so much what he ate but how it was presented that mattered. "You can serve shit on a shingle, but as long as that shingle is bone china, no one'll notice," he liked to say. As if to prove his point, we were walking up Broadway past Burger King on One-Dollar Whopper Night. Not one to pass up junk food, especially if it was a bargain, he peeled off into the restaurant. At home, he pulled two burgers from the sack and set them on a plate. He arranged fries around the rim and sat down to wait for me. I foraged in the kitchen cabinet for the box of Fiber One cereal I'd stashed there, and grabbed a matching china bowl, a spoon, and a quart of skim milk. "Yes, yes," he said, motioning for me to eat, his falsetto quavering in his best Julia Child impression. *"Bon appétit!"* From the satisfied smile splitting his face into two, you would have thought he was eating at Buckingham Palace. Afterward, even though the couch, *Roseanne,* and my laptop were calling, I lingered. For him.

But I was screwed. Losing and keeping off all that weight for those five years had required Herculean discipline. *Not* lingering at the table was one of the ways I prevented myself from swallowing donuts and spiral hams whole. So was pattern eating. Every morning on my way to the ad agency, I grabbed a bagel and orange juice. Lunch was a tuna-salad sandwich and a Diet Coke at my desk. Dinner consisted of either a bowl of cereal or, occasionally, pasta with low-calorie sauce. That was it, for a long time.

Restricting what I ate wasn't just about remaining thin, but also about how it made me feel: light, like I had been carved hollow. My senses snapped into high-definition—smell and taste especially. At the most unusual times—when I was walking to the subway, or sitting in a meeting at work—a euphoria would sweep through me, carbonating my insides. Alan didn't understand why anyone who wasn't overweight would want to limit consumption. All of his life he had tried to gain weight: gulping shakes and wolfing down high-fat foods, candy, and carbohydrates. Yet there we were: he on one side of the table, stuffing his face with burgers; I on the other, making do with three-quarters of a cup of sticks and twigs.

He undid me, meal by meal. Not because he was a great cook; he wasn't. His mac and cheese came in a blue box. He had an unapologetic love for Velveeta and cakes with fruit cocktail baked inside. It was his act of cooking for me, along with his steadfast desire to make me happy, that released something inside—what I imagined the slow, seductive unlacing of a corset must feel like, and I could breathe again.

Love Food, we called it. The handful of dishes we made each other that autumn, as a way of nurturing ourselves and the affection we felt but didn't want to jinx by naming. His weekend place, a sweet ranch house in Barryville, New York, was a stone's throw from the Delaware River. On our way up, we'd pass patchworks of orchards and stop to pick apples and buy fresh-squeezed cider, apple butter, and, if I was feeling particularly svelte, cider doughnuts.

One Saturday afternoon I woke from a nap, the angled autumn light long gone, and walked down the hall. I heard the rhythmic *toc-toc-toc* chopping of a knife. Something was spitting in a pan. That damned Kenny G playing on the boom box. I leaned against the kitchen doorway, watching.

"Hello, *mon cher!*" He said it as if he hadn't seen me in a week, and I liked that. I walked over to him, and he gave me a kiss, a wooden spoon cocked in his hand. I wrapped my arms around him as he stood at the stove. "What are you making?"

"Pork roast with sautéed apples." It was a recipe he'd learned a few years earlier and made every autumn. I turned my head to the side and rested it on his shoulder. The movement of his arm as he stirred the skillet lulled me, and I closed my eyes. The sweetness of the apples and the sting of the onions tamed by heat and butter wafted through the kitchen. I was hungry. Not just for dinner, but for cooking, which I had forsaken for so long. For the primitive, intimate connection it forges. For the way it says, "You matter to me." For the naked vulnerability of hoping you'll please another. I'm convinced the reason I recall that moment, that room—when so many others have slipped from memory—is the food. It anchored me to that spot: head on his shoulder; white walls, cabinets the color of pumpernickel; the coils of the electric stove glowing red, like giant branding irons.

My contribution of a sour-cream apple pie would be, in my estimation, a far more monumental addition to the night than a skillet supper, because it required baking, the prissy and unforgiving sister of cooking. Earlier that day, I had heaved a bag of apples onto the counter. Alan watched me from the kitchen table.

"What are you making?" he asked.

"Never mind," I answered. "Just go—leave me alone." I shuffled him out of the kitchen.

"Is that for me?" he said, glancing over my shoulder at the apples, his eyes lighting up. I shot him my mother's look, the one that levels people, the one that says, *Don't mess with me, fellas!* He held up his palms in surrender and headed for the living room. Moments later, Kenny G's saxophone began worming its way into my head.

At the counter, I stared at the ingredients for the piecrust—flour, butter, and salt—giving them the same withering look, but I wasn't able to bully them as I had Alan. I mixed everything by hand in a big country bowl, drizzling in ice water, just enough, as the recipe said, to make a ball. From the moment I wet the flour, it wanted to wrestle. "Sonofabitch!" I muttered. When the dough came together,

I wrapped the clump in plastic and tossed it in the fridge for an hour. Alan poked his head into the kitchen and saw the mess I'd made.

"You can use my grandmother's rolling pin." He placed it on the counter and slipped backward out of the room, leaving me in my dust storm of flour and indignation. After some pounding and slapping, I managed to fit the chilled dough into a pie plate and shove the whole thing back into the fridge while I made the filling.

The apples have to be easier, I figured. And they would have been, if it hadn't been for the paring knife: a small wooden handle with a nicked, rusty blade sticking out of it.

"It's all I have," he said with a shrug.

"Let me guess—your grandmother's."

About an hour later, two pounds of apples had been peeled, cored, and sliced. I tossed them in the egg-and-sour-cream mixture, scraped the whole mess of it into the crust, and sprinkled it with a streusel topping. While baking, the apple slices jostled together in layers, interspersed with tangy cream. What had looked like an ugly-ass strewing of crumbs had baked to a handsome pebbly topping. I slid the pie onto a rack to cool and went to take that nap.

I was ashamed to be so clumsy in the kitchen. It was more than just being out of practice. While I made the pie, anxiety had idled, low and threatening, in my rib cage. For too long, cooking had acted as an antidote to feeling miserable. It was a simple prescription: Walk into a kitchen sad and despondent, whether at the Hollises or my first apartment in Brooklyn, and walk out feeling full and better. Cooking and eating did that; it blunted the pain. Now, after all this time, I discovered I was terrified to stand at the stove. Scared I would hurtle back and become that morose and desperate version of myself, as if within the action of stirring sauces, pounding cutlets, and chopping vegetables lived an emotional memory that, like muscle memory, I could slip back into without ever noticing. And, of course, there was the fear I'd let go and pig out back to 240 pounds.

A normal person would just have gone to the gym more. Logical and appropriate. Here's the thing: For several years before meeting

Alan, I had availed myself of the facilities at my gym—namely the steam room, sauna, and whirlpool—after a workout. And when your gym is in the middle of the West Village, New York's gayest mecca, those amenities take on a different purpose: sex. David Lindsey and I had spent endless uncomfortable hours parsing whether this was sexual compulsion, boredom, a death wish, or a way to relieve the incessant stress of work at the agency. That last one got both our votes, although I never told him I was drawn to the gym even when I wasn't at the office. Still, he kept hammering away at the risk/reward ratio of it all: Were a few minutes of happy slapping worth flirting with AIDS, getting bashed and bloodied by a straight guy caught in queer crossfire, or having my butt hauled off for public indecency?

After Alan and I had been together for several weeks, a famous actor who was electrifying Broadway at the time parted his towel, much like the curtain on a stage, and though I was momentarily honored to be that day's solo audience member, I flustered out of the steam room. Driven by guilt, I confessed.

"Did anything happen?" Alan asked.

I told him the truth: "No."

"Then there's nothing to worry about, is there?" That was it. With that one statement he closed the issue. The graciousness with which he extended his trust was so striking, so gentlemanly, I never abused it. But that meant not stepping foot in a gym again, even in a different part of town. Gay men, even famous ones, were everywhere. And as far as exercising on my own, well, that was never going to happen.

Before dinner that night, Alan slipped two Fiesta plates from his collection of more than two hundred pieces onto the warped oak table, and tucked colorful napkins to their left. On top went a fork and steak knife. He poured wine, lit candles, and lowered the lights. He served me a thick slice of pork and a spoonful of roasted apples, all drenched in cider-butter sauce. He watched. I took a deep breath and cut into it. "Excellent!" I said, and it was. He nodded his appreciation, and only then did he turn his attention to his plate. I ate all of it, every last butter-laden bite, for him. Afterward, I cut him a generous piece of pie and sliced a sliver for myself. He ate it and then, holding out his empty plate, asked for more. I was deeply pleased that I had pleased him.

Throughout that autumn, pork and pie became our weekend dinner. And from the repetition and sanctity of that meal, even though our menus ultimately changed and grew, came our first tradition: Sunday supper.

28

THEREiN LiES THE LiE

Mrs. Young reminded me of a strand of antique pearls—luminescent skin over round, smooth cheeks—and even though she was well into her eighties, she carried herself with an elegance and class you don't see much these days. When I spoke to her, she nodded and smiled, listening to everything I said in a way that made me feel I was the highlight of her day. Alan told me she had a remarkable ability to remember birthdays, favorite colors, and your latest infatuation. I had just met her, but I was smitten.

She and her two daughters, Susan and Emily, had invited Alan and me to their home on Shelter Island for Thanksgiving. It was momentous, because it was our first holiday together. Since Mrs. Young assured us she could wrestle with the turkey and attend to the various pots burbling on the stove—"I've been doing it for decades, after all"—the rest of us went for a walk along the water, at Alan's suggestion.

"Really? It's so cold," I said, hoping Susan or Emily would back me up.

"Must like the beach in November." He reminded me of the line from my ad in a way that sounded like it was time to pay up. I could feel irritation tightening around my neck. In the best of times, I was inadequately dressed. I didn't see the point of spending money on a raincoat or boots—you use them maybe a dozen times a year—and I hadn't worn gloves and a hat since my mother had dressed me. I'm genetically blessed with hot hands and a helmet of hair. The last thing I'd expected was a stroll by the bay on one of the coldest Thanksgivings on record, so I'd made no provisions. Alan, on the other hand, looked like a Macy's balloon, wrapped in layers of clothes, a scarf, a hat, gloves, and boots.

As we walked along the beach, the wind pulled at our jackets and snapped my pants against my legs so hard, it felt like my shins were being caned. Eddies of sand swirled around us. Undaunted, Alan forged ahead over driftwood and along frothy lips of foam left behind from white-capped waves lapping the shore. Susan and Emily, easily twenty-five years my senior, were keeping up with him, talking and laughing as if they were in a General Mills International Coffee commercial. I lagged behind, unable to hear anything over the incessant howl. "Are you frigging kidding me?" I muttered. Finally, I had to say it: "Can we get the hell out of here? I'm freezing." It came out harsh and bludgeoning. Alan looked back at me oddly, like he suddenly didn't know who I was, and shame thundered through me. I tried to make a joke of it, bluffing that I was fine, really, we could go on, but Susan and Emily had picked up on the anger in my voice, and we all turned back.

On the way to the house, I understood something: Alan wasn't built to withstand the gale force of someone like me. If he saw my temper, my *veneta*, he'd walk. So I would lie, I decided. I would hold in all the horrible, the untoward, the negative. I'd hug the horrendous to my chest like it was an unexploded bomb, and turn away to protect him from it. Who I am had to become invisible to him.

At dinner, which Mrs. Young had laid out while we were at the beach, I was wiped from the energy it took to keep the conversation

tinkling and interesting. While passing mashed potatoes and talking about tide charts, I tried to drown my pique and rage. I knew
well enough, after all these years, that this had little if anything to do
with Alan, or going out in the cold. It wasn't about control or loss of
it, as David Lindsey often asked. These periods just descended, and
all I could do was dig my nails into my palms and wait for them to
pass. So I complimented. I smiled. I laughed, sometimes too hard.
Through it all, Alan kept watching me, evaluating me. Every time
someone said something, he glanced over to check my reaction. How
could I become transparent if he wouldn't stop staring?

I excused myself and went to the bathroom to escape. I sat on the
closed toilet seat, feeling drained. With my head against the wall, I
closed my eyes and breathed deeply. Everything grated: Susan's im-
patience, Emily's restraint, Mrs. Young's generosity. And, especially,
Alan's incessant looks. I felt a bottomless sorrow open up, because I
had believed that once you met *that* person, The One (my nickname
for Alan), you're not supposed to feel miserable anymore. But it was a
lie—*another* lie. I felt as irritable, tired, and heavy as I ever had. More
so, maybe, because I couldn't blame being single or dating an ass for
my wretchedness. No matter how much I tried not to catastrophize,
I was convinced that when we left the next day, Alan would break up
with me in the car. "You know," I imagined him saying, "this isn't going to work." He had seen me—the broken, unsalvageable me—and
there would be no second chance. No opportunity to gouge those
images out of his brain with my thumbs, to blind him to the worst
parts of me.

When what felt like a reasonable length of time for a good dump
had passed, I flushed the toilet and ran the water, to make it sound
like I was washing my hands. Looking at my reflection, I fixed a smile
on my face—my mother's Courtesy-Booth Girl smile—and whispered, "Please try harder."

After we cleared the table, Emily, Alan, and I played Scrabble at
the card table pushed up against the stairs. I couldn't concentrate. It
was as if my eyes were backward, looking in, searching for answers.

No matter how many times I rearranged my tiles, no words emerged. But I was certain no one could pick up on it now. I had managed to become invisible, to arrange myself—my body, my face, the tilt of my head—in such a way that I resembled someone who was enjoying himself. I don't recall what word Alan was trying to pass off as English, but Emily, who was wicked smart, wouldn't let him off the hook. I jumped in, too. He knew he was on thin ice, but he kept trying to bluff. The more he bluffed, and the more Emily and I pushed back, the more he laughed.

I had never encountered this in my life, but Alan laughed so hard, he started crying. Huge tears rolled down his face, and the more he scrubbed at them with the cuff of his sleeve, the more they came. Emily and I began laughing, which only fueled his, causing more tears. I'd never fallen in love with someone's laugh until then. Suddenly, something let go inside, and I was overcome with the desire to grab his face and kiss him all over. His laughter had short-circuited whatever was going on with me. No one had ever done that before, and it was salubrious. My appetite, which had absented itself all day, found me, and I asked Mrs. Young if I could make myself a sandwich. She was delighted, I can only assume at the change in me, and unwrapped leftovers and put together my sandwich. I took it back to the card table, and handily trounced Alan and his imaginary English, only to be bested by Emily.

On the way to Barryville the next morning, he said, "Can I ask you something?" My stomach pitched. Here it was, the brush-off.

"Okay."

He didn't take his eyes from the road, which was just as well. I didn't want him to see me. I stared forward, too, waiting. "You're really moody, aren't you?" He had studied me all Thanksgiving afternoon, gathering proof I was unfit. I was stung by what he'd said. It didn't jibe with how most people would characterize me, I was certain. *Moody* was someone who moped, was depressed, lifeless. I considered myself passionate, deeply emotional, exuberant, and opinionated. I was Portuguese; it was my cultural birthright. But moody?

No. That was the domain of the poet, the writer, and that kid in high school who was never the same after his father was murdered in New Orleans. He pressed into the lockers going down the halls and bled into the bleachers in gym. He was a ghost. *That* was moody.

Before I could say anything, he added, "The good thing is your moods don't last." He turned quickly and shot me a smile. I de-escalated. He wasn't looking to break up after all. This wasn't a car ride that would end with him dropping me off at the Greyhound station near Barryville, an apologetic, halfhearted smile on his face. His was an observation, nothing more.

That week in therapy, I mentioned what Alan had said. David Lindsey watched with that amused look of his. "What?" I said, "I'm sure you have some bitchy comment to make."

"Do you remember in the first few months of therapy, I said to you, 'I think you might be depressed?'"

"No, because you didn't."

"Ohhhh, yes I did, sir. I have the session notes to prove it."

"So what of it?"

"Do you remember your response?"

"Apparently not."

"Let me refresh your memory. You took your fists and hammered down on my mission chair—Lord, I thought you were going to break it—and shouted, 'I am not nor have I ever been depressed.'"

"I don't remember that, and for the record I *don't* think I'm depressed."

"Then what do you think Alan was picking up on?"

I couldn't come up with a good answer, so I stared at the spider plants dying in his window.

"Well, you can continue lying to yourself, David Leite. Denial works." He took a look at the clock above my head. "Our time is up." Sometimes I thought he planned his last words so that they would circle around me all week like vultures, waiting.

29

WHEN i FALL iN LOVE

Alan sat at dinner, pushing chicken around his plate, preoccupied and silent. It was early December, and he'd just returned from visiting his mother and sister Diane in Baltimore. I was beginning to log his patterns: Every time he returned, he was out of sorts for a while. "Remind me never to spend more than two days there," he had asked me the last time he came home. He'd ignored my warning this trip and, again, wound up glum at the table. I fought my inclination to plunge my hand into the quiet and fish out whatever was bothering him. *If something happened while he was down there,* I reasoned, *he'll tell me.*

Suddenly: "Do you think, if this thing is real," he finally said, pointing his fork back and forth between us, "you can promise me forever?"

I set my bowl of Fiber One aside. *Here we go,* I thought. The Conversation. By that time, thanks to my Coterie of Penises, I'd spent the previous five years serial-dating and getting any romantic notions of forever kicked out of me. I also knew how Alan had been shunted from his mother to his grandmother to their pastor and back to his mother when he was growing up, and how much it had devastated him. The idea of permanence was paramount to his happiness. Yet I didn't want to lie.

"No, *mon cher,* I can't."

Suddenly he looked like a five-year-old whose Big Wheel I'd accidentally backed over with my car. "I *want* to promise forever," I rushed to say, trying to cheer him. "But neither of us has any idea who we'll be in twenty years. We could grow apart."

You'd have thought I'd run over his dog, too.

"Or—or—or, on the other hand, we could grow closer. Right? That's a possibility. . . ."

He traffic-copped me, putting up his palm and cutting me off. "I get it. Don't worry about it."

I struggled to find a way to express my hopes for us. I tried journaling, to see if I could unearth something. I verbally wrestled with David Lindsey, blaming him for making me a romantic pragmatist— so realistic and clear-eyed about love that I couldn't indulge in a little forever fantasy for the poor guy. I asked advice of friends who'd been together longer than us. All nonstarters.

Alan said nothing more about it, but his silence shouted: *I can't feel safe with you.*

"You have a passport, right?" he asked a few nights later, while clearing the table.

"Yes . . . why?" I was intrigued.

"Oh, no reason." It was his playful voice again, the one shaded with possibility and surprise.

"Let me guess: You're an international jewel thief, and you need an extra orifice to stash the loot when you escape."

He just smiled and continued washing the dishes.

"Tell me!" I demanded.

"There's nothing to tell." *Nothing* turned out to be a weeklong trip to Paris to celebrate New Year's Eve with his friends Giles and Larry, who lived there.

Larry, an American, was plump, with mischievous eyes and a re-markably athletic laugh. It could soar to high titters and then plum-met to thunderous tugboat blasts. He was all twittering fingers, elastic eyebrows, and hands cupped over his mouth after letting slip his newest morsel of gossip. It took all of a few minutes before he was pulling me into a corner and taking me into his confidences, which, I later learned, included everyone. It was hard not to be taken with him.

Giles, on the other hand, was trim and compact, with dark hair and eyes. From the moment he greeted me, he seemed constricted and dense, as folded in on himself as Larry was expansive. A black hole to a supernova. Giles was always shushing Larry or exploding over the slightest offense. And he had a terrible habit of pulling on his eyebrows when he talked to you, then opening his hand and look-ing at his quarry. Trichotillomania, I remembered from psych class. I didn't like him, but I made an effort.

He was a sensational cook, though, and the poster child for the French Paradox: Despite the prodigious amounts of food and wine he consumed, he never gained weight. *Le bâtard!* I watched him pre-pare New Year's Eve dinner: foie gras he'd ordered fresh from the farmer; duck breasts cooked slowly in a pan with only their own fat to sear them to a deep, crusty brown; salad with a luscious vinai-grette that hugged the leaves; side dishes I can't remember; cheeses; and *gâteau au chocolat* with ultrarich crème fraîche, which I thought was whipped cream and heaped onto my dessert in mounds. Cham-pagne, wine, and Calvados flowed freely. Whatever Giles lacked in tact, he made up for in generosity.

Toward the middle of dinner, he leaned unsteadily in my direc-tion. *"Calvados ouvre votre trou Norman,"* he said, a bit lasciviously.

"I beg your pardon?"

"Calvados opens your Norman hole," he translated.

"Oh . . ." I wasn't about to let this boozed-up Frenchman any-where near my Norman hole, whatever that was. I later discovered he hadn't been making a pass. He was referring to how knocking back a shot during a long meal makes room for even more food—which was his intention, because sometime around one in the morning the courses finally stopped.

I rang in 1994 with my first case of a wicked *crise de foie*. My normally parsimonious diet had done nothing to prepare me for Giles's Napoleonic assault of rich French food, and I spent the day in bed, moaning, craving nothing but twigs and leaves—any roughage to get this stuff out of me.

Once I recovered, and my stomach and fat became reacquainted, Larry, Giles, Alan, and I never passed up an opportunity to dine out. We lingered long over brasserie tables splotched with the oceanic liquid of *moules marinière* and splattered with murderous-looking drops of blood from Alan's *steak frites*, which made it look like a crime scene. Or in a clubby restaurant swathed in red leather, where children sat erect, reading menus almost as tall as them, and I had foie gras for the third time. Or, as a thank-you to our hosts, a dinner at Jacques Cagna, the most formal and expensive restaurant I had ever been to, where an appetizer of a tiny puff-pastry box of three scallops cost more than twenty-seven dollars. And we all had it. (For those who are bad at math, that's $180 in today's bucks—*just for appetizers*.)

Toward the end of our visit, while Larry went to French class and Giles was at work, we were alone in their huge, magnificent apartment. I flipped on their five-figure sound system and stopped dead in the enormous living room. From the ceiling speakers wafted lyrics to a song—"When I Fall in Love"—that gave voice to what I hadn't been able to all those weeks earlier.

We had yet to profess our love for the other, but this song syncopated two ways of loving, equal but different. "When I fall in love, it will be *forever*, or I'll never fall in love" was all Alan. Those words would comfort him, make him feel safe. "When I give my heart, it will be *completely*, or I'll never give my heart" spoke to me. I couldn't promise him forever, but I could promise that I'd love him completely for as long as I could. It was my own personal forever.

"ALAN?" I shouted through the labyrinthine space.

"WHAT?" he shouted back from our room, the maid's room, on the other side of the apartment behind the butler's pantry.

"C'MERE!"

"FOR WHAT?"

"WOULD YOU JUST *PLEASE* COME HERE?"

I reset the song and waited. When he entered, I positioned him under a speaker as the opening strains embraced the room.

He began to speak. "Shh! Listen."

As a man's voice crooned the "forever" verse, I laid my hand on his chest. "This is you." Then, as a woman glided through the "completely" stanza, I took his hand and placed it on my heart. "This is me."

I waited. For that movie moment. For him to break down crying and hug me, because he understood how much he meant to me. For us to say "I love you." For Olympian sex, the sounds of which would carry through that cavern of an apartment, and make Larry and Giles smirk at us during dinner and ask, "So what did *you* two boys do this afternoon?" We were halfway there: The song, I later learned, was from the freaking soundtrack to *Sleepless in Seattle*. Instead, he nodded and smiled. That was it. A nod and a smile, which made me rush in and proclaim, "This is our song!"—pointing to the speakers as Clive Griffin and Céline Dion kept singing. "Don't you get it?"

"I do." I looked at him in disbelief. "I do, I really do!" He said he understood that although he needs to be loved forever and I need to be loved entirely, we were committed to each other in our own way. *Cut! End of scene.*

Deflated that he didn't see divine intervention at work, the historic synchronicity of that moment, I brushed past him and dropped onto our futon in the maid's room and pouted.

I tried again on our last afternoon.

As we ambled along the Left Bank munching on crêpes (he *jambon et fromage*, I Nutella), I pointed toward the river. "Let's walk down there." The Seine on a dreary, cold day in January wasn't the beach in November, but at least he'd be near water. The minute we made our way down the stone steps, I regretted it. Lapping at the edge of the embankment was a raft of garbage—plastic bags, cups, cigarette butts, condoms.

"Gross."

"Ignore that," I said, "it's our last day in romantic Paris. Let's enjoy it!" Chipper didn't come naturally to me. Under normal circumstances, I would've complained about the flotsam, the overcast skies, the cold, but I had a plan, and dammit if it wasn't going to unfold exactly as I had envisioned it the moment Alan had surprised me with news of our trip.

I'd been bursting to tell him I loved him since Thanksgiving. But considering my history of cranking through boyfriends in fewer than three months, I figured it'd be prudent to wait until that milestone had passed. All I had to do was hold out until January fifth, *today*, and then I could say it—unless he said it to me first, which he had chosen not to do while Céline sang her heart out.

"You've got to be kidding me," I said.

"What?"

Ahead of us was a riverboat disgorging its contents. Tourists, mostly Americans, were swarming the embankment, trying to shoulder their way through the collected crowd waiting to board.

"What's wrong with you?" he asked.

"Fine." I turned toward him. "I love you, all right? *That's* what's wrong with me."

"I love you, too."

"But this isn't how it was supposed to happen." I explained it was supposed to be sunny, and there wasn't supposed to be a herd of lowing Americans making it sound like we were back home, and there certainly wasn't supposed to be trash, especially condoms, all around us.

He stopped and turned me toward him. "Did you hear what I said?"

Deep breath. Let it go. "I did. And I love you, too."

"I know," he said. "You just told me."

We both grinned a goofy smile. I knew him well enough after three months and one day to know he was a deeply private person, and recoiled from any kind of public affection. There would be no swell of music, no grand embrace where he bent me backward and kissed me, prompting the American cattle to start cheering. No free ride on the riverboat, with us at the prow arm in arm, waving to the Parisians lining the banks above. Maybe there was no such thing as a movie moment, the kind Becca and I devoured every Love Day. And maybe that was okay, because I would always have his words.

When we returned home, we started looking for a place together. I called off the search after a month, because we argued something fierce. Out of the blue, this man who I loved and thought was perfect suddenly had opinions and ideas about living spaces that I didn't particularly agree with, and he wasn't willing to reel them in. We tried a few more times that winter and spring, and each time we stormed off in opposite directions, lobbing a few choice word grenades before parting. Exhausted by the whole proposition, Alan finally said, "Why don't we just find you a place near me; that way you can have exactly what you want."

"Oh, that's rich. So you can once again lure a boyfriend out of Brooklyn so you're not inconvenienced?" I asked. I reminded him that when we'd met he had made a point of saying that we'd spend equal time in Brooklyn and the Upper West Side, because he had rarely visited his previous boyfriend's place and felt bad about that. Not so bad, though, that he hadn't gotten the poor guy to move uptown, a few blocks away from him.

"Fine!"

"FINE!"

With a moratorium in place, I forgot about cohabitation. One afternoon in August, Alan called me at the ad agency and told me to meet him at his apartment. He explained that he'd found a place that he thought was right for us, and that he had been searching since April on his own to avoid more fallout.

"Just do me a favor," he said, "and say nothing. Don't get excited if you like it."

"I promise."

The minute Norma, the landlady, opened the door, my mouth dropped, which, unfortunately, she noticed. And she knew how to play me. It was like watching an old-timey stripper revealing her goods, slowly, piece by piece. The apartment was a triplex in a brownstone on West Seventy-Seventh Street. She teased me by walking us through the first floor, pointing out the balcony, wood-burning fireplace, and dishwasher.

Boom, chicka, boom.

Up half a level was a full bath with a separate commode. Another half-level up was the bedroom—actually, two smaller bedrooms combined into one, giving it an L-shape, so half could be used as a TV room.

Chicka boom.

"Tired yet?" she asked.

"Not me," I said.

Another half-level higher was the largest landing I'd ever seen in New York. "This is going to be my office!" I squeaked with excitement. She just smiled as Alan mouthed, *Stop it!* behind her back.

On the top level, she said, "And up here is—"

"Is this for real, Norma?" She'd been slowly building to this, pulling on the anticipation, until I was face-to-face with the sweet spot of the apartment—the pasties and G-string of it all. We stood on a landing almost as large as the one below, looking out a sliding glass door that opened onto a wraparound roof terrace.

Chicka boom, boom, boom!

I didn't smoke, but I felt like I needed a cigarette.

"Well, I guess there's no point in trying to negotiate the price, is there?" Alan said to Norma as he pointed at me.

The day we moved in, a heaviness descended. I was crossing Broadway with a friend of Alan's, and I could feel the street telescoping. As he talked about his new gift store in Rhinebeck, New York, his voice grew distorted. It was like I was in a diver's suit—all I could pay attention to was my breathing and heartbeat. The whole day, on and off, I felt dizzy and had the worst headache. A sense of dread kept eating away at the edges of what was supposed to be the happiest day of my life—back then, the gay equivalent of a wedding. Several times I sat down on the stairs.

"Are you okay?" Alan asked.

"Sure. I'm just winded. All these freaking steps."

As soon as we were finished and settled in, boxes broken down, friends gone, the anxiety started to swell. I was sitting in the wing-back chair, Alan on the couch.

"I think I made a mistake," I mumbled.

"What?"

I could feel the old need to run, to flee, rising. "I think we rushed moving in together."

"No, let's be clear here," he said. "*You* pushed for this. I just let go of a rent-controlled apartment I had for thirteen years that I loved."

"I know, I'm sorry," I said, ducking my head as if he were going to hit me.

Standing up in the middle of the room, he turned to me. "So what do we do now?"

"I don't know. Let's just get through the night and see how I feel tomorrow."

I slept very soundly, which was surprising: Sleep was evasive when I was anxious. This felt different, though. It was pinioned to

something, like a butterfly to a board. It was causal. Despite my proclamations of wanting to set up home, something I had been panting
after for years, I discovered I was mortified of it all.

"Fear of intimacy," David Lindsey said when I told him, later that
week. "Fear of commitment. Fear of being seen. Take your pick."

"I just feel so bad that I told him. Now he's hurt and paranoid."

"That's understandable. What's important now is you don't say
or do anything else that you're going to regret until we talk through
this."

"When will I finally stop sticking my head up my ass?"

"When you get tired of smelling your own farts." Oddly, it made
me feel better.

30

PROUST WASN'T DELUSIONAL

I decided to become a therapist.

After six years in advertising, I was tired. Of the insane hours and stupid clients. Of being greeted in the morning by projectiles of vomit from my art director, who would stay out all night drinking and snorting coke with other creatives in the agency. Of saying to those same creatives the night before, "No, taking me to a strip joint and buying me a lap dance isn't fun; it's actually harassment." I felt I'd be happier in the supportive world of feelings, rather than one filled with bodily fluids and naked women. So the month after Alan and I had moved in together, I enrolled in Hunter College and took an undergraduate night class.

One Saturday, I was lying on the couch with my *Psychology of Personal Adjustment* textbook propped up on my chest. Alan stood behind the wide expanse of counter that divided our raspberry-red kitchen from the living room with exposed brick. Spread out in front of him were index cards he had plucked from a metal recipe box.

"I'm going to bake a pineapple upside-down cake," he announced over the classical music curling from the radio.

"Knock yourself out."

"Wanna help?"

I flopped the book onto my chest and gave him a look. Even though I'd begun eating most everything again, cooking still pretty much fell to him. In the year we'd been together, I'd gained only five pounds. My clothes still fit, and that wasn't changing.

"Suit yourself," he said.

Baking was Alan's comfort. Because his stepfather had refused to go to work and would lie on the couch all day watching TV, his mother had to make ends meet by baking desserts and decorating cakes after work and on weekends. He'd grown up with naked Winnie the Pooh, Mickey Mouse, and Easter Bunny cakes cooling on wire racks; with piping bags that had wriggles of rainbow-colored frosting spilling from their tips; with the scent of vanilla extract and melting chocolate wafting through the house. By the time I met Virginia, those days were long gone. She was hunched over—a tiny, bony comma—her trembling hands reaching for her pack of Viceroy cigarettes. If Alan wanted to taste his childhood, he'd have to bake it.

He pulled out a mustard-yellow hand mixer and began beating something. The stuttering of the metal against the big Fiesta bowl drilled into my head. It was hard to concentrate.

"My grandmother's!" he shouted over the noise and music, waggling a beat-up silver spoon in the air, its edge worn so thin it curled over itself.

"Of course it is."

"The cake'll never come out if I don't use it."

"That's wonderful, love," I said from behind my book. He scraped the batter into the pan with the spoon and slid it into the oven.

"You want to lick the bowl?" Because of his incessant interruptions, I'd read the same section about Maslow's hierarchy of needs over and over; I just gave up.

"Fine," I said, exasperated. I swiped my finger around the inside of the bowl and licked it. Something murmured inside of me. I took another swipe. This was familiar. The flavor hovered over some memory, looking for a place to land. The harder I chased it, the faster it evaporated. I picked up the bowl and held it to my face, sniffing.

"I know this taste," I said. "This smell."

"From what?"

"I . . . don't know." But the homey scent of vanilla, the egginess, even how the batter dripped down like long exclamation points with big, fat drops beneath, were connected to some memory. *But what?*

Still haunted by that taste, I called my mother a few days later. "Ma banse."

"God bless you," she answered.

"Ma, did you ever bake cakes?" I knew the answer. With the exception of occasional Pepperidge Farm frozen turnovers or slice-and-bake cookies, she never made desserts.

She *tsk*ed her tongue. "Banana, you know better than that."

"Did Dina or Vo?" The only sweet I recalled my godmother making was chocolate pudding.

"Not Dina so much, but Vovo did."

"She did?"

"Don't you remember? You'd stand on the chair next to her at the stove."

The chair.

The scrapping sound as she dragged it across the floor. My grandfather's enormous red-plaid shirt she put on me backward. Resting my hand on her breast as she rolled up the sleeves. The stove, white. She had to light it with a match. The clock in the middle of the back panel; it didn't work. The stand mixer that looked like a rocket; I think she'd borrowed it from Dina. Cream-colored, with pale green glass bowls. The electric smell of the motor when it warmed up. I think it was a cake mix she used to make. A blue-and-white box. Jiffy. It was Jiffy.

For almost thirty years I'd forgotten that I used to cook and bake with my grandmother. In my attempt to disown my heritage, I'd disowned her memory. I suddenly ached for her and for the foods she'd made me. But Vovo was gone; she had passed two years earlier, in 1992. She'd had a stroke and eventually died of old age at eighty-nine. She'd stopped cooking years before, although she'd kept one eye on the stove for as long as her health permitted, rattling lids and my mother. When she died, so did some of her specialties. My mother had her versions of Vo's classics, but they were merely that. No one could match her *sopa de galinha* (chicken soup) or sausage stuffing, which we ate like a side dish; they were always the highlights of Sunday dinner.

"Ma, do you still have your green cookbook?" When my parents had married, my mother had taken an old three-ring telephone binder and typed up my grandmother's recipes. Behind the "B" tab, the only tab in the book, are the recipes—ingredients in red, the method in black—for Portuguese baked beans, baked codfish with tomatoes and potatoes, octopus, Portuguese fava beans, her chicken soup and stuffing. All the foods I'd refused when I was a kid.

"Yes, I do." she said. "And why?"

"Can I have it?"

My mother paused. She sensed something. Then, softly: "Of course, sweetheart."

Proust wasn't delusional, after all. That one lick of cake batter crowbarred open more than just the past. The more memories flooded me, the more I surrendered. It was similar to what I had felt when Alan made me roast pork and apples the first time, but more urgent, more primal. A tendril coiled around me and tugged me toward my grandmother, and toward the joy of being with her, of being fed, being loved. My fear of food and cooking and eating had betrayed her.

I slowly began taking a deep and serious interest in baking. I elbowed Alan out of the way, too preoccupied to see his hurt and disappointment as he quietly put aside his family recipes for the ones that I was mining on the computer through something called the World Wide Web. I'd sit for hours, hunched over the blue glow of my laptop, trolling for fancy pies, extravagant cakes, and delicate pastries.

Both of us were recovering churchgoers; still, on Sunday mornings in Barryville, we engaged in our own particular kind of worship. We'd wake up early and flick on the old portable TV with the manual dial that chunked into place. We got two, maybe three stations up there in the woods. First we'd watch Bob Vila on *This Old House*. I'd become keenly preoccupied with Alan's weekend place. I bought armloads of DIY books and started all kinds of projects, abandoning many of them. Bemused, he'd lie on the deck, his body turning clockwise from morning to midafternoon to follow the light, lounging like a sun-starved Newfoundlander. Me, I was on the roof cleaning gutters, painting bedrooms, throwing up a dust storm in the kitchen as I sanded and refinished cabinets, furiously scrubbing at permanent rust stains in the toilet bowl from the iron in the water. I had boundless energy that needed an outlet, and the Barryville house, with all its dings and dents, was one enormous project.

After Bob Vila came the main attraction: Martha Stewart. We'd lie there watching. Alan was slack-jawed at the perfection pouring from the screen as I frantically scribbled down recipes, kitchen tips, gardening dos and don'ts. "We need to get her magazine," he finally said. And thus began the great onslaught: *Martha Stewart Living, Bon Appétit, Gourmet, Food & Wine, Saveur, Cook's Illustrated.* Over the next year, cookbooks crowded out novels and biographies on our shelves. I rooted through boxes of kitchen utensils from his mother and grandmother, and scoured flea markets for what we didn't have. Macy's, Bloomingdale's, and Bridge Kitchenware cluttered our credit-card bills as I bought doubles of everything: two sets of cake pans in every size, two food processors, two stand mixers, two sets of knives. One for the city, the other for the country.

We began entertaining and cooking elaborate, over-the-top meals.

On Saturday mornings, we'd rummage through Oelkers General Store. I'd paw through produce in the walk-in cooler while he'd scour the grocery aisles. Once I forgot myself, excited over some find, and called out through the open door, "Alan, look what I found, sweetheart!" A woman who was considering a head of lettuce gave me a curious look, to which I added, "Ellen, sweetheart? Did you hear me?" as I walked out of the cooler. Most weekends we'd drive miles into Pennsylvania for what Oelkers didn't carry.

We rarely cooked the same dish twice, which infuriated me, but Alan's philosophy was "Why make the same thing again and again when there's so much to experience?" But now that I had returned home to the kitchen for good, I wanted to learn, to master, to earn the right to stand there. That meant repetition and failure. Flirting with the unfamiliar until I could bend it to my will, until I could turn out a flawless dish without glancing at a recipe. Just a few was all I wanted, so I could feel accomplished. That's when I began taking classes in culinary basics at Peter Kump's New York Cooking School.

Ingredients we'd never cooked with started appearing on our counters: wasabi paste the color of our backyard in spring; fish sauce, with its nauseating smell; fresh handmade ravioli; anchovies; salty-sour capers; bison. We went to the Eldred Preserve nearby and bought fresh rainbow trout; other fish and meats came from Citarella and Fairway in the city.

During the week, we would plan our country feasts: whipped carrot soup from Le Cordon Bleu; a French daube that took two days to make; Lidia Bastianich's tagliatelle with sweet shrimp and leeks; luscious white beans; orecchiette with broccoli rabe and sausage; and Alan's roast chicken. His chicken became our new Sunday supper, that last meal of the weekend before we closed up the house and headed back to the city for another round of counting the hours until we could be away alone, cooking. And it would, in time, come to act as his Love Food when my periods of dark hollowness descended.

I ate, unabashedly. I bought larger jeans, but I didn't care. I was in love, well fed, and finally free.

What's this all about?" David Lindsey asked me, when I told him of the activity humming in the country. He sat there serenely, his eyes on me.

"What are you talking about?"

"I smell somethin'." A favorite phrase of his. "All that sanding and painting and cooking?"

"What?"

"I don't know; you haven't told me yet." I'd been working with David Lindsey long enough to know that when something I said didn't jibe, he heard it, even if no one else did, like a dog whistle. And he became a bulldog, and like a bulldog, he wouldn't let go.

"Well, it's called happiness," I said, irked that my good mood and sudden domestic interests were suspect. "You should try it."

"And I'm happy you're happy," he said. "I really am. But I'm not convinced."

"This is just one of my extroverted times," I explained. Early on in therapy, years before I'd met Alan, I'd explained to David Lindsey how I categorized my days or months by where they fell on the continuum of introversion and extroversion. Introverted times were when I ducked out of going out with friends, felt tired, closed my door at the agency, couldn't care less about dating. At those times, all I wanted to do was burrow into a book in my apartment and be left alone. Extroverted times were all about bouts of creativity at work, long nights of boy craziness, carousing with friends, dancing, drinking, and making delicious spectacles of ourselves at gay-pride events.

Even while I defended myself to him, I was aware of a thin thread of irritability that was knitting its way into my days.

During spring semester, I was taking two psych classes, plus volunteering as an LGBTQ peer counselor, all while still working part-time. At my latest ad agency, a large, has-been shop where I'd sold out for even more money, everything rankled. At performance evaluations, my boss classified me as "ornery," "difficult," and "not a team player." I classified him as a shit, because he had on more than one occasion stolen my work and passed it off as his own. To cope, I'd escape to the cookbook section of Rizzoli bookstore during lunch to catch up on homework and plan dinner parties. If I couldn't get my assigned reading done there, I'd burrow into a corner of the school library until it closed, then grab the crosstown bus back to the West Side, willing myself not to fall asleep.

That was work and school and life; they were supposed to be stressful. But not cooking—that was my refuge, my meditation. Yet I grew even more ambitious with our entertaining. I'd plan too many courses, especially on weeknights, even though Alan kept trying to pull me back. I'd insist we make not only every dish but a lot of the ingredients for the dishes, as we did in class. Tagliatelle Bolognese wasn't the same unless I simmered the sauce for hours *and* made and cut the pasta myself. Homemade butter had to be slathered on homemade bread. Hamburgers were made from hand-ground meat; the pickles were ones we had put up ourselves. Even our ketchup was house-made.

Obsession itched my skin from the inside. Classic puff pastry, which I had folded and rolled into 1,457 faultless layers of butter and dough, was measured and cut into exact ninety-degree angles using a ruler and triangle. Because I was always running late, something would get messed up—a pie dough was overmixed, or a salad dressing broke—and I'd scream, "Tonight's going to be a fucking disaster!" and throw it in the trash and start over.

"It doesn't have to be perfect," Alan would say, laying his hand on my arm, trying to turn me from the counter. "It's only dinner." I would shoot him a look that pinned him to the wall. Fed up, he'd lift his hands in the air and mutter, "Fine, whatever you want," then walk to a safer part of the apartment.

Guests became superfluous. Dinners weren't about getting together with friends anymore; they were an opportunity to showcase my growing talent, and I wanted praise. And when that praise came, as it always did, I'd bat it away, outlining for the table—point by point—every flaw in the meal that they were too stupid to notice.

"Well, I thought it was just great!" or "I could never cook like this—it was wonderful," were the usual replies. *What asses,* I'd think as I smiled at them and cleared their plates.

After everyone left, I could sense Alan keeping to the sidelines, careful not to walk into my crosshairs. I'd inevitably apologize and blame school, or my workload, or exhaustion.

"Go to bed, you look awful," he'd say. "I'll clean up."

Full of remorse, I'd lace my arms around him, and he'd pull back, just a little. "Thank you," I'd whisper.

Lying in bed listening to the clinking of dishes, I'd be seized with fear that he would leave me. I imagined waking up the next morning, feeling his side of the bed, and finding it empty. Propped up on the breakfast table would be a piece of light blue stationery lipped in dark blue. On it would be just one line: "I can't do this anymore."

31

THE OLD ONE-TWO PUNCH

I paced the kitchen, twisting my fingers into knots. Millions of nerves stretched like elastic bands until they snapped, stinging my legs, arms, neck, back. I closed my eyes and tried breathing deeply, but the air shuddered in my lungs. My heart was beating so hard, my body rocked, as if it were keening. *Flee, defect, escape, cut and run.* The claustrophobia of knowing that I couldn't bolt—that Alan and our life had nailed me to that spot—left me dizzy. Instead, I slammed pans onto the stove and rummaged through cabinets to distract myself.

The noise brought Alan down the stairs. "What's the matter?"

Shame prickled my cheeks. "Nothing."

Again, this time emphatically: "What . . . happened?"

I battled telling him. Once he knew firsthand, once he saw the effect, I'd forever be branded the sick one in the relationship, the *pobrinho:* poor little thing.

Finally: "I had a panic attack." A full-price, premium-brand panic attack.

Early on, I'd told him about them and my breaks while we were lying in bed in my old apartment, the darkness allowing us to talk unfiltered about our childhoods, the dents in our lives, our disappointments.

"Oh." He just stood there, arms by his side, useless. I hated him fully and without remorse. At last, he added, "When?"

I walked him through it like a crime scene: I had been with Becca at the movies, having a good time. We were feeding each other popcorn and goofing at ads for real estate brokers who looked like flight attendants. Then—*slam!*—no reason, no provocation, no warning. Machine-gun rounds discharged. Somehow I stopped myself from running out of the theater, but I couldn't stop the offensive my body had launched. What fueled the high-fidelity screaming inside was the terror that I would again be staring down sleepless nights and lead-heavy months of agony. I reminded him that there were times it had taken years before I felt better.

"Don't put the cart before the horse." I hated him even more. I needed to burrow into him, tumbling over myself like a cat until I found just the right position to rest, but instead, he was offering me platitudes. And then the elevator free fall of realization: He couldn't take care of me. He had never experienced a panic attack; he knew nothing of the horror, of how it atrophies a life.

How could this happen again?" I demanded of David Lindsey at an emergency session. It was a bald-faced indictment of his abilities. I don't recall his measured response, but he mentioned depression again.

I leaned forward in the chair, screaming, "I am *not* depressed. Why do you keep bringing that up?"

"Depression and anxiety are sometimes two sides of the same illness."

"I have *nothing* to be depressed about." The more I yelled, the more he seemed rooted in place, an oak against a storm. "Do depressed people have full-time jobs while going to school at night? Do they get A's in every subject? Are they witty and charming and do they host fabulous dinner parties? Do they have a successful relationship that even *you* have to admit is great? No—they don't."

"Some do." He said it so quietly, with such compassion, I broke. I cupped my hand over my mouth and sobbed, my gut convulsing, and then a long, pitiful howl of sorrow. In that moment, I allowed myself to know.

"I want you to see Jack Constantinides." I could sense the plea in his voice. Jack was a psychopharmacologist he often worked with.

I shook my head. "I don't believe in drugs," I said. "You know I refused Valium when I was a kid."

"This is different."

"How?"

"You're not a kid," he said gently, "and you have too much to lose."

That was it: I had too much to lose. I'd thought the stakes had been high at Carnegie Mellon, where I'd refused to consider the unimaginable defeat of dropping out until I couldn't imagine the pain of continuing. But if I'd chosen, I could have started again, a clean slate. There was no do-over now. Ever since I was sitting on those side steps on Brownell Street, I'd been waiting for something special, something amazing, that was rightfully mine. After thirty years, I knew it was this one man and this one life.

"Get the medication so that we can take anxiety and depression out of the equation and see what's going on." Reluctantly, I agreed.

Later that week, I left Jack's office with prescriptions for the antianxiety drug Ativan and the antidepressant Prozac. I filled them that night, put the pills in my underwear drawer, and refused to take them.

Instead, I tried to work it out on my own. I walked to and from work, thinking the exercise would help. Something about a brain chemical that's released when you move. But too often, I ended up sitting on a bench, head in hands, crying as I stared at the pavers between my sneakers. I doubled up on therapy. I took a yoga class, but kept finding myself staring off into the middle distance, forgetting to change positions. "Are you okay?" the teacher whispered, laying her hand on my arm. I looked at her and blinked. I grabbed my jacket and, summoning all the *veneta* I could, slammed the door on my way out. *Who the hell does that deodorant-phobic, granola-munching bitch think she is?* I ran down the stairs and out onto West Seventy-Second Street. At Gray's Papaya across the street, I ordered the Recession Special, two hot dogs and a coconut drink, and stuffed my face.

A s it had before, a switch flipped, and just like that it was over. I was back to my Extroverted Self. My joints felt scrubbed and newly greased. I glided through my day, easy and unruffled, like I was on a flowered parade float, my hand oscillating a greeting to on-lookers below. My grade-point average was still bulletproof at 4.0. Over the summer, I felt so good, I quit my job and registered for a full load of classes for autumn. To give myself something to do in the meantime, I took a statistics intensive for experimental psychology that squeezed a semester's worth of material into just four weeks. I got a one hundred on every test, including the two-hour-long final.

"No one has ever done that before," my teacher confessed over her second glass of the precocious white wine she brought. I'd invited her to dinner, and she and Alan were sitting at the table on our roof terrace as I grilled tuna burgers on a small hibachi.

"Really?" I asked, not because I didn't believe her, but because I wanted to hear it again.

"Are you kidding?" she said. "*No one* came close." I poured her an-other glass of wine and passed the wasabi mayonnaise.

I had drop-kicked anxiety back into the past where it belonged—on my own, without the crutch of chemicals. I had one thing left to do. I went up to our room and fished out the pills from my under-wear drawer. In the bathroom, I poured them slowly into the toilet and flushed.

I had won. I was victorious.

After my last class of fall semester, I was crossing the skyway that connected two academic buildings on either side of Lexington Avenue when I suddenly stopped short, fear nail-gunning me in place. Students passed, some muttering and staring—a sudden boulder in a river. A thought flooded me, causing me to involuntarily gulp for air: For the next month, I wouldn't have any schedules or routines, the barbed wire that sharply defined the perimeter of my days. Now, suddenly, they would be shapeless. The impending inactivity felt like death. What made it worse was that Alan was going to visit his mother for Christmas, while I stayed in the city; I felt too scattered to visit my parents. I'd be alone. Since I was a kid, I'd never liked being alone. There was always something sinister and dark about it. I collected myself and continued to the library to return my overdue books.

With so much time on my hands, I had to do something. So I created lists. Pages and pages of lists. And along the way something happened. I was no longer writing the pedestrian lists of ordinary people, but the exalted lists of the Revered and Admired. I wrote about defeating the ignoble, championing the silent, being One's True and Highest Self. (The Capital Letters were back, and I felt almost as electric as I had back in the Carnegie Library.)

Emboldened, I sat on the bed with the phone in my hands. My stomach swilled; my throat kept catching. I took a deep breath and dialed my parents. As we talked, I imagined the Christmas tree blazing in the living room. My mother's plywood Santa Claus painting now under their mattress for support. In its place, a giant spotlighted banner that read: "Jesus Is the Reason for the Season."

I hadn't told my parents about Alan, out of cowardice. I'd met his family, and the only reaction I'd gotten was from his sister, who blurted, "Does that make you my unofficial brother-in-law?" as Virginia was putting dinner on the table. For my mother, whose embossed Bible had been worn smooth from all her thumping, being gay in the abstract, and from a distance, was one thing. But to know that it was real—and in the form of another man who gets all jiggy with her son—was something entirely different.

It was time.

Finally: "Mom, I've met someone." And to make clear this wasn't going to be any long-awaited come-to-Jesus moment, I added, "A man."

Silence. I couldn't tell if it was frostiness, or if she was trying to gather herself. Then, "Oh, really?" Yup, frostiness.

"Yes. We've been together for more than two years."

"Is that right?"

"Yes."

"Well, I'm very happy for you," after which followed a series of hollow *thunks* as she dropped the receiver and let it clatter against the kitchen wall. I could hear her voice, tinny and distant: "Manny! David wants to talk to you."

My father picked up the extension. "Dave?"

"Hi, Daddy. Dad banse."

"What's happening—?"

"And let me tell you something else." It was my mother again. "That man will never, ever step foot in this house. I don't care if you've been together two years or two hundred years. Do you hear me?"

"Loud and clear, Ma. And neither will I." I slammed down the phone.

"It's okay," Alan said later that night from Baltimore. "She probably just needs to get used to the idea of me. Up until now she always thought of you as alone."

The idea of him. If she only knew of his kindness, his patience, his good humor, of how he had changed me, she couldn't possibly remain implacable.

"Come home soon," I said when we were hanging up. "I miss you."

"I miss you, too."

For the rest of the holiday, I wandered through the apartment.

Barryville was out of the question; the isolation, even with our cats
Ariadne and Maxine, would crush me. The city with all its distrac-
tions was a better place; I just didn't want to go anywhere. I cooked,
not for the pleasure of the food but for the comfort of the act, yet it
eluded me. When Alan returned, we spent New Year's Eve in the
country, as we always had, alone over an elaborate dinner that included foie gras and Kenny G, and we rang in 1996 in bed, watching
the ball drop ninety miles downstate in Times Square.

February. I was sitting in an experimental-psychology lab, listening
to the professor explain populations, statistical significance, and
blind and double-blind studies. For the first time since I'd started
classes eighteen months ago, I was disinterested. Bored was more ac-
curate. What was preoccupying my thoughts was the bag in front of
me on my desk. Inside was a madeleine pan. I'd never baked a madeleine, never even eaten one, I was sure of it. I wondered how many
homemade madeleines I could knock back in one sitting. I bet *that*
would be statistically significant.

I had doubts about becoming a shrink, too. "I don't think I want
to make eighty grand a year," I said to Alan as we prepared dinner
one night. Advertising salaries were astronomically high, especially
for freelancers. Therapists made so little in comparison. I had made
a mistake; I just had to face it. Nonetheless, I was determined to get
my bachelor's degree, after almost twenty years. So I trudged along,
dutifully conjugating French verbs, collecting data for experimental psychology, comparing and contrasting different theories of the
mind. And the drudgery, the banality of what I was learning, pulled
on those nerves, stretching them tighter and tighter.

One Friday, Alan double-parked the car in front of our brownstone
so we could load it for our weekly pilgrimage to Barryville. When
I came out, a policeman was giving us a ticket.

"Hey, what are you doing?" I said, trotting down the stairs. "We *just* pulled in."

He pointed to the parking sign with his pen.

"I know what the sign says, asshole, I can read." He tore the ticket out of his book, lifted the windshield wiper, and, while looking at me, let it snap back.

"Fuck you!" I screamed into his face. Then I thought better of it and ran to the top of the stoop, in case I had to duck inside. Distance steeled me. "Fuck you!" I yelled louder, as mothers with strollers looked on, stunned. The cop kept walking. "Yeah, fuck you, you fat fucking pig!" He raised his hand and waved without turning around.

I was yanked back into the building. Alan slammed the door. "Are you crazy? Do you want to get arrested?"

I ripped my arm away. "It's not my fault. Did you see what he did?"

"I don't care what he did."

"He gave *you*," I said, stressing the word *you* as a way of implicating him and pulling him to my side, "a ticket for double-parking." I was certain he'd see the logic of my actions and start running down the street to talk the cop out of it.

But instead he said, "God, what's *wrong* with you?" He was unaware of it, I was sure—he'd never be so intentionally hurtful—but he looked disgusted. It was the same look he had in my dreams when he walked out on me.

In the car on the way upstate, I lolled my head against the window. The vibration was soothing. I was too tired for conversation; I just made sounds in response to his occasional questions. That was the problem with *veneta*—afterward, sometimes, you're wiped. When we arrived it was after dark. I didn't even bother unloading the car. I just unlocked the front door, plodded down the hallway, and slipped into the bed in the guest room, where I slept until Saturday afternoon.

On Sunday, I sat on the counter and watched while Alan prepared his roast chicken. He carefully wiggled his fingers beneath the skin of the bird to loosen it.

"It's going to be okay, *mon cher,* you'll see," he said, hugging me with his elbows, his hands up in the operating-room-doctor position because he'd touched the raw chicken. I wrapped my legs around his waist and kissed the top of his balding head. "And," he added, "that cop was probably an asshole, right?" He mixed chopped rosemary and thyme with butter and smeared it under the skin.

"I don't care how hard you fight me," he said, "I'm making your favorite potatoes." I started to laugh. "Nope, sorry. I'm making 'em, and that's that." He knew I love cubed Yukon Gold potatoes that have been tossed in oil and roasted with the bird, so they soak up all that flavor and their sides turn the color of bronze tourmaline.

"You're a good man, mister," I said.

He looked square at me: "Damn right I am, and don't you ever forget it." Then he kissed me and slid the chicken into the oven.

For weeks, I couldn't shake this funk. It went beyond the run-in with the cop; that had just been a footnote. The narrative itself was sad, bereft. Things were spinning out of control again. I didn't want to be me anymore. I smiled through meetings with my advisers, the dutiful straight-A student who would make the department proud. I didn't give a rat's ass for them, or what I was learning. As long as it looked good on paper, no one had to know how miserable I was. The only book I wanted to stick my nose in was a cookbook. By now, one wall of my office was lined with them, and every night, instead of learning about dementia praecox or schizoaffective disorder, I was reading about Lynne Rossetto Kasper's journeys in Emilia-Romagna, and getting lost in Paula Wolfert's exotic and strange Morocco.

And then it happened. I was bored, so I slumped on the floor and watched a documentary on World War II. A film clip of Hitler and Eva Braun in the bunker flashed on the screen, a clip I must have seen a million times; nonetheless, that familiar nuclear blast erupted in my chest. As if back from vacation, all the attendant insomnia, pain, panic, and dissociation showed up and punched in for work.

I can't say this siege was any worse than the others, because it wasn't. But what made this *different,* and therefore far more devas-

tating and dangerous, was that it led to a crippling sense of hopelessness, like in those dogs that stand in a box getting shocked even
though they can escape. Since age eleven, I'd built a Theory of Explanation that with each attack grew more fantastical, as I tried to
encompass this mutating affliction. At first, I'd thought the cause was
simply scary movies. Remove the cause, remove the symptom. False
logic. After two years of not getting any better, I'd assumed therapy
would root out these attacks. And relief had come, and I was guile-
less enough to believe I was cured. When I'd been struck down at
Birch Grove and CMU, I'd thought that it might have been the stress
of being gay, and that if I could turn straight, I would finally find
peace. But that wouldn't be the case. And so I'd embraced my sexual identity, wrapping my arms around it and hugging it close to my
heart, and that had done the trick. I was finally free. Until a decade
later at Hunter, when for no apparent reason, I had been cut down
again. But after a few torturous months, I knew I had mastered it. All
it had taken was a pair of titanium balls and the right shrink. Why
else would I have rebounded in record time?

But here I was, less than a year later, clear out of explanations.

"I want medication," I told David Lindsey the next morning, in
yet another emergency session.

He looked at me, confused. "You're *on* medication."

I explained how I'd hidden them and then thrown them away.

"Oh, David Leite, you've got your tits caught in the wringer now."

32

BAD CHEMiSTRY

Stuffed animals, colored blocks, dolls with missing limbs, and miniature versions of the chair I was sitting in were strewn on the floor around me. I felt absurd and disproportionately large. As I waited, I nervously squished the decapitated head of a Barbie doll under my heel.

David Lindsey was flabbergasted that I'd lied. For the past year, he'd thought I was popping pills that were giving me what he called a "floor," a baseline I couldn't fall below. Technically, it hadn't been a *lie*. I'd never said I took the pills, just that I'd filled the prescription. "This time," he said, "I'm calling Jack myself, and if you don't take those fucking pills, I'm going to kick your ass up between your shoulder blades."

That was how I'd ended up here, staring at Dr. Orenstein's diplomas in child psychiatry. Jack was away on vacation, and Orenstein was covering his cases. I'd have to endure an hour of questioning before I could get my hands on medication.

"Hello, David," she said. Then, after looking around the room, she tossed me a glance that apologized for the mess. "Occupational hazard." I was expecting someone all pinched, with hard edges and points, wearing a Chanel suit. She came across more like a kindergarten teacher, slightly plump with billowy clothes. The pile of hair on her head looked as if she'd misplaced it. I liked her immediately.

"Dr. Griffin didn't tell me very much, just that he wanted you to be evaluated. If it's all right, may I ask you a few questions?" She even sounded like a kindergarten teacher.

"Sure."

She dragged over her desk chair, and we sat knee to knee. As she went through the evaluation, asking about family mental illness, suicide attempts, moodiness, odd behaviors, I kept looking at my watch. I was on lunch break from an advertising job. I'd had to drop out of school again, but unlike at CMU, I was determined to return.

After I'd cataloged my history from *House of Wax* to practically that morning, she offered up her diagnosis—the same as David Lindsey's: depression with anxiety features. I didn't have the strength to fight it any longer. I nodded in agreement. She went on to describe the process of starting psychotropic medication, which would screw with my brain chemistry, in a way that made it seem like I was embarking on some grand and magical journey, like Huck Finn or Peewee Herman. Finally, she patted the top of her desk until she found a prescription pad.

"This," she said, scribbling, "is for Prozac." The same drug I'd tossed in my sock drawer the year before and never taken. *Could all of this have been avoided?* When she saw my face, she misunderstood and gave me an empathetic pout: "Oh, David! Don't worry, it's not the end of the world. I'm sure you'll be back to your old self in no time."

She handed me the piece of paper and stood, a Buddha smile on her face. "It was a pleasure to meet you," she said, shaking my hand. I half-expected her to offer me a lollipop. "And good luck!"

When I was almost out the door, I turned around. "Where's the nearest drugstore?"

"There's a Duane Reade on the first floor of this building."

I waited in line at the pharmacy. If it was true that one in five people take drugs for mental illness, there had to be at least one other nut here, but they all looked normal. I was sure I had "MENTAL DE-FECT" scrawled in fire-engine-red lipstick across my forehead. When it was my turn at the register, my face burned. I handed the prescription to the clerk who looked at it: the first person who would know my secret.

"It'll be a half hour." That was it. No judgment, no hooded glance to a coworker. Just annoyance that I didn't step out of line quick enough.

When I got the medication, I ripped out the bottle and tossed the bag in the garbage can on the street corner. Then I thought better of it and stuffed it in my pocket. I didn't want to take a chance that anyone I knew would find it and know I was on Prozac. (As if I had friends who rummaged through Midtown trash bins.) My hands shook as I popped a pill in my mouth.

I leaned against the wall and waited. I knew there was a six-to-eight-week ramp-up time, but there were exceptions. I closed my eyes and tilted my face to the sun, waiting for the drug to wash through me like an excellent Malbec, soothing my jangled nerves. I imagined that floor David Lindsey had talked about reassembling itself under my feet. "Three-quarter oak," I remembered my father saying of the floors he'd laid down in our house. I wanted to be stand-ing on a floor built by my father. The thought made me feel better, hopeful. Or was it the Prozac?

It wasn't. Nor was it Remeron, which replaced Prozac a few months later courtesy of a patronizing shit of a doctor, when I re-ported I wasn't feeling much better. I think he had more of an issue with the fact that the dispensing doctor had been a child psychiatrist and a woman than the drug itself. Wellbutrin, Serzone, and Desyrel were also crossed off the list.

While I waited for relief, my thoughts turned dark and violent. When I spoke to people, I terrified myself, imagining what a knife jabbing into their rib cage would sound like. When writing, I kept seeing my fingers being chopped off by a cleaver.

I became fixated on my looks. I spent hours staring at myself in the mirror, like I'd done when I was a teenager. I was convinced a face-lift would make me feel better. I imagined my face slit open and peeled back. I curled my lips so that they didn't look so full; I wanted a tight hyphen of a WASP smile, nothing too ethnic. Turning my head to the side, I ran my fingers over the bump of my Neanderthal brow. I wanted it smashed and reconstructed, so there would be just the slightest divot at the top of my nose. Speaking of noses, it would be whittled flat and pointy, something you'd see on *General Hospital* or *The Young and the Restless*. The widow's hump would be snapped, and I'd have the posture of a sixteen-year-old ballet student.

David Lindsey was worried, I could tell. During the eight years I'd been seeing him, he'd never seen me like this. I looked awful. I was getting too little sleep—not because it felt like my veins were pumping with quicksilver, like before, but because I couldn't stay asleep. Even the sleeping medication didn't help much. In the middle of the night, I'd slip out of bed and step out onto the roof deck. Standing there in my underwear, I'd look down and wonder if five stories were enough.

Alan tried to help. As with my parents so many years ago, distraction was his tack. We went for walks through Central Park, which was stained with fear, as I'd had unrelenting anxiety at the band shell, by the boat pond, along the Mall while walking back and forth to work. He pulled out the Scrabble board. He surprised me by taking me to a foreign movie, which he hated, and forcing himself to stay awake. He even tried to get me to laugh by playing Joan Collins in bed. He'd fluff up a pile of pillows and lean back gingerly while holding a book and speaking with a proper English accent, calling himself "Joon Colons." Nothing.

One night over dinner, which he'd made, because I couldn't focus in the kitchen anymore, I said, "I have to move out."

It was as if I had struck him. "Why are you doing this?"

"Because I can see how much this is killing you. You didn't sign on to be with some crazy person."

"It's none of your business what I signed on for," he said, raising his voice. He then reached over and held my hand. "You don't have to leave."

"I can't do this anymore." The words hung in the air between us. All these years I had imagined he would be the one to say them while ending our relationship, and in the end it was me.

We had started couples therapy a few weeks earlier with, in a bit of irony, the niece of Julia Child. I had waved the white flag and admitted defeat. The relationship had been staggering for months, but the added stress of my moods toppled it.

As I packed my bag, he sat on the bed, his eyes blurred with tears. I tried to explain that it was more painful to stay together than to split. What he didn't understand was that activities that usually bring joy to anyone—a terrific meal, a funny movie, meaningful sex—only served as reminders of just how sick I was, because I derived no pleasure from them.

"Where are you going to stay?" he said, wiping his face with his sleeve.

"Alice's apartment." Becca's mom lived a dozen blocks north of us, and she was spending the summer on the Jersey Shore. "Look, I have no idea how long this will be, or if it's permanent. Just give me time to get back on my feet."

He nodded and reached around me, burying his head in the crook of my neck. I'd always complained to him that he wasn't physically affectionate, but now he wouldn't let go. So I stood there and embraced him, and let him hold me for as long as he needed.

"I'll see you in couples therapy," I said at the front door. He had walked me down to the stoop.

"I love you, you know," he said.

"I love *you*." As I looked at him standing there, he reminded me so much of my father that day at Bradley Hospital, helpless and bewildered.

was reduced. When I was living alone at Alice's, stripped of everything that held meaning or gave me comfort, my existence became circumscribed. It was about three things: work, food, sleep. Anything else was too exhausting to consider, and I knew I would collapse under its weight. A phone call pressed; making dinner crushed. I didn't cook, didn't feel the impulse. On my way back from yet another agency where I was freelancing, I stopped at the grocery store in the bottom of Alice's building and bought packages of Buddig turkey and ham, Kraft American cheese, Pepperidge Farm bread, Doritos, Ben & Jerry's ice cream, and Diet Coke. I'd watch TV for a bit, eating a sandwich and drinking from the bottle. I didn't give a shit about my weight now. I'd managed to keep it under 190 for several years, but it began creeping upward, one or two pounds a week, because of the medication and my apathy.

But again, there was Julia. After dinner, which was usually six-thirty, I'd take my sleeping medication and crawl into Becca's childhood bed with my copy of *From Julia Child's Kitchen*. Scrawled on the title page in a wobbly hand was *"Bon appétit* to David—Julia Child." David Lindsey, who was friendly with Julia, had asked her for this favor years earlier. I would read the book over and over again while the summer sun streamed through the curtains. Just like when I was a child and watched Julia in *The French Chef,* and the pain disappeared for a half hour, I was finally calm. It was like Julia's writing was tapping my brain like a keg and draining my head for a while. And I'd inevitably feel a sense of relief, happiness almost, because I knew that in a matter of an hour I'd drift, the book slipping from my hand, and turn from the window, on fire with the evening sun, and slide into blessed, obliterating blackness.

A few weeks later, I arrived at couples therapy early, and Alan wasn't there yet. Rachel, our therapist, motioned to the sofa in the living room and told me to make myself comfortable. On the coffee table was a book, its cover divided in half horizontally, black on top, white on the bottom. But it was the small picture of a young woman that caused that old inversion feeling in my head, bumping me outside of myself. I felt sucked out of that room and down through the black-and-white of the picture. Her expression—pensive, detached, a faraway otherness—was so viscerally familiar. That was not her face, not her expression. It was me, my face, my expression. I knew this woman.

An Unquiet Mind, shouted the title. I checked the author's name—Kay Redfield Jamison—then settled back, losing myself in a page filled with phrases I could have written: "For as long as I can remember I was frighteningly, although often wonderfully, beholden to moods." She described herself as I always had: "intensely emotional as a child." Her words, her descriptions, wrapped themselves around me, tightly, supporting me, whispering fellowship and understanding— of me and by me.

On the next page:

> My manias, at least in their early and mild forms, were absolutely intoxicating states that gave rise to great personal pleasure, an incomparable flow of thoughts, and a ceaseless energy that allowed the translation of new ideas into papers and projects.

Suddenly I was back at the Carnegie Library in Pittsburgh, thoughts pouring out of me like rainwater, the pen moving so fast I couldn't keep up; riding the rush of energy from shift after shift at Windows on the World; gliding along DeKalb Avenue as a staggering and prodigious production of a Dvořák symphony unfurled in my head. I was so overwhelmed, I didn't hear Alan walk in, or notice they were standing there, amused, waiting on me.

"May I borrow this?" I asked Rachel.

"Of course."

That afternoon while Alan was at work, I slipped under the

covers of our bed with the book. Somehow, I'd needed the safety of our home to face Jamison's words. Ariadne curled up against me in that upside-down way she had, like Rusty had so many years before. When I was done, hours later, I picked up the phone and dialed Rachel.

"I think I'm manic-depressive."

A very long pause. "Bipolar disorder is a serious diagnosis. If I were you, I'd be very careful about whom you talk to; there are consequences to something like this." My medical records, she explained, would forever show I was manic-depressive, which could be reason enough to deny me life insurance and disability insurance, affect employment, and more. "Are you ready for something like that?"

I was too worn out not to be.

I sat in David Lindsey's office, with my own copy of Jamison's book on my lap. It was the first time in months I'd felt good in a session. "David Leite, you are *not* manic-depressive," he said.

"But there are so many similarities," I protested, offering the book. "You should read it."

"I don't need to read it." He said that, yes, there had been times when I'd walked in wired and spoken of effortless flows of creative ideas, as well as times when I had looked and sounded depressed, despite my refusal to acknowledge it. "But that doesn't necessarily make you manic-depressive. I've behaved like that, and I'm not manic-depressive. Now, if you want to tell me you think you suffer from a depressive disorder, I'm all ears. *That* I could see, and I've been saying it till I turned blue in the face. But I haven't witnessed one episode of mania in all the time you've been coming here—unless there is something you're not telling me."

I persisted: "I really think I might be." One thing David Lindsey did better than Dr. Copley or Kim Mueller was protect me from myself. He'd helped me see that I always harbored a secret belief that I was sicker, more frail, more broken, than I was. There were times I was willing to abdicate myself, or as he poetically described it, "You're all too quick to throw up your hands and fall through your own asshole." But he was wrong this time.

"Don't you think if I'd smelled even a whiff of mania, I would've said something?"

"Of course, but—"

"Have you written a novel this thick"—he held his fingers several inches apart—"from start to finish in two weeks?"

"No."

"Well, one of my bipolar patients has. Have you spent entire nights cleaning your apartment—ceiling to floor—washing walls, waxing floors, using a toothbrush to clean the grout and moldings?"

"No." I was almost belligerent.

"Another bipolar patient. These things are all about degrees, about where you draw the line."

"But David Lindsey—"

"Look," he said gently. "I'm willing to consider it, but you're going to have to prove it to me."

Veneta swirled in my chest. But it was the good kind. The kind that propels, rather than destroys. The kind that, when focused, is unstoppable and magnificent. "Fine," I said. "I will."

My self-diagnosis made sense. Manic depression was that single, elegant Theory of Explanation I'd been searching for since I was a kid that summed up everything. I'd suspected it; the book confirmed it. Nothing before had ever made so much sense to me. *Nothing.* Now, I had to find a way for it to make sense to him.

There's a yellow-and-black sign on the corner of West Seventy-Second Street, high above Gray's Papaya. It reads, "Depression is a flaw in chemistry not character." It offers an 800 number to call. I had looked at it every time I went to the subway, disgusted that it gave an easy out to people who didn't have the balls to deal with life. Blaming your mood on chemistry was just another way of exonerating unfinished projects, failed marriages, people with rotten dispositions. But now, after having read Jamison's book, I secretly hoped that the sign was true, and that it might be true of me. Maybe I wasn't broken. Maybe I just had bad chemistry.

33

DiAGNOSiS: MENTAL LiTE!

Neil De Senna was a professor of psychiatry at Columbia University Medical Center. He was also an acquaintance. Alan and Neil's wife were friends, which is why it hadn't dawned on me to reach out to him for a psychiatric evaluation. I only knew him sitting across tables filled with half-empty glasses of wine, plates pushed back, as I licked my fingers and dotted the tablecloth to pick up the last crumbs of bread.

"Yes, of course," he said over the phone. "Meet me at my office."

I settled into a chair across from him. I was suddenly glad David Lindsey had asked me to prove I was manic-depressive, because if I was it would be something *I* had discovered, and that could never be taken from me. I'd walked into a shrink's office, not unlike this one, when I was fourteen, looking for answers. I couldn't think of a better way to honor the courage of that scared, freaked-out kid.

Neil turned to me, pen hovering over a pad. *Here we go.*

Did I ever have rapid, repetitive thinking?

Yes. I told him about all those times in the shower, or walking to work, or lying in bed awake, the force building in my head as so many thoughts and ideas pressed on one another, like a trash compactor, threatening to crack my skull.

Did I ever talk fast, sometimes so fast people couldn't understand me?

"They called me Chatty Cathy in high school," I said. When I was in our senior plays, I'd had to work with a woman to slow down my speech. She wasn't successful. "Yes."

Had I ever been so irritable, I shouted at people or started fights or became violent?

The cop came to mind, of course. But there were also all of the arguments I instigated with my parents, Alan, friends. Then there was the time I'd bitten my cousin Barry so hard he was bleeding. "Yes, plenty."

Had I ever had a decreased need for sleep? If I slept just a few hours, did I feel great?

He nodded as I recounted the four to five hours of sleep I'd gotten at CMU and Hunter, and even at Birch Grove summer camp.

Did I ever engage in risky behavior that endangered my life?

I hesitated. Neil was a friend, someone I would see again socially. Did I have to be completely honest? *Screw it.* I told him of my adventures of the flesh at the gym. *It isn't like I'm the only guy doing it* was how I had justified it to myself. The steam room and sauna were packed with bodies, giving new meaning to the term "cheek by jowl." It had never occurred to me it could be part of some larger issue, something that had nothing to do with being queer or horny.

I looked up. He met my gaze, level and nonjudgmental. "Next question, please."

Had I felt unusually self-confident in myself and my abilities? Did I ever experience grandiosity?

Let's see, where to start? Believing I could direct a film based on an F. Scott Fitzgerald story, when I knew nothing about directing? Or film? I'd say yes. Thinking I was part of a divine group of people chosen by God to protect the planet would certainly count. Since I'd been a teenager, I'd started small companies only to abandon them when I lost interest, or when it finally dawned on me I lacked basic business acumen. And there was that time I'd finagled my way into an important position in advertising when I wasn't qualified.

Then came the questions that made me queasy: Had I ever had morose, violent thoughts?

I explained imagining vomiting on people, plunging knives into their rib cages, cutting off my fingers with a cleaver.

Had I ever contemplated suicide?

A quiet "Yes."

Had I ever attempted it?

"Thankfully, no."

Had I ever lost interest in things because nothing gave me pleasure? Were there times when I was very interested in being with people, and other times when I wanted to be alone? Did I have crying jags, anxiety and panic, trouble falling asleep or staying asleep, bad feelings about myself?

Yes. Yes. Yes. Yes. Yes. Yes to it all. David Lindsey had been right: I'd been depressed, many times, and seriously.

As Neil questioned, I could feel something give inside, like those push puppets, their muscles elastic strings running through limbs and body, and when you press on the bottom of the toy, they collapse. I didn't have to strain anymore, always bracing for impact. My mind was lighting up, new connections and relationships suddenly shaking hands.

It was a long evaluation. When it was over, he said, "I think it's safe to say you have bipolar disorder. Specifically, bipolar II." He said the medical community no longer used the term *manic depression*. It felt it was stigmatizing.

He explained that there are two types of bipolar disorder. Bipolar I is the more severe form, what Kay Redfield Jamison, the author of *An Unquiet Mind,* has. In it, the manias are screechingly amped up and oftentimes dangerous. They're emblazoned with inflated self-esteem and billowing grandiosity, a marked decrease in sleep, a pressing need to talk, sometimes with odd features such as "clanging," where speech loses meaning and follows a pattern of rhymes or sounds. Someone suffering from full-blown mania can be grossly distracted; battle racing, looping thoughts; and engage in potentially dangerous and deadly activities, such as unchecked buying sprees, risky or anonymous sex, foolish business dealings, and reckless driving. All the while, psychosis—a disconnection from reality—can be skulking in the background, just waiting for a pause, an opening. These manias can disrupt a person's life to such a degree that jobs are lost, relationships implode, families disintegrate. Hospitalizations usually follow.

"What you have, bipolar II," he continued, "is a milder form of the illness." While the depressions can be just as deep and disabling, he said, what makes the difference is the quality, degree, and length of the high times. With bipolar II, a person suffers from hypomania. Elevated, expansive moods that are seductively attractive to the sufferer and the people around him, hypomanias are a watercolor version of bright-neon manias. Through it all, life isn't disrupted to the same degree, and there's never a psychotic break. Hospitalizations aren't common.

"It can be very, very difficult to diagnosis hypomania," Neil said. "Especially in type-A people who are normally goal-oriented, high energy, and creative. Their personalities can mask the illness at times."

"Where on the continuum do you think I fall?"

"From what I've seen of you at dinners and parties, you're very high-functioning, and my gut is you're probably more on the depressive end of the spectrum, with occasional periods of mild hypomania." *It's all a matter of degree.*

Then he joked, "I'm envious. I wish I had a jolt of hypomania once in a while. I could use it when I'm on deadline for writing a grant."

I smiled, I think for the first time that afternoon.

"Here's the name of a colleague who might be a good match," Neil said, writing on a prescription pad. He handed me the paper, and I slipped it in my pocket. As with all the other psychiatrists I had seen, Neil's guy dealt only with medication management. "So if you want to work through this in therapy, which I recommend, you should continue with your shrink," Neil said.

It was hard to look him in the eyes. "Thank you." He nodded. I would like to think he understood what he had just done.

Sitting on the subway hurtling back home, I could feel the relief that I was finally understood, demystified, and categorized being edged out by sadness and *veneta*. How could it have taken twenty-five years, and more than a half-dozen doctors, before a proper diagnosis was handed down that explained what was wrong with me, as far back as that dark movie theater in Fall River? There was Dr. Copley. Had there been signs then? I think so. He knew that I heard breathing and saw that demon face in the window. He knew of those blissful times in high school when, without reason, a heavy, musty tarp lifted, and I could breathe again and everything became easier. And Kim Mueller of the Eames Chair? She'd definitely seen me down, although I have no recollection of her ever uttering the word *depression*. She most certainly knew of the Magical Mystery Tour I took in the Carnegie Library, when I came to believe I was one of God's Elite Task Force. Her response? Nothing. She was tying herself into knots, trying to get me to admit I was punishing my mother by being gay.

What of Jack Constantinides, Dr. Orenstein, Dr. Patronization, and a few others not worth mentioning? All of them medical professionals—board-certified psychiatrists—trained in differential diagnosis: the art and science of distinguishing between conditions that share similar symptoms. Even after evaluations as long and as detailed as Neil's, they had all come to the same conclusion: anxiety and depression. *No surprise there.* They had expected to find anxiety, because I'd walked in telling them I was riddled with it. They were sure they'd excavate depression because of what David Lindsey had told them over the phone even before I said hello. I hadn't been withholding information—*they'd never asked the frigging questions that had needed to be asked.* They hadn't gone deep enough into me, their patient, the person who was paying exorbitant amounts for their expertise. They'd stopped the moment they found what they expected. Then they'd treated the symptoms, not the patient. Scripts had been dutifully scrawled for benzodiazepines and SSRIs, and when the anxiety and depression hadn't evaporated as they had assured me they would, they weren't just flummoxed; they were annoyed. My lack of psychiatric response was looked upon as a challenge to their unassailable medical authority. It wasn't just David Lindsey who had missed the mark—it was every doctor I'd ever seen.

As I turned onto West Seventy-Seventh Street, I remembered Dr. Bercoli, Neil's colleague, and stepped off my soapbox and into hope. If he was half as kind and insightful as Neil, I would be in good and, finally, medically responsible hands.

That next week, I sat in David Lindsey's office, smug, and began flaunting the proof he'd demanded, even though I knew he'd already spoken to Neil.

"Before you start, I have business I need to clear up." He scooched forward in his chair, like he wanted to whisper a secret. I did the same, so our knees were almost touching. I'd never seen him so vulnerable. "I failed you. I apologize. I hope you can forgive me, and that we can work through this together and focus on getting you well."

He was making hating him so hard. Isn't this what he'd always taught me? To take responsibility, to admit when I was wrong, to change my behavior? These weren't just words filtered down to me from a twelve-step program he'd been in for decades; it was how he lived his life. His humility gutted me. We sat there, both crying. Both waiting, unsure of whether our relationship was over.

I was the first to lean back. To begin again.

PART III

PROPHYLAXiS

REFERS TO THE MEASURES TAKEN TO PRESERVE HEALTH AND PRE-
VENT THE SPREAD OR WORSENING OF AN ILLNESS. OTHERWISE
KNOWN AS BETTER LIVING THROUGH MEDICATION.

34

SHiTS AND GiGGLES iNC.

It was as if I'd been handed a giant Christmas present, but after opening it had discovered it required big-ass assembly. I didn't know how to wear this official mantle of bipolar disorder, which I preferred to call manic depression—it was more exact and descriptive of what I felt. At times, I was elated. Whenever I went up to Alan—we were back living together by this time—I'd say, "Do you realize you're in love with a crazy person?" I think it was my way of getting comfortable, test-driving the diagnosis to see how it fit. I suspect I was also testing his limits, to see if he would finally run, giving him ample reason if he did. But at other times, I'd be horrified that my greatest fear, which I had carried around in a hard, shiny place deep inside since I was a kid, was true: I was mentally ill.

While I waited to see Dr. Bercoli, David Lindsey and I decided my course of action should be to tell the people closest to me. Although this was the second time I would come out, it was by far the hardest.

"Mom," I said into the phone. Alan stood next to me, holding my hand. "Can you put Daddy on the extension?"

"Why? What's the matter?" It was her panicky voice.

"I'll tell you in a minute."

"Mannnnn-nnnnny!" she shouted, I assumed into the backyard, where he was tending his grapevines.

A click as he picked up. "Hello?"

How do you tell your parents something like this? I explained that I had been feeling really poorly for a long time, and had gone to a doctor for an evaluation. "I was diagnosed with manic depression."

"Manic what?" my father asked.

"Manic depression," I said. "They also call it bipolar disorder." I gave a lay definition: mercurial moods, anger, irritability, sadness, fast speech, everything. I heard my mother weeping.

"Why are you crying, Ma?" I tried to hide my exasperation.

"Did I do this?" It was matter-of-fact and martyr-y.

"This isn't about you, Ma," I said. "This is about me." Alan pulled me back somehow. Blowing up at my parents while floating the idea that I'm mentally ill by them wasn't exactly the best timing.

"How do you get this, this bi-polo sickness?" my father asked. His voice was smooth and even, oil on her turbulent high seas.

"It's hereditary," I said, then waited for the sobs. "They say it's often from the mother's side." Right on cue.

"I'm sorry." She gulped into the phone.

"Ma," I said softly, "unless you can control your genes, you had nothing to do with it."

"Son," my father added, "do what you have to do to get well."

"I will."

For my first appointment with Dr. Bercoli, I arrived early. Too early. Sitting there in the waiting room, I reviewed the list of questions I wanted to ask him. The first was: *How does anxiety fit into all of this?* I had an idea, because I had read Patty Duke's book *A Brilliant Madness*, in which she outlines her illness, from her childhood to being in her midthirties and finally being properly diagnosed and treated.

When he came to collect me, I stood and shook his hand. It's odd. I have no recollection of what he looks like. For the two years I saw him, it's like his face was blurred and his voice mechanically manipulated, like those witnesses to a crime on the evening news.

Apparently, Neil had done the heavy lifting of diagnosing. It was Bercoli's job to keep things tidy with medication management. After hearing me out—much of the same information that I had already given to Neil—Bercoli wrote a prescription for a pink pill, an anti-seizure medication given to epileptics. "It also acts as an anti-manic," he said. "Very stable drug, very stable. Been around for years." He wrote a prescription for an antidepressant sleeping medication as well, saying that lack of sleep is a major contributor to manic episodes.

The side effects of the pink pill were awful. My weight ballooned. I was now 220 and counting. An intense and crushing pain clamped down on my head whenever I stood up. A fog descended, slowing my thoughts—entire days were lived in that midafternoon slump, which no caffeine or sugar could rouse. I would start sentences, but the meaning would meander so that by the end of them I'd forgotten what I was saying. The names of ordinary objects, like "pencil" or "water" or "television," escaped me, even though I was looking right at them.

I lost control of my body, too. My hands trembled slightly almost all the time, and my bowels went on strike. One afternoon, I was walking through Central Park on my way home from work. My gut began to spasm. The nearest restrooms in the park were padlocked. I ran over to the West Side and into Café des Artistes, but the manager sneered at me as I begged to use the bathroom.

"For customers only," he said.

"I'll buy something," I pleaded, as he shunted me out of the way with his arm to make way for a couple.

With no other choice, I walked back into the park—heel toe, heel toe, heel toe—trying not to jounce my swilling insides. I stood in the bushes, my hands over my face, and let go. Then I walked the fifteen blocks home, head down, the legs of my jeans and socks wet and reeking, ignoring anyone's complaints of smell.

For months, I saw no improvement in my moods, although the physical symptoms abated some. "These kinds of things take time," Bercoli said, visit after visit. "Everyone is different." And as I sat there, despondent, he would lean back in his chair, his eyes heavy-lidded and bored, as if he couldn't wait for me to leave so he could get back to bidding on a *Knight Rider* denim jacket on eBay.

Therapy was the only place I saw progress. I culled my journals, highlighting passages, running a thick red marker under others, making big exclamation marks in the margins. And then twice a week I discussed it all with David Lindsey, turning each item over like an antique plate, examining it for potential. Questions that had hovered in the air between us for years were beginning to be answered. Some of my introverted and extroverted periods weren't just the moods of someone with an artistic temperament any longer; they were the shuttling between the highs and lows of the disease. My sudden onslaught of weekend activities in Barryville—cleaning gutters, painting kitchen cabinets, scrubbing rust stains—which David Lindsey had always held as suspect, were now seen as hypomania, mingled with the ecstatic flush of new love. Slowly, we recast reactions, renamed thoughts, recategorized behaviors. I drew diagrams that looked like enormous bell curves, curves that explained in the most elegant, concrete way what had happened to me since I was a kid.

I traced my index finger along a flat line hurtling ahead to the right. Slowly it rose; this was the hypomania just beginning to take hold. Well-being squared. As it continued to rise, the smooth vertical side of a sugarloaf or anthill, this was where I felt marvelous. Words came easily, charm and sociability bubbled (*this* was when you wanted to get invited to our house for a dinner party), connections that startled my bosses and me were made here. *I'm a genius,* I would say to myself. As the curve reached its crest, life swirled, energy crackled, I needed little sleep. But something else began whirlpooling under the surface. Irritability and anger swelled, and a hot, screaming frustration took root. *Why is everyone so stupid? Why is everything so fucking slow?* And, suddenly, fences broke, and anxiety and panic galloped wildly through every artery and muscle in my body. Anxiety, I came to see, wasn't the problem. It was the exhausted, pitiful reward for all that hypomania. And it acted as a switching station for the descent, which wasn't a curvaceous, gracious slope downward, a mirror image of the exhilarating, addictive ride up. It was almost a vertical drop. A free fall into depression. I often think of it now as a half-built roller coaster, the tracks ending at the apex, two metal rods poking the sky. Below, boulders and scarred earth—nothing to break the plummet.

35

COPE iS A FOUR-LETTER WORD

The circle of people sitting on metal folding chairs looked glum. I stood in the doorway, about to back out, when a woman's voice from behind said, "Welcome! Join us!" Like a rogue wave, her unrelenting buoyancy pushed me into the room. I took a seat on the far end, away from her, and waited. A heavy woman across from me, dressed in a ratty skirt and T-shirt dotted with what I could only assume were food stains, worried her hands. The twisting and knotting of fingers was causing a bubble of nervousness to rise inside. I took deep breaths, trying to keep calm.

I had joined a bipolar support group at David Lindsey's suggestion. "It's important to see where you've been, where you are, and where you're going," he liked to say of the benefits of being in a group. Looking around the room at the slumped bodies, restless knees and feet, shifting eyes, frightening cheerleader smiles, I didn't feel particularly confident in a sunny future.

"Who would like to start?" asked the Rogue Wave. I could feel the group move back a bit, as people suddenly took an interest in their sneakers or fingernails.

"I will."

"Great!"

The speaker was a small, doleful woman with loose steel wool for hair. Her face was slack, as if it needed a puppeteer to pull strings to make it express anything.

"I still can't work," she said in a monotone. She explained that no matter how hard she tried each morning, she couldn't rouse herself from bed to find a job. She'd get as far as the bathroom and have to turn back, all freaked out, and sleep until midafternoon. Only then could she face the day. I understood that. When I was depressed, mornings were the worst. Only as the day passed, and bedtime with its merciful blackness drew closer, did I start to feel better, knowing there was an inevitable end to the pain. But, still, I forced myself to go to work.

The group murmured its empathy, and a few people offered resources. The woman nodded robotically. "Thank you."

Can't hold down a job, can't afford medication, boyfriend/girlfriend left me, parents kicked me out, am thinking of suicide again, swirled through the conversation. Hands rubbed backs, faces burrowed into a nearby neck, shoulders hitched with tears.

At the break a young guy, in his twenties I'd guess, came up to me.

"Pretty intense, huh?" he said, smiling.

I looked around to make sure I was out of earshot of everyone. "Are you kidding?" I whispered. "This is enough to make me want to put a gun to my head." I leaned in. "Of course, I mean that in the most figurative of ways." I didn't know if gallows humor was allowed.

He stifled a laugh. "It isn't always like this. When people are on the upswing it's more positive and fun." I looked at Rogue Wave. "But when they're feeling *too* good," he continued, "they take off. They think they don't need the group or their meds. Then they end up back here." He pointed to the cluster of lumpy, sagging bodies. "Like this."

"You're in a pretty good mood," I said. "Will you be taking off soon?"

He shrugged his shoulders. "Depends. I got a mild case, and I take my meds."

Was that possible? Could that be me? Could my pink pill do that for me, too?

Rogue Wave spoke, in great swells, after the break. She'd been sitting on her hands and rocking, an impish smile on her face. She said she knew she was feeling good and just wanted to enjoy it a little bit longer before she had to put the kibosh on it and get back to taking her medications. As she flitted in and out of how she was feeling, she suddenly recounted her first time having a manic episode.

She balanced her ass on the edge of the chair, her legs jumping as she pumped up and down on the balls of her feet. "I was seeing a revival of *Gone with the Wind* in a theater," she began. My gut lurched. *A movie? You've got to be fucking kidding me.* The last thing I needed was to hear another story of madness kicked off by a movie, but to hear it from her—this knot of insanity—was just unfair. I needed to think I was better than her, healthier, that we shared nothing—*nothing*—but a diagnosis.

Her hands fluttered in front of her as if she were drawing the scene for us, erasing, sketching, shading. She had walked into the theater hunched and sullen, she said, barely able to follow the story as one scene bled into another, colorless, even though it was Technicolor. As Scarlett, played by bipolar compatriot Vivien Leigh, pushed herself off the red clay of her ruined plantation and lifted her fist to the sky, vowing, "I'll never be hungry again," Rogue Wave was infused with a renewed strength and resolve. When she exited the theater some four hours later, she was giddy. "I had no idea why, but I was joyous, spinning around and talking nonstop"—not unlike what she was doing now—"about how absolutely! marvelously! tremendously! positively! happy the movie made me feel."

It was like she was a human electroshock machine. The rest of us looked on, some reinvigorated, others dazzled; the woman with steel wool for hair was even smiling.

When I spoke after Rogue Wave, I brought down the mood of the room to mildly depressed. I talked about how I didn't think my medication was working. A chorus rose, punctuated with Latin-sounding words: *Try lithium! You can't beat Topamax! Ask for Tegretol! Lamictal will do the trick! You can get Prozac from China for practically nothing!*

I sat in David Lindsey's office and recounted my night.

"*That's* why I said you weren't manic depressive," he said. "You never presented like that."

"Then I don't know what to do," I said. "I'm not crazy enough to relate to most of those people, and I'm *more* than crazy enough to have to quit school—twice—destroy relationships, quit jobs over and over again when I'm on top, not complete things—"

The hand again. "It will not always be like this."

"How do you know?" I suspected he was right, but I wanted to drag him around the block and make him say it, plainly.

"Because this medication or *some* other medications will help, and you'll learn how to cope."

There was that word again. I'd heard it since I was a kid, from my family, school counselors, Kim Mueller of the Eames Chair, and now him. *Cope.* One of the most hateful words in the English lexicon. It comes from the ancient Greek word *kolaphos,* which means "a blow with the fist." A strike down in battle. I didn't want to cope anymore, because I was over getting my ass kicked. I'd never thought I'd get to the point in my life when I would beg to be ordinary, average. But I had. I wanted to be in the emotional fiftieth percentile, right in the middle, lost and safe.

36

MEET THE LEiTES

I eventually returned to school, taking one class a semester so I could keep the stress to a minimum. At David Lindsey's suggestion, I hired a tutor. Although I still had a 4.0 GPA, new math was threatening to topple it. (Why old math wasn't good enough was beyond me.) Finally, when I was thirty-seven years old, I graduated with a B.S. in psychology, four schools and nineteen years after starting.

My parents came for the ceremony, which I hoped would go better than their previous visit to the city, almost a decade before. Then, as I'd toured them around Manhattan and Brooklyn, my mother had sat in the front seat screaming almost the whole way. Back at my apartment, she collapsed on the couch, exhausted. "Too much traffic," she said, looking up at me as I handed her a glass of water. "All those people. It was like an obstacle course. I don't know how you do it, Son." Visiting this time meant facing what I hoped wasn't an insurmountable obstacle: Alan. Although I don't recall this, he told me my parents had had several phone calls with him before their trip.

It was my mother, he said, who had reached out. They were cordial talks, never addressing the lavender elephant in the room, except that once she did floor him by saying, "Let me tell you something, Madison," her nickname for him, because I'd told her he sold high-end real estate, "I'm not suddenly going to jump up and join PFLAG." How she'd known about the largest parents, family, and friends organization that supports the gay community, he had no idea—and he knew it was better not to ask.

When they arrived, I flung open the front door to the apartment and kissed and hugged them.

"Mom banse, Dad banse."

"God bless you," they said together.

My mother was in her tan trench coat over a flowered print dress, both redolent of Chantilly, her perfume for years. My father looked dapper in his blue sports coat and tie.

While my father admired the apartment, leaning back and looking up the staircase and out at the view from the balcony, I noticed my mother was standing motionless, as she darted her eyes over the living room and kitchen without moving her head. Something she does when she's nervous.

Upstairs, rustling in the bedroom. My mother pulled her purse to her chest and began backing up slowly, as if away from a rabid dog, until she'd wedged herself into the corner of the living room. She stared at the top of the stairs, waiting. I have no idea what she expected—bugle beads? studded leather? Liberace?—but her preemptive expression of horror unsettled me. When Alan descended, wearing a broad smile, an oxford shirt, and khakis, relief rippled across her face. I caught her sizing him up out of the corner of her eye as he talked with my father. I couldn't ferret out what she was thinking, and I wasn't about to drag her into the bathroom giggling and say, "So . . . whaddya think?" You just don't do that sort of thing with my mother.

At graduation, my parents, Alan, Becca, her sister, and her mother all sat together in the theater. I had also invited Danny Pring, our next-door neighbor in Washington Depot, Connecticut, where we'd bought a country house. Danny and Alan were extraordinarily tight, and having her there was a bit of an emotional bolster for him. As I waited in line for my diploma, I watched them. Finally graduating from college wasn't the greatest accomplishment that day. (By this time, I was certain I wasn't going to graduate school to become a shrink. I'd had enough of pain, depression, and hopelessness in my life, thank you very much. I was now looking for joy.) Seeing my parents sitting next to Alan—my mother obviously enjoying his company, because she kept leaning across my father to speak to him, just like she and I did in church—just about did me in. The secrets were no longer. There was no need to hide who I was or parry questions from anyone, especially my parents.

As the ceremony dragged on, the crowd grew rowdy. Loud shouts and whistles rose when the names of many of the graduates were announced.

"David Joseph Leite," thundered through the hall. I caught my mother as she stood and shouted, "We love you, Son!" Then she slipped her little fingers into her mouth and let out a piercing whistle, that clarion call that had summoned me all my childhood, which caused most of the auditorium to turn toward her, laughing. Some even applauded.

"What can I say? He's our kid!" she yelled.

My mother was never outdone.

Afterward, I spotted David Lindsey, whom I'd also invited, sitting by himself.

"Congratulations," he said, hugging me.

"Thanks. Just a minute." I returned with my parents and introduced them.

He stuck out his hand, "Manny and Elvira, it's a pleasure meeting you." Only he pronounced my mother's name El-*veer*-ra, even though I had corrected him a million times. "El-*vye*-ra," I'd say, "it's El-*vye*-ra." He liked to get my goat that way.

My father choked up. "Thank you for what you've done for our son all these years."

"I'm going to let you in on a little secret," my mother said, leaning in. "Every morning, we pray for you and the work you do." She then reached out and touched his arm. "May God bless you."

And to my shock, he replied, "Thank you. God bless *you*." That man never stopped surprising me.

After a late lunch at a local restaurant with views of Lincoln Center, my parents hugged everyone goodbye, including Alan. I walked them down the street, past the screaming kids in the school playground, to their car.

"Thank you so much for coming," I said, wrapping my arms around my mother. "Dad banse," I said, kissing him.

I wanted to gush. I could feel the excitement of the day dovetailing with swelling hypomania; words were pushing against my teeth, trying to get out. All kinds of over-the-top movie goodbyes, weepy rococo thanks kitted out with emotional embellishments that were way out of proportion to the moment. A bravura performance just waiting for the curtain to rise. That's the seduction of my illness, I came to see: I feel it, and because I feel it, it's real. But I'd fought back. I was slowly learning to stay in the moment—not the chemically manufactured fantastical version of the moment exploding in my brain, but the unadorned moment between me and my parents, who had come so far in their own lives—and in their faith—to be standing here with me.

"Oh, no!" my mother said, fishing in the shopping bag she was holding. "I forgot my coat in the apartment." Now, my mother doesn't forget things. She's the person who'll remind everyone else not to forget their things, regardless of who they are.

"I'll get it," I said, turning back up the street.

"No, that's okay." She laid her hand on my arm. "I'll get it next time." Even though my hopped-up brain was whirring, constructing magnificent homo-bejeweled bridges between us, I was shocked. She knew exactly what she was doing and what this meant. She had never offered to come visit before. It was her way of saying, "I accept, I approve." I thought of offering to bring it to her on our way to Martha's Vineyard the next month, but I didn't want to wrest the moment away from her.

37

TWO THOUSAND PiNK PiLLS LATER

A year after graduation, the anxiety and hypomania were gone, but I was still often depressed. But the kind that doesn't prevent only impedes. So I was never too ill to have a dinner party, but I was ill enough to not enjoy it. I was never too sick to bake, though—one of the few activities that grounded me when I felt rootless. And with each cake or pie or brownie, my spirits rose, but only imperceptibly.

Tired of the ineffectiveness of Bercoli's approach, I made a suggestion during one of my appointments. "What if next time Alan and my shrink come with me, so that they can report what they experience. Maybe I'm not giving you a full picture." What I really wanted to say was, *Why the fuck am I not getting any better?* During those two years, I'd ingested bottles and bottles of his pink crazy pills, and I was still limping through life. There had to be something I was missing, I figured, and if I brought in Alan and David Lindsey, perhaps they'd say something that would prompt a flashbulb pop of insight, and he'd try something different. Anything different. A blue pill, or a yellow pill, or a green pill. Where's the medical logic in offering a patient the same course of treatment—more than two thousand pink pills—and, even though they weren't working, holding out for a sudden change for the better? And *I'm* the one who's supposed to be mental.

Bercoli bristled. "I don't think we need to go to that extreme," he said. Then, smiling, "You're a very good reporter, David." A nod of his head, then he leaned back in that bored way, as if to let me take in his compliment.

"I want them to come."

"David—"

"Dr. Bercoli, please? It might just help."

Next time I had both of them in tow. "Dr. Bercoli, this is Alan, my partner; and Dr. Griffin, my therapist for ten years." They shook hands. We three crowded on one side of the desk, Bercoli on the other. I could practically smell his disdain.

As Alan answered questions, I felt a gush of gratitude. To have both of these men, two of the most important men in my life, in this one room together for my sake was humbling. When it was David Lindsey's turn, Bercoli grew more uncomfortable. Unlike with Alan, now it was David Lindsey who did the questioning. He grilled Bercoli on my moods, the arc of the illness, other modalities that might help me. And then the big question: "Do you think psychotherapy can help David get better?"

This was Bercoli's trump card. To a medical doctor like him, who parsed patients by neurotransmitters, therapeutic blood levels, and side effects, mental illness is nothing more than a fifteen-car pileup in the brain that can only be fixed by someone trained in the mysteries of medicine.

"This is a chemical issue, not an interpersonal one, Mr. Griffin. All psychotherapy can do is help David deal with the illness."

Bercoli didn't catch it, but David Lindsey had dismissed him. On the spot and completely. For the last few minutes of the session, he sat there, palms tucked between his knees, a smile plastered on his face, nodding obsequiously. Bercoli seemed pleased.

In the taxi on the way home, David Lindsey let loose. "I hate that pompous motherfucker. First he's patronizing to Alan, then he thinks psychotherapy can't help you? I've been in practice longer than that little shit has been alive." I looked at Alan and waited. Three, two, one: "And who the hell does he think he is, calling me *Mister* Griffin? I wanted to take that desk lamp and shove it up his ass." All three of us busted out laughing, and suddenly Bercoli didn't seem like a problem anymore. It wasn't just me; they saw exactly what I'd been dealing with for two years.

At the end of my next appointment, after Bercoli's usual volley of questions about dosage and side effects, I said, "Tell me, Dr. Bercoli, will I get any better?"

He looked up from his notes and leaned forward, like we were finally going to cut the crap and speak the truth. "This is as good as it's going to get."

A tsunami of *veneta* began gathering, and I did nothing to quell it. I stood up, placed both fists on his desk, and leaned over him. He clearly didn't like the submissive position I was putting him in. "Let me tell you something, Dr. Bercoli," I said slowly. "*Fuck you*. You hear me? I *will* get better, and I *will* lead a productive, fabulous life. And I don't need you to do it."

On my way out, I slammed the door for dramatic effect—I am my mother's son, after all. I walked to the subway, feeling the lightest I had in years. It wasn't mania or hypomania or medication-induced euphoria. I was feeling powerful. I'd reclaimed my ability to take care of myself *in a way that felt right for me*. I had no idea what I would do next, or whom I would see, but I knew, more than anything, that at that moment I wanted a big, thick, bloody steak. A victor's dinner.

38

i AM HERE

For a while something had been scratching at the underside of my defrosting brain, demanding attention. Writing. Until then, it had been something I did for others, for their benefit, for their gain. Now I sensed it wanted me to turn inward, to find expression there. I thought of that little kid kneeling at the side of his bed, determined to write a story about pirates—something he knew nothing about. The subject that insisted on itself this time I knew intimately and missed terribly: Vovo Costa. The continental drift I had set into motion that separated me from my heritage felt almost unnavigable, and I needed to do something declarative and permanent to close that gap.

I wrote for weeks about growing up in a Portuguese home, about our huge, raucous dinners, the dishes my mother and aunts would stake out as their own, and about how when Vo died, so did a lot of our heritage. Her food had been the embrace that kept us close. I surprised myself by how much I longed for what I had forgotten. As I kept writing, trying to give shape to this new insistence, I decided to turn it into an article. To my surprise, it was accepted by the *Chicago Sun-Times* and ran on the front page of the food section. *With a byline.* Although I'd worked on ad campaigns that had appeared in national newspapers and magazines, and on television, my name had never been associated with them. The idea of creating my own work about subjects I cared about—and having my name appear on it—was almost too easy of an answer. Without any more consideration than that, I left advertising and became a food writer.

More of my articles made the front page of the *Sun-Times,* one of which was a six-thousand-word treatise on the foods of the twentieth century. In February 1999, I started a website called Leite's Culinaria as a way of posting my writing, hoping editors would see it. My first food essay was for *Bon Appétit,* in which I wrote about my eight-year search for the perfect stove—our beloved Viking range, which we installed in the Washington Depot house and nicknamed Thor. Eventually, I added the *New York Times, Los Angeles Times, Gourmet, Food & Wine, Saveur,* and *Martha Stewart Living* to my résumé.

I'd found my niche, with the help of modern chemistry. After Bercoli, I rooted out a psychopharmacologist who added a white pill, an anticonvulsant that also works as a mood stabilizer for manic depression. I don't remember exactly when it kicked in, but it didn't take long. I was sitting in the dining room of our new apartment, just one street south of the triplex, which Alan had made sure included a swinging kitchen door with a round window in it. He'd bought it for fifty bucks from a neighbor who was throwing it out.

I was writing when it struck me that something was different. If depression was a deficit, a debit that kept draining my resources, I was no longer in the red. I was a perfect zero. It may sound odd to be so happy about feeling nothing, being on the fulcrum of negative and positive. But it was this lack of depression, which had burrowed so deep, it was crowding out everything as it grew—a tumor crushing organs—that allowed for other emotions to rush in and take its place.

A slow state of delicious forgetfulness descended. I'd lift my head from my computer and see from the light, low and slanting across the apartment, that it was late afternoon, and I hadn't even thought about my mood. Or I'd be cooking all Saturday with Alan, only to be waving goodbye to guests near midnight, and it would dawn on me I hadn't once felt depressed. And then there was the hysteria on the morning of the Great Conflagration, up in Washington Depot.

Wrapped in the thick blue terry robe I had gotten him during our first few months together, Alan was standing at Thor, stirring a skillet of homemade corned-beef hash and chatting with me about our agenda for the day. Alan likes agendas; they make him feel productive on what are supposed to be lazy Saturday mornings. As he reached over the stove, the front of his robe went up in an enormous burst of flames.

His ear-splitting six-year-old-girl scream filled the house. "David! I'm on fire! I'm on fire!"

I froze. Not out of fear or shock. I was dumbstruck to see him running around the kitchen beating at his chest with the spatula. All I could think of was the Scarecrow in *The Wizard of Oz*.

When the flames died out, he leveled a dead-serious look at me: "I could've died, you know." He said it as if he'd narrowly missed being hit by a falling chunk of concrete, or escaped a pack of pit bulls. I tried biting back laughter—the man needed his dignity, after all—but it was useless. "It's *not* funny."

I nuzzled my nose into the lapel of the robe and took a whiff. The culprit? Although he was nearly bald and sported a hard top, Alan had a sartorial need to drench his head in hair spray every morning. Over time, the ridiculously flammable spray had built up on the front of his bathrobe; hence his human-torch act.

"C'mere," I said, bringing him into the light from the window over the sink. I pulled his face close and ran my fingers over his eyebrows. Tiny bits of frizzled hair dusted his cheeks and nose. That unhinged me. I looped my arms around his shoulders and pulled him close, as much to comfort him as to lean on him, so I wouldn't topple. As my chest was hiccupping with laughter, he mumbled into my neck, "No, really, I could have died. And think how bad you would have felt not helping me." I'd forgotten how long it had been since I'd lost myself in such gut-busting abandon.

We began traveling again. We went to Lisbon on assignment for *Bon Appétit,* my first travel story, where I wrote about the burgeoning food scene in my newly adopted country. We returned to Paris and made our own food discoveries: Poilâne bakery, Pierre Hermé, Bistrot Paul Bert, the street market on Rue Poncelet, and a marvelous throwback to seventeenth-century France at the restaurant Aux Anysetiers du Roy, on Île Saint-Louis. In Italy, we stayed at our friends' home in Trastevere in Rome, as well as in a villa a bunch of us rented in Panzano in Chianti. We ate fried zucchini blossoms, guaranteed to have been snipped no more than an hour before, followed by plates of hand-cut pasta, in sun-burnished piazzas; platters of rabbit and carafes of house wine in an out-of-the-way farmhouse in the country; and gelato everywhere. Oh, how I adored the gelato. Wales was all about pasties and Welsh cakes. Russia was a blur of borscht, pelmeni, and caviar and blini.

As much as I begged my parents to come with us to the Azores, where they'd met, they demurred. My father couldn't bear to be reminded of the poverty he'd left behind. When I insisted that things had to have improved over the past four decades, he said it would be just as painful to see what had disappeared.

"There's nothing left for me there," he said, cupping my face in his hands. "My life is here with you and your mother. But go in my place, Son."

After getting lost several times one morning, Alan and I find the town my father's family is from. Maia, on the north side of the island. We stand on the top of a street. Above us, set into a wall, is: *2a Travessa da Rua dos Foros.*

Second Lane of the Road of Privileges. The blue-and-white tile sign, yellowed and chipped like a smoker's teeth, is inset high on the brilliant white of the stucco. Some careless painter, perhaps full from too much wine at lunch, or distracted on a hot Saturday afternoon by a young woman with full hips, had thwacked the tiles with a roller, leaving patterned splotches that mar the blue scroll design framing the neat serif letters. As Portuguese tiles go, it's not a beautiful specimen. The lane, nothing more than a crossing from one street to the next, is named for Rua dos Foros, the road we're standing in, which slopes down to the sea. But still, I'm moved.

"What are you thinking?" asks Alan, nudging his chin down the road. I'm thinking of travel brochures.

When I was in elementary school, my mother, in an attempt to rouse her depressed eleven-year-old, would stop by the travel agency in Somerset and pick up armfuls of heavy catalogs. In my room, I'd flip through them endlessly, having conversations with the models in the pictures. I knew it would be people like this man in sharply creased pants at a café; or that woman in a colorful dress and a hat that looked like a red bowling ball, waving from a double-decker bus, who would someday be my friends.

"Who are you talking to?" my mother would ask through the closed door.

"No one!" I'd shout, shooting up from the bed and shoving the catalogs underneath, as if they were *Playboy*.

When the pages were dog-eared and the ink smudged from too many greasy fingers, I cut out the pictures of Westminster Abbey, Buckingham Palace, the Coliseum, the Eiffel Tower, and taped them into a spiral-ring notebook. There was not one picture of the Azores.

In the intervening years, as I visited each place in that secret notebook—standing in front of soaring arches, meticulously painted fences, crumbling ruins, and sweeping steeples of iron—I would whisper over and over again to myself, as a way of marking the moment, imprinting it on some neural pathway, so that years from now the memory of once having been there would be as powerful as the act of standing there: "I am here, I am here."

"I am here," I say to Alan. Here is the street in the old part of the tiny town where my father's family lived for generations, where my parents honeymooned, their bed a pile of hay with a sheet on top. Here are the whitewashed houses, their windows painted with thick eyeliner of blue, green, or gray; impossibly narrow sidewalks— twelve inches at their most gracious; a flow chart of grass sprouting between rows of basalt cobblestones in the street, so infrequent is the traffic. Beyond, the ocean that I no longer use to separate me from myself. Standing here marks the end of running, of hiding, and the beginning of inching toward something worthy: my identity.

I knock on the door of the house once owned by my family. Voices inside, then shuffling. The sound of a game show. The door opens slightly; a white face with floating wisps of gray peeks around it.

"Sim?"

"I am David Leite," I say in Portuguese. "The son of Manuel and Elvira Leite." The woman looks toward Alan, then back to me. Then, recognition.

"Ay, Da-veed!" she screams, yanking me down to her bosom, even though she is a good foot shorter than me. She is Elvira Tomás, my fa- ther's cousin, who bought the house from my grandfather, Vu Leite.

She pulls us inside and introduces us to a man sitting in front of a huge wide-screen TV. We shake hands, and he nods, then goes back to his show. The room is nothing like I imagined. I have heard of dirt floors, exposed rock walls, the simple loft above where my father and his four siblings slept. The wall oven in the kitchen and the pig- sty right outside the back door. The outhouse where chickens would peck at your ass while you did your business. But now sleek white tiles with a scroll design cover the floor. The walls are plastered a pristine white. In the kitchen, a yellow electric range, sink, cabinets, appliances.

In no time, the house is filled with family. Señora Elvira has called her two daughters, Fátima and Teresinha, who speak English, and from there the phone tree sprouts. Outside the two windows, neigh- bors gather. The stern-faced old man who watched our car go down and up the hill as we looked for the town pokes his face in the win- dow. He, it turns out, is a distant cousin.

I ask Teresinha, "Does the wall oven still exist?" She translates for me.

"*Sim*," Señora Elvira says proudly. She motions for Alan and me to move the range forward and remove a metal panel. I clasp a hand over my mouth and begin to sob. There, cut into the wall, is a hole, charred black, where Vo Leite made do with so little for so many years.

"That's where she made everything, your grandmother," says the daughter. "Breads, meats, fish, stews. Everything."

And as the defenses I erected so long ago against my family, my hometown, my heritage, my identity, lose their grip, I'm overcome with regret. I whitewashed myself so much, ethnically cleansed who I was, that I am ashamed. I never afforded my family and all Azoreans back home the respect and dignity they deserved. I thought of them as uneducated, ignorant immigrants with at best a second-rate culture. Yet it was in this room, this house, that humble, honest people beat the odds and survived, and by going to America, with my father leading them, thrived. They searched and worked for decades for a better life, to surmount the obstacles thrown in their way, just as I did. If it were possible for roots to sprout from the soles of my feet and curl their way into the volcanic soil and rock of that tiny island, they would.

I am here, I think. *I am home.*

39

AN ASYLUM TO CALL MY OWN

In December 2006, we moved from Washington Depot and bought a large home one town over, in Roxbury. As much as we loved our sweet little Dutch colonial, our neighbor Danny had moved, and Pete, on the other side, had a bad habit of dropping in, oftentimes without knocking. The day he surprised me while I was in the shower was the day we put the place on the market.

I wasn't too keen on the new house: It looked like the love child of Tara from *Gone with the Wind* and the suburban Colonial from *Leave It to Beaver*. Four spindly columns stood guard in front of a white shingled façade with small midcentury windows.

The moment we entered, an oppressive energy emanated like a foul odor. That was when most intelligent buyers would've high-tailed it to the next property. But not Alan. Just like those fools in horror movies who trip over the hacked-up body of the head cheerleader and decide to press on, we stayed. Being exquisitely attuned to my own melancholy, I'd become sort of a high-fidelity depression detector, and I sensed a profound sadness that penetrated every stud, every floor slat, every doorframe.

Our broker whispered that the owner, Audrey, had lost her husband just before moving in. Then I understood. Living here, trying to honor her dead husband, Audrey had been trapped in grief like an insect in amber. That explained the neglect, the family room whose wood planks and window frames had been chewed by their dog, and the horrible condition of the yard, its gardens overtaken by thornbushes, and trees nearly strangled to death by vines thick as forearms.

Undeterred, Alan bought the place. (After leaving advertising and refusing to make a pathetic eighty grand as a shrink, I'd decided to turn to food writing full-time, in which, in my best year, I pulled in a whopping thirty thousand. All I could afford was a good attitude.)

I wanted to respect Audrey's loss, but the last thing I needed was to suck up her sadness like an emotional wet/dry vac. So a week after we closed, we threw a demolition party. As we refreshed glasses of prosecco and tried to assure our friends that the bloodred bedroom was not a portal to hell, we also passed out pencils. We instructed them to write well wishes to us all over the walls before they were painted over. We wanted a happy home, we said, and we couldn't think of a better way to achieve that than to imbue it with their love.

Everyone scattered and took to the walls. Some scrawled their well wishes in huge block letters a foot high; others scribbled hopes for us so small, you had to lean in to read them. Later that afternoon, as Alan and I walked through the house picking up empty paper plates and plastic cups, we stopped every so often, heads tilted like a pair of hard-of-hearing cocker spaniels, to read the wishes and wisecracks. The kitchen was festooned with messages that foretold many fine meals. In what would be my writing studio were various wishes for a lifetime of creativity, joy in my work, and pots and pots of money. (Alan had written that last one.) In our bedroom, witty and smutty suggestions, not to mention a few somewhat explicit—and flatteringly out-of-proportion—illustrations, covered the walls.

To combat the lack of light, Alan came up with the idea of exploding open the outside walls with huge French doors and rows of big windows. So now I write in a studio that looks out onto almost four manicured acres of parklike land, and is flooded with light from sunup to sunset—which, if my psychopharmacologist is to be believed, is restorative and healthy for manic depression. Something about vitamin D.

Post-renovation, the kitchen houses three James Beard awards and acts as the setting for my food writing as well as for my blog, *The David Blahg.* The title was meant as a gentle reminder of the accent I had all those years ago back in Fall River. But most people seem to think I meant it to sound erudite, upper-crusty, British even. You just can't win.

For a year and a half, the kitchen was also where I developed recipes for my cookbook, *The New Portuguese Table.* After our trip to the Azores and my father's childhood home, Alan and I spent more time in Lisbon and traveled to the Ribatejo, Alentejo, and Algarve—three of the eleven historical regions in Portugal, the rest of which I visited over the next several years. The book was meant to honor the food of my heritage by recounting some of the stories and dishes that came out of that small, cramped kitchen on an island in the middle of nowhere, and to re-create some of the lost recipes of Vo Costa. (I succeeded, with the exception of her pink chicken soup. She's probably looking down and chuckling every time I try to make it.)

Most important, what the house became for me was an asylum. And like all nuthouses worth their monthly payments, it had 1.) gorgeous grounds for strolling and for sitting under a tree with a book; 2.) therapeutic activities—in my case, writing, cooking, and crafts; and 3.) quietude.

As I wrote my cookbook, I began spending more time in Roxbury. The book was a ruse, really. "The kitchen here is so much better," I'd say to Alan, as an excuse to stay an extra few days or the whole week. Eventually, I moved there permanently. Our almost twenty-year routine of riding up and back to the country, two hours each way, which Alan and I used as a way to decompress and reconnect, was over. I saw him from Friday afternoon until Monday morning. While the move brought great peace to me, it caused incredible disruption to us. We fought more than ever. Everything became a flash point.

After a dinner of *frango na púcara*—a boozy dish from my cookbook of chicken cooked in wine, brandy, and Port—on one snowy Saturday in February, we began talking finances. I bristled. I always bristled when we discussed money. When I'd blindly launched head-first into a writing career, I'd naturally assumed I would succeed, and that meant financially, too. No one had told me I would have years of making less than ten thousand dollars. After my savings, CDs, and IRA evaporated, Alan supported me.

"It's just until I make it," I kept telling him.

On this night, the conversation again snaked around to my piss-poor income.

"Look," I said, "it's getting better, right?" I was referring to my advance for my cookbook. "It's just until I make it."

I'm not proud of it, but I can bully Alan, making it hard for him to speak up, and it allows me to slip out of uncomfortable situations. But this wasn't one of those nights.

"David, you *have* made it," he said, barely controlling himself. "You've won awards. You've written a cookbook. You've been in all the magazines. This is as good as it's going to get." The same line Bercoli had used a decade earlier.

"I don't want to talk about this," I said, picking up plates and throwing them into the sink.

"You never want to talk about it," he said, following me lockstep into the kitchen. He was never this insistent, this dogged. "This is *not* what I signed up for."

That was it. I spun around to him, screaming: "Do you think being a fucking lunatic is what *I* signed up for?" And to drive home my point, I added, "I have an illness!"

"Yes, you do, but what's worse is you have an attitude about your illness. You feel that since you're manic-depressive, you're entitled to annihilate anyone within a fifty-foot radius. Do you have any idea how exhausting it is to be on the opposite end of this?" He raised his hand and pointed at me. "Your moods and rages? Do you know how hard I have to work not to upset you? Or rattle you? Or trigger you? I walk on eggshells every day in our own house. You're not the only one affected by this."

I grabbed the All-Clad skillet that was on the stove and slammed it down on the countertop three times. "Stop it! Stop it!! STOP IT!!" The granite shattered, and two dents traversed the bottom of the skillet. The conversation whiplashed from sixty to zero.

We had had only one rule from day one: Violence = The End of the Relationship. I had broken it. I held my palms up, a sign of surrender, and said, "I'll take the car to my parents' tonight, and when you go to the city on Monday, I'll come back and move my stuff out."

As I brushed past him, he grabbed my arm and stopped me. "Let's talk."

I wrenched away. "I don't see what good it'll do." I didn't mean it. I said it to strike back, to punish him.

"David?" He led me into the family room, and we sat on the couch looking at each other. He seemed almost relieved, as if goading me into shattering the safety that defined us (and a very expensive granite countertop, in the process) had been the only way he could speak up for himself. For years, I had been the heart and voice of our relationship, he the head and hands. I felt and talked for us; he reasoned and acted. We each needed to do all of it—feel, talk, reason, act—for ourselves if we were to survive as a couple.

The blowup uncovered a bunker of unexpressed feelings that had festered longer than either of us had the balls to admit. For hours, we sifted through the debris of his resentment over my lack of money, his frustration about always having to put my illness first, even before him. I confessed my exhaustion and confusion, how my life had drifted off course, one degree at a time, until I felt marooned by my choices and my solitude. He countered with how wounded and alone he felt with me being up here all the time. It was as if there had been a death, he said, and he was in mourning.

How could we solve this? Staying in the country meant risking my relationship. Returning to the city meant risking my mental health. For years, living in New York had been a thrill. The energy and excitement of being in the greatest city in the world—*I am here!*—would pulsate through me, careening me from place to place, from day to day. Since my diagnosis, though, the city rankles. I feel jangled, sharp, and irritable when I'm there. I can't shut out the world around me, and I can't turn off how it makes me feel. My asylum was becoming a prison, where I was trapped by my illness.

I wish I could say there had been a deus ex machina denouement, in which the heavens opened and some benevolent (and rich) God laid her hand upon our troubled hearts and empty wallets and made it better. But that's not what happened. The solution is still ongoing, and it's inelegant at best. What's good is that I haven't thrown up my hands and fallen through my own asshole, as David Lindsey loves to say. Or left Alan, or, worse, had him leave me. Or sunk so low into depression, I can't writhe my way out of it. Some weeks, I spend a day or two in the city; other weeks he stays on in the country. I tried to get him to use Skype or FaceTime, so we could have virtual dinner time together and I could see that beloved face, but he's still figuring out texting. Technology isn't in his blood.

It's tempting to say food saved us, but that would be grand and blustery—and in our food-fetishistic society, a cliché. We don't play golf or tennis, or belong to bowling leagues, or take macramé classes, like some folks. Food and cooking are our one shared passion and a big part of our bond. And at times it has brought us together; at other times it has melted the knots that threatened to choke our relationship—from that lick of cake batter so many years ago to dinner last night. But I've learned it's not just food, but what we say and do at the table, how we use that precious time, that matters most.

I've kept the dented skillet, as a reminder of everything I have to lose.

40

THE LAST SUPPER

March 1, 2014. A blisteringly cold, clear day. Snow still covered the yard, and in places was piled waistdeep. The early-morning light was just beginning its tour across the room; in just a few hours it would splash on the table in the family room—set up in a giant T-shaped configuration to accommodate fourteen graciously. Burlap runners with three red stripes on both sides raced down the middle of the tables. Vases of tulips, a hope for an end to the endless winter, were set everywhere. At each place setting, silverware was tied with raffia and fanned out on the plate. Draped over the back of the chairs were champagne-colored napkins with a woodcut print of a duck. On the wall above where I was to sit later that day—in the glorious, swirling center of it all—was a giant vintage poster of the jolliest, most contented fat man at a table, on each shoulder an enormous goose.

Looking at the room, I couldn't help thinking of my parents. How they'd transform our kitchen or, if the guest list was large enough, our garage or backyard with long rows of mismatched tables. Chairs pulled from every room in the house, and sometimes borrowed from my godparents. Jugs of my father's homemade wine never more than an arm's length away from anyone. Towers of white paper napkins held in place by bowls of olives—green, never black. My mother joking with my father, "We've got enough food to choke a horse, Manny Brown!" To which he always added, "Here's to you, Mrs. Leite." It was always the same, whether we were celebrating a birthday, an anniversary, a graduation, or just Sunday supper.

This table was for our annual cassoulet party. It started as the brainchild of our good friends Cindi Kruth and her husband, Martin Goldberg. After several years, Alan and I took over as hosts, with me cooking and him, as usual, working his magic with the lighting, table, music, and ambience.

This year, though, was going to be different.

I'd been feeling upbeat for five months—not manic, hypomanic, or grandiose. Nor expansive, cocky, or delusional. None of the moods medication was created to bitch-slap into submission. Just *good*. Truly well. I'd decided that this time I wanted to do everything myself—invitations, shopping, cooking, decorating, entertaining, and hosting. I wanted this dinner to be an expression of me entirely—and I wanted Alan to be my special guest. It was to be a private gift to him, a show of thanks for putting up with so much for too long. So with the help of my friend Annie, I planned in secret. We scoured Pinterest and tore out piles of pages from magazines for ideas. Went shopping together and then pissed off sales clerks by returning most of what we'd bought—none of it had the right feel. I was going for classic, comfortable, relaxed; not these over-the-top, hyperstylized, Martha-Stewart-on-crack decorations every home blogger under thirty seemed to love. I didn't feel like copying, and I was tired of competing. Instead, I did something I hadn't done since I was a kid. I whipped out a pair of scissors, and some iron-on transfer paper, ribbon, cardboard, and ink, and created.

"Oh, you'll see" was my standard retort whenever Alan asked how things were going. "You'll see."

On a Friday a few weeks before the dinner, a truckload of boxes from D'Artagnan had arrived. I hauled out two huge stockpots from the basement and set them on the stove. I let the twenty-five pounds of duck necks defrost, then slicked them lightly with olive oil and roasted them until they were the color of rosewood. Half went into each pot, along with carrots, onions, smashed garlic, handfuls of fresh thyme, and a slug of tomato paste. Covered with water, the necks simmered for six redolent hours until they fell apart. I strained the stock and let it rest in the fridge until needed.

Rory, our cat, sat patiently, softly lifting first his left paw, then his right. Left, right, left, right, in a procession that went nowhere. It was his way of saying, *I want.* I picked some of the meat from the bones, now just a heap of vertebrae, because all the marvelous, slick collagen from the connective tissue that had held them together had melted into the glistening, gelatinous stock.

It was one in the morning, and Alan was upstairs, dead to the world. He has a strict no-cat-on-the-table policy. *Eh, he'll never know.* I picked up Rory and put him on our red Formica kitchen table, and I saw it for the first time: Our table, which we had bought earlier that year, was just like the ones from my childhood—Dina's, Vovo's, my mother's. I'd inadvertently re-created Brownell Street. Rory, oblivious to this, hunched over his bowl of meat, and I sat there petting him, the black windows steamed over. Peace.

A few days later, I laid the duck legs on sheet pans and massaged them with a mixture of crumbled bay leaf, dried thyme, ground coriander, minced garlic, allspice, nutmeg, ginger, and plenty of salt and freshly ground pepper. The smell was heady, rich, like spice cake, but with the unmistakable bite of garlic and the calming stroke of bay leaves. After a day in the refrigerator, they were ready to be confited.

Into our largest enamel pot, I scooped quarts of white duck fat. I watched as it started to puddle, becoming transparent. I thought of icebergs melting and of global warming. *Morose.* I thought then of the pleasure of carrying casserole dishes filled with shredded duck confit, pork and duck sausages, and Tarbais beans cooked *and* soaked in my elixir-like duck stock, and I smiled. I slipped the cold duck legs into the warm fat, and the edges of the skin began to curl, just slightly. I covered the pot and let it burble slowly until the duck was meltingly tender and had no use for a bone anymore. Once cooled, the pot was covered and slipped into the refrigerator for two weeks, to allow the flavors to meld and the meat to continue to break down and tenderize.

That's the thing about cassoulet. It's an enormous undertaking if done from scratch—and it should be, because that's where the satisfaction comes from. But when this behemoth is stretched out over several weeks, and broken down into its smallest constituents—simmer, chop, rub, burble, chill, simmer again—the work isn't rushed, and the pleasure isn't lost. To make cassoulet is an act of faith. You believe that what you do today will shake hands with what you'll do next week, and the week after that, and in the end, the result will nourish and sustain and delight.

It was a lesson I was learning to apply to my life, post-diagnosis.

The night before the party.

"Close your eyes," I said to Alan.

"You know I don't like surprises," he warned.

"Yeah, well, tough," I said, doing my best imitation of my mother. "Get over it."

"Oh, Mamma Lee's in da house." That was *his* nickname for her.

I led him into the family room, coaching him up the step and positioning him so the whole room, cast warm by the dim lights overhead and the flicker from the fireplace, was in view. "Okay, you can open."

He gasped. His look was incredulous. Annie, who was standing off to the side, smiled at me.

"Do you like it?"

"I think it's amazing." He walked around, picking up the name cards, with their red satin ribbons looped through a hole in the top. He ran his fingers along the edges of the plates, the runner. I began crying because I had made this man happy. This dear, sweet, kind man, who had put up with every single thing my illness, my often-unchecked narcissism, and my Portuguese *veneta* could throw at him.

Annie left us, and we sat on the couch, which had been moved out of the way to make room for the tables, and talked. Nothing important, or that I can remember. It was the warm murmurs of unspooling our week for the other, wineglasses in hand.

"It really is beautiful, David."

I slipped my hand into his. "Thank you, *mon cher*. For everything."

Guests arrived the next day, beginning at one in the afternoon. Bottles of prosecco were popped. "We always begin a party with bubbles" was my motto, and our cassoulet parties were no exception. As Alan filled glasses and stoked the fire, I moved from one knot of guests to another, offering a platter of gougères. Annie kept sidling up to me, asking me if there was anything she could do. "Yes," I said. "Enjoy yourself. Now get lost!" She and her husband, Tony, peeled off and chatted with Dan, our contractor, and his wife, Mamie, a local chef, and our photographer friends, Bob and Linda.

"Everything is so beautiful," Cindi whispered, reaching for a gougère. "It's magical. Alan did a wonderful job." I smiled to myself; I had no desire to correct her.

"I think you've forgotten something, sir." That was Martin, and knowing Martin as I did, I figured he couldn't get through the day without ribbing me about something.

"And what is that, Mr. Goldberg?"

"This." And he wrapped his arms tight around my rib cage. He was shorter and older than me, but there was the sweetness and innocence of a ten-year-old to his affection. It was like getting a hug from Boo-Boo Bear.

Carlos and Jeffrey admired the Hershey chocolate cake gracing the sideboard. I had originally planned for a seasonal apple cake steeped in plenty of cream and butter, but it was Aurora's birthday, and, with apologies to the French, birthdays and the Hershey cake trump everything at our house.

Bob called Alan and me over to the poster of the fat man and his geese, and held up his camera. I rested one hand on Alan's shoulder, the other on his arm. Laurel and Hardy. Fat and skinny. Throughout my life, I'd battled a whole hell's worth of demons, but weight was the one that had eluded me in the long run. *Tomorrow,* I keep telling myself, *tomorrow.*

"I want a picture of us, too," said Kate, one of my closest friends and a longtime editor in chief at a publishing house.

She sat on my lap, and I scooped her close as she leaned her head against mine. For years she'd been encouraging me to write a book, but my answer was always the same one I'd given my father so long ago: *I have nothing to say.*

"I think I finally know what I want to write about," I whispered. That's when Bob snapped the picture.

To people who've seen the photo on Facebook or Twitter, it looks like nothing more than two friends, heads together, smiling at the camera. But I see the moment of resolve, the decision to tell my story.

I stood and walked over to Alan in front of the fireplace. I threaded my fingers through one of his belt loops, like I'd seen my mother do so many times to my father, and pulled him close. I called out: "Everyone . . ." The room quieted, and heads swiveled in our direction. "Let's eat."

EPILOGUE

I am untethered from my heavy, cloddish body and soar, with the daring, stomach-lurching swoops and dips of those flying dreams I loved when I was young. I hover near that eleven-year-old boy pacing outside of a movie theater, wringing his hands as he tries to make sense of what just happened to him. He doesn't see me, because he can't; I haven't happened yet. But I float up to his ear and whisper softly, so softly he can't hear it, but his heart feels it: "You will be okay. You will grow to have an astounding life. Just hang on, Banana. Just hang on." He looks at the clock on the wall and walks bravely back into the theater, back into the hell he just escaped. But he has a gift he doesn't yet know how to unwrap.

I stand in the center of a running track. It's morning. I watch that young man bolt from a cafeteria. He's trying to outrun his fear. I shake my head. He doesn't yet understand that wherever he goes, fear is. He hasn't figured out that fear topples in the face of authenticity and truth. "You must become your real self, imperfect and glorious," I thrum into his burning lungs. "Only then will you be able to stop running." But he's too frantic, screaming at the sky, cursing God as if it were His fault this happened, pleading to be healed. I plunge my hand into his gut and plant a small seed of quiet. It's too tiny for him to notice. But it will take root. "It will grow," I assure him, although all he hears is his hoarse shouts, "and you will eventually have the courage to be yourself, to love the way you were born to, and you will persist. I promise."

That man, now a few years older, lies restless in bed. His head is full of guns, pills, and nooses. The threat of death comforts him. I lie down beside him. I spoon him. He, too, can't see me. But he feels something—he is too exquisitely sensitive not to. I take my fingers and comb them down his body, untangling his exhausted and depleted nerves. "Death is not yours to choose," I tell him. He thinks of a smiling face of pills. He imagines swallowing them, but I stop him from taking all of them. "It is not your time." He struggles and cries; the relief of death is so seductive, he just wants to let go and float down into dark, cold water until he is no longer. But he grows sleepy because of my stroking. He doesn't know it yet, but sleep will always, always be his greatest gift. It was the gift he once didn't know how to unwrap. He is learning.

Last, I stand next to that same man, fully grown, in love, and out of his mind. He shits his pants, he abandons his one true love, he wants to give up. He believes, incorrectly, that he has succumbed to his enemy. What he doesn't know is I have been whispering in his ear for years, "You are not at fault. Your body, your DNA, is to blame." And like a mantra I sing, "Manic depression, manic depression, manic depression." He doesn't hear. I persist: "Manic depression, manic depression." One day, out of the blue, while at the stove cooking too much food for too few guests, he tells his beloved, "I know what's wrong with me." Joyous, I kiss this man gently on the lips. He finally knows I'm here, understands I have always been here, but he waves me off. He's too excited about the possibilities.

RESOURCES

BEING GAY / COMING OUT / BULLYING

Dawson, James. *This Book Is Gay*. Naperville, IL: Sourcebooks Fire, 2015.

Huegel, Kelly. *GLBTQ: The Survival Guide for Gay, Lesbian, Bisexual, Transgender, and Questioning Teens*. 2nd ed. Minneapolis, MN: Free Spirit Publishing, 2011.

Owens-Reid, Dannielle, and Kristin Russo. *This Is a Book for Parents of Gay Kids: A Question-and-Answer Guide to Everyday Life*. Thousand Oaks, CA: Chronicle Books, 2014.

Savage, Dan, and Terry Miller, eds. *It Gets Better: Coming Out, Overcoming Bullying, and Creating a Life Worth Living*. New York: New American Library, 2012.

Signorile, Michelangelo. *Outing Yourself: How to Come Out as Lesbian or Gay to Your Family, Friends, and Coworkers*. New York: Simon & Schuster, 1996.

BIPOLAR DISORDER

Cheney, Terri. *Manic: A Memoir*. New York: HarperCollins Publishers, 2009.

Duke, Patty, and Gloria Hochman. *A Brilliant Madness: Living with Manic-Depressive Illness*. New York: Random House, 1997.

Jamison, Kay R. *An Unquiet Mind: A Memoir of Moods and Madness*. New York: Knopf, 1995.

Miklowitz, David J. *The Bipolar Disorder Survival Guide: What You and Your Family Need to Know.* 2nd ed. New York: Guilford Publications, 2011.

Papolos, Demitri F. *The Bipolar Child: The Definitive and Reassuring Guide to Childhood's Most Misunderstood Disorder.* 3rd ed. New York: Crown Publishing Group, 2007.

RECOVERiNG FROM CULTS

Lalich, Janja, and Madeleine Tobias. *Taking Back Your Life: Recovering from Cults and Abusive Relationships.* 2nd ed. Berkeley, CA: Bay Tree Publishing, 2006.

Langone, Michael D. *Recovery from Cults: Help for Victims of Psychological and Spiritual Abuse.* New York: W. W. Norton & Co., 1995.

Professional organizations: The International Cultic Studies Association (ICSA), ICSAhome.com.

Singer, Margaret Thaler, and Janja Lalich. *Cults in Our Midst: The Hidden Menace in Our Everyday Lives.* San Francisco, CA: Jossey-Bass Publishers, 1995.

ACKNOWLEDGMENTS

It takes enormous courage, and a certain amount of ballsiness, to write a memoir. It takes even more to know you're being written about and not to complain. No one exemplifies that more than my parents, Manuel and Elvira Leite. They're extremely private people, yet when they knew our world would be cracked open for others to see, they responded with: "If writing about our struggles can in some way help others with theirs, you have our blessing." Thank you for your kindness, understanding, and generosity of spirit. I love you both.

To Alan Dunkelberger, thank you for answering that ad in 1993 and for every year since. For allowing me my obsession, for following me down every dark and frightening alley as I wrote this book, and for making sure I always found my way home. I couldn't be who I am if it weren't for all that you are. I love you, too.

To my agent, Joy Tutela, I don't deserve you, but I'm so happy I have you.

To everyone at Dey Street Books: My amazing editor, Denise Oswald, who gently and with great insight guided me and the text and who reminded me I was funny. To the publicity and marketing gurus, Shelby Meizlik, Michael Barrs, Sharyn Rosenblum, and Emily Homonoff. I never cease to be amazed. To my publisher, Lynn Grady, for adding me to Dey Street's roster of jaw-dropping authors. (I'm still shaking my head.) To Mumtaz Mustafa, art director and designer, and Joel Holland, illustrator and hand letterer, who created a cover that still causes me to sigh with pleasure every time I see it.

To Marion Roach Smith, for her guidance in class and in life. You are a friend, truly. To my fellow writing students, Suzanne Fernandez Gray, Cheri Gregory, Susan Kayne, Sheila Siegel, and Dan New. I hope you see a little bit of yourself in here. And to my writing group closer to home, Cindy Eastman and Trudy Swenson, I'll always be indebted.

To my early and not-so-early readers, Ellen Kroner, Kate Morgan Jackson, Deb Turcotte, Jeanine Bova, Roy Trimble, Danny Pring, Martha Engle, Jenifer Monroe, Gigi DiBello, Jeffery Stockwell, Carlos Rodriguez-Perez, and especially Suzanne Fortier, who read the manuscript—what?—seven times. To Ned Nunes, for his careful and critical eye.

To Renee Schettler Rossi, Beth Price, Tracey Gertler, and Dan Kran, who kept Leite's Culinaria fresh and vital in my absence. To Annie Musso and Kelli Willis, both of who kept my life this-side-up for more than five years. I can't thank you all enough.

To Janet Mitchko, for your love and friendship and our endless phone calls. To Edith Gould, who helped put the pieces back together. To Dan Harris, who encouraged me early and consistently. To Anne Goudreau, Joe McDonald, Beverley Loranger, and Greg Martin, for research help. To Joyce Johnson and Sydny Miner, for their sound advice. To Ann Stamler, for her warm encouragement and kindness. To Elizabeth Alvarez, who suggested I write a little book of essays. (I guess I don't do anything little.)

To those whom I may have forgotten, blame my aging brain, not my full heart.

THE BANANA PROJECT

In honor of my mother and her inventive notes on bananas—something she still does whenever I go back to Swansea, Massachusetts—I've created The Banana Project, and I hope you'll join me. Simply grab a banana and write a message of love, support, encouragement, good wishes—whatever—to a loved one. Slip it on the table, like my mother did, in a lunchbox, on a desk—you get the idea. And, in turn, ask them to do the same for others. I'm hoping that this small act of kindness mushrooms to reach as many people as possible and becomes a movement of compassion, thoughtfulness, and love. Consider taking a picture of your banana creation and sharing it on social media using #NotesOnABanana. Momma Leite will love you for it.

David, AKA "Banana"

ABOUT THE AUTHOR

DAVID LEITE (rhymes with "eat") is a food writer, cookbook author, and web publisher. He founded Leite's Culinaria (leitesculinaria.com) in 1999. In 2006, he had the distinction of being the first winner of a James Beard Award for a website, a feat he repeated in 2007. His writing has appeared in the *New York Times, Martha Stewart Living, Saveur, Bon Appétit, Food & Wine, Pastry Arts, Men's Health,* the *Los Angeles Times,* the *Chicago Sun-Times,* and the *Washington Post,* among other publications. His first book, *The New Portuguese Table,* explored the food of his heritage and won the IACP's 2010 First Book: Julia Child Award. David is also a frequent correspondent and guest host on public radio's *The Splendid Table.* He has been heard on NPR's *All Things Considered* and has appeared on *United Stuff of America, Beat Bobby Flay,* and the *Today* show. When no one is looking, he still dances in his underwear in the kitchen.